The Prisms of Gramsci

Historical Materialism Book Series

The Historical Materialism Book Series is a major publishing initiative of the radical left. The capitalist crisis of the twenty-first century has been met by a resurgence of interest in critical Marxist theory. At the same time, the publishing institutions committed to Marxism have contracted markedly since the high point of the 1970s. The Historical Materialism Book Series is dedicated to addressing this situation by making available important works of Marxist theory. The aim of the series is to publish important theoretical contributions as the basis for vigorous intellectual debate and exchange on the left.

The peer-reviewed series publishes original monographs, translated texts, and reprints of classics across the bounds of academic disciplinary agendas and across the divisions of the left. The series is particularly concerned to encourage the internationalization of Marxist debate and aims to translate significant studies from beyond the English-speaking world.

For a full list of titles in the Historical Materialism Book Series
available in paperback from Haymarket Books, visit:
https://www.haymarketbooks.org/series_collections/1-historical-materialism

The Prisms of Gramsci

The Political Formula of the United Front

Marcos Del Roio

Translated by
Pedro Sette-Câmara

Haymarket Books
Chicago, IL

First published in 2015 by Brill Academic Publishers, The Netherlands
© 2016 Koninklijke Brill NV, Leiden, The Netherlands

Published in paperback in 2017 by
Haymarket Books
P.O. Box 180165
Chicago, IL 60618
773-583-7884
www.haymarketbooks.org

ISBN: 978-1-60846-693-1

Trade distribution:
In the US, Consortium Book Sales, www.cbsd.com
In Canada, Publishers Group Canada, www.pgcbooks.ca
In the UK, Turnaround Publisher Services, www.turnaround-uk.com
In all other countries, Publishers Group Worldwide, www.pgw.com

Cover design by Jamie Kerry of Belle Étoile Studios and Ragina Johnson.

This book was published with the generous support of Lannan Foundation
and the Wallace Action Fund.

Library of Congress Cataloging-in-Publication data is available.

Entered into digital printing October, 2017.

The same ray of light passes through different prisms and yields different refractions of light: in order to have the same refraction, one must make a whole series of adjustments to the individual prisms.

GRAMSCI 1975, p. 33; 1992, p. 128

Contents

Foreword: Identity and Diversity in Gramsci's Thought   IX
Acronym List   XIII

Introduction   1

1   War, Revolution and the Communist Scission in Gramsci   12
   1   Communist Scission and Communist Refoundation in Lenin and Rosa Luxemburg   12
   2   Liberalism, Revisionism and the Problem of the Scission (or Cleavage) in Gramsci   22
   3   The Organic Scission of the Workers' Movement and the Foundation of the Communist Party in Italy   38
   4   The Origins of the United Front Policy in the Communist International   50

2   The Paradox between Communist Scission and United Front   58
   1   How the Communist Scission in Italy Consolidated Itself over the Dispute within the Communist International and the Fascist Offensive   58
   2   The United Front Policy in the Communist International and in the USSR: Theoretical Weakness and Political Defeat   68
   3   Gramsci in Moscow and the Solution to the Dispute between the PCd'I and the Communist International   77
   4   Gramsci between the Communist Refoundation and the Theoretical Regression of Bolshevism   87

3   The Communist Refoundation and the United Front in Gramsci   104
   1   The Influence of the Theoretical Regression on the Political Actions of the Communist International   104
   2   Gramsci in Vienna and His Confluence with the Communist Refoundation   112
   3   Gramsci in Rome: The United Front Policy and Anti-Fascism   121
   4   On the Way to the Third Congress of the PCd'I   131

4   The Strategy of the Anti-Fascist United Front   140
   1   The 'Lyons Theses' and the Theory of the Socialist Revolution in Italy   140

2   The Third Congress and the New Lines of Division   150

3   Gramsci and the Russian Question   161

4   The Agrarian Question as a National Question, and the Problem of
     the Southern Intellectuals in the United Front   174

Conclusion   186

References   201
Index   205

Identity and Diversity in Gramsci's Thought[*]

Marcos Del Roio provides us with a sober and careful analysis of Gramsci's political and intellectual activities, but it is also forceful and determined, proposing a strong and radical thesis: namely, that there is a continuity between political action and philosophical thought throughout the *whole* of Gramsci. I recall a statement to this effect expressed in no unclear terms by Battista Santhià, the worker who was the leading figure of the *biennio rosso* ['two red years' of 1919–20], when I carried out a long interview with him at his home in Turin in 1987, a few years before his passing. Santhià was not an intellectual by profession, even though his approach was that of the 'organic intellectual' as defined by Gramsci in his speech to the Political Commission at the 1926 Congress of the Italian Communist Party [PCd'I] in Lyons. Disputing the preference given to intellectuals by Amadeo Bordiga's extreme left, he said: 'the intellectuals were the most politically and socially advanced elements, and were therefore destined to be the organisers of the working class. Today, in our view, the organisers of the working class must be the workers themselves'.[1] It must be highlighted that, according to the language used in the *Prison Notebooks*, the term 'organisers' refers to intellectuals in a broad sense.

At the time, Santhià's words seemed to me to be filled with 'triumphalism'. Yet as I reconsidered them, I saw that he was very much in the right. To insist upon the unity of Gramsci's whole work does not imply underestimating the change, transformation, or even the ruptures that occurred in his brief but densely-layered existence. Conversely, today we know that it is impossible to study the *Notebooks* without using the analytical tools of a genetic and evolutionary method of research – and this does not mean wiping away their internal unity.

As we read Gramsci, certain key ideas come forth, and they determine in unitary fashion the rhythm of his thought, at least from the time of the factory councils to the writing of the last notebooks (Gramsci himself points out the path of this continuity in a strategic note in the *Notebooks*).[2] I am referring to the key ideas that constitute the identity of his thought, throughout and beyond the diversity of its manifestations, that identity which is the usual hallmark of all great thinkers.

---

[*] This foreword was translated from Italian into Portuguese by Alvaro Bianchi.

1 Gramsci 1999a, p. 430.

2 Gramsci 1977, vol. 4, p. 328 ff.

Both the title and subtitle of Del Roio's book remind us precisely of the counterpoint between identity and diversity, which Gramsci theorised in highly imaginative terms in *Notebook 1*, and which we can, perhaps with a little more audacity, apply to his own thought:

> The unitary elaboration of a collective consciousness requires manifold conditions and initiatives ... The same ray of light passes through different prisms and yields different refractions of light ... Finding the real identity underneath the apparent differentiation and contradiction and finding the substantial diversity underneath the apparent identity is the most essential quality of the critic of the ideas and of the historian of social development.[3]

The subtitle's essential category, as well as the contents of Del Roio's work – the 'united front' – direct us to an identical problem dealt with in Gramsci's political action, namely that concerning the radical Leninism that guided him in his confrontation with Bordiga.

Del Roio recalls the birth of this 'political formula' – in the Germany of 1921 – which was central to Lenin's mature thought, shows the various ways in which it was interpreted, and analyses Gramsci's cautious attitude. An important aspect of this latter is the fact that it is the practical necessity imposed by the united front strategy that explains the monumental prudence and flexibility Gramsci displayed towards Bordiga, both when Bordiga established the party line, and later, when Gramsci's supremacy began to take shape.

The metaphor-image of the ray and the prism allows us to approach the guiding thread that accompanies the transition from Gramsci's final year at liberty to the genesis of the *Notebooks*. In this respect, Del Roio picks out some important elements, particularly from the incomplete and then-unpublished 1926 essay on the 'Southern question'. However, it was both the political and theoretical elaborations of Gramsci in that year that broke the ground for the construction of his thought as it matured in prison. To recall the main stages, we have the Lyons Congress and the corresponding theses (21–26 January), his letter to Togliatti on the situation within the Bolshevik Party (October), and *Some Aspects of the Southern Question* (in the months before his arrest on 8 November).

---

3 Gramsci 1977, vol. 1, p. 33 ff. In the second draft of this passage, in Q24, §3 (the special notebook dedicated to journalism), the 'unitary elaboration' becomes 'the national unitary elaboration', and the 'quality of the critic of ideas' becomes 'the more delicate gift, albeit misunderstood, but still essential, of the critic of ideas', among other changes.

The *Lyons Theses*, written by Gramsci with Togliatti's help, are probably the best and most complex document in all the theoretical and political history of the communist movement in Italy. These theses, read together with Gramsci's aforementioned words to the Political Commission of the Congress, constitute an admirable instance of that 'spontaneous philosophy' he would find again and again in Lenin's and Machiavelli's political formulations.

Forming the basis of the 'united front' policy, Lenin's alliance of workers and peasants is specified as identifying the two 'motor forces of the Italian revolution', whose 'development' and 'speed', as the theses explain, 'cannot be predicted without an evaluation of subjective elements'.[4] It is opportune to highlight at this point how the combination of the categories of 'force' (and obviously the associated physical-biological and technical metaphor) and 'subjectivity' (the humanist and historicist element) represent a tensional arc that would circumscribe Gramsci's prison reflections as a whole.

In his words to the Political Commission, Gramsci shows clearly and unmistakably the antithesis between Bordiga's conception of the party as an 'organ' and the party's congenial conception as 'part' of the working class. In order to highlight the distance between abstraction and concreteness, between sharing and instrumentality, Gramsci writes: 'the party is united to the working class not merely by ideological bonds, but also by bonds of a "physical" character'.[5] The argument goes on to say that 'party organisation must be constructed on the basis of production and hence of the work-place (cells)'.[6] Gramsci's historicist subjectivism, if deprived of what we could call the technical-naturalistic implications of his argument, would necessarily have led to a one-way idealistic road.

The guiding thread in Gramsci's discourse is far from a straight, homogeneous line. Gramsci needs to harmonise two complementary aspects, even if they stand at a distance from one another: the *centrality* of the working class and the organisation of the party (hence Bordiga's idea of the party as a 'synthesis of heterogeneous elements', and polemic against factionalism) and *internal democracy*, that is, the anti-authoritarian nature of the party itself, which appears in the dialectical relation the party must establish with the mass organisations and also within itself, between centre and periphery.

The central problem resides in the hegemonic role of the proletariat (as indicated in the *Theses*) with regard to the peasant masses (who are by defini-

---

4　Gramsci 1999a, p. 483.

5　Gramsci 1999a, p. 429.

6　Gramsci 1999a, p. 494.

tion amorphous and lacking in cohesion), the intellectuals and also the other strata that can be 'hegemonised'.

'The ray and the prism' symbolise the main methodological question that accompanies and guides the evolution of Gramsci's thought in the *Notebooks*. We could name this question as research on both the strengthening and weakening of dialectics.

Dialectics strengthens and at the same time weakens itself by exalting its relational origin or matrix. The conceptualisation throughout the *Notebooks* is shot through by dichotomous pairs; polarities that are not necessarily antinomic, but nevertheless lack any third term representing a possible or necessary synthesis. A lexicological examination would be required to illustrate this thesis, which we here again mention on account of its obvious relation to the *animus* of Del Roio's research. I will restrict myself to drawing attention to the peculiarity of the use of dichotomous pairs throughout the *Notebooks*, such as: history and nature, humanity and animality, intellectuality and life, hegemony and power, production and culture, reform and revolution, the evolutionary-temporal dimension and territorial-spatial dimension of the vicissitudes of humanity (beginning with speech and languages ...).

Passing from the language of wakefulness to that of sleep, we could say that the prisms harmonise with one other as if standing in counterpoint. They may give rise to consonance as well as to dissonance. The question (philosophical as well as political) is why the various refractions required the identity of a ray. The unity of counterpoint has a source that is different from the counterpoint itself. There is only one front – a united front – because it has a centre.

> *Giorgio Baratta* († 20/01/2010)
> Professor of Moral Philosophy at the University of Urbino
> President of the Italian Section of the International Gramsci Society
> Author of *As rosas e os Cadernos: o pensamento dialógico de Antonio Gramsci* [*The roses and the Notebooks: Antonio Gramsci's dialogical thought*]. Rio de Janeiro: DP&A, 2004.

Acronym List

CGL	Confederazione Generale del Lavoro [General Confederation of Labour]
CI	Communist International
CNI	Confederazione Nazionale dell'Industria [National Confederation of Industry]
ECCI	Executive Committee of the Communist International
ENIOS	Ente Nazionale Italiano per la Organizzazione Scientifica del Lavoro [National Italian Board for the Scientific Organisation of Labour]
FIOM	Federazione Italiana degli Operai Metalmeccanici [Italian Federation of Metalworkers]
IWW	Industrial Workers of the World
KAPD	Kommunistische Arbeiterpartei Deutschlands [Communist Workers' Party of Germany]
KMU	Kommunistàk Magyarországi Pártja [Communist Party of Hungary]
KPD	Kommunistische Partei Deutschlands [Communist Party of Germany]
KPP	Komunistyczna Partia Polski [Communist Party of Poland]
KSC	Komunistcká Strana Ceskoslovenska [Communist Party of Czechoslovakia]
NEP	Novaja Economiceskaja Politika [New Economic Policy]
PCd'I	Partito Comunista d'Italia [Communist Party of Italy]
PCF	Parti Communiste Français [French Communist Party]
PNF	Partito Nazionale Fascista [National Fascist Party]
PPI	Partito Popolare Italiano [Italian People's Party]
PSI	Partito Socialista Italiano [Italian Socialist Party]
PSU	Partito Socialista Unitario [United Socialist Party]
RKP(B)	Rossijskaja Kommunisticeska Partija (Bolsivikov) [Russian Communist Party (Bolshevik)]
SFIO	Section Française de l'Internationale Ouvrière [French Section of the Workers' International]
SPD	Sozialdemokratische Partei Deutschlands [Social Democratic Party of Germany]
USPD	Unabhängige Sozialdemokratische Partei Deutschlands [Independent Social Democratic Party of Germany]

Introduction

Gramsci is certainly one of the most controversial authors of the politico-cultural tradition initiated by Marx. This mainly owes to the very nature of his written work as an early publicist and organiser of working-class culture. It is a work that encompasses newspaper articles and party documents and that was always open to debate, to discussion with the other side, to polemics. Even a considerable number of his letters were aimed at the goals of politico-cultural action, including his private correspondence. Gramsci thus always bore the profile of a politically revolutionary agent, the 'communist man' of the philosophy of praxis.

However, the work he produced after being imprisoned by the fascist régime is far more studied and disseminated. Many commentators have portrayed the *Prison Notebooks* as a self-contained work, allowing for interpretations that do not take into account the author and his political theory as a whole, which in its turn becomes a mere provider of ambiguous and unclear concepts, and thus useless from a scientific standpoint. Gramsci is, at times, also reduced to a mere political tool, even if this is done with the best intentions. Whether as a living author or as a deceased one, Gramsci has always been contested.[1]

Gramsci's work follows the trajectory of the communist party, which he had helped to found and consolidate, and which provided him with vast theoretical and cultural material. Gramsci has been seen as a great 'Leninist', but also as a great national-popular intellectual, understood as a precursor of the 'Italian road to socialism' and as the theoretician and strategist of the struggle for hegemony inside the bourgeois democratic order.

The influence of his work and his ideas in Italy increased together with the influence of the PCd'I, especially after 1956. By that point, the publication of the first version of the *Prison Notebooks* had been completed, and, starting with the Twentieth Congress of the CPSU and Togliatti's elaboration of the 'Italian road to socialism', the politico-cultural turn of the communist movement was underway. However, Gramsci's work reached its greatest influence as the explosion of socio-cultural protests by workers and youth in 1968–9 unfolded, even if the so-called 'New Left' did not generally draw from the work of the late Gramsci, restricting itself to the experience of the factory councils in 1919–20.

---

1 Liguori 1996. This title provides us with an excellent overview of the intellectual and political debate in Italy around Gramsci and his work from 1922 to 1996.

The fact remains, however, that the expansion of the PCd'I caused an ever greater wave of discussions of the Sardinian revolutionary, both encouraging the studies that would culminate in a new edition of the *Prison Notebooks* in 1975 and feeding from them, thanks to the initiative of a group of intellectuals, some connected with the PCd'I, others not, led by Valentino Gerratana. The publication of the so-called critical edition coincided with the historical zenith of the PCd'I. The political strategy then known as 'eurocommunism' was aimed at the struggle for hegemony within the terrain of liberal-bourgeois democracy, attempting a change of direction in favour of the working class and the popular masses. The political leadership and the intellectuals tried, with undeniable merit, to travel theoretically and practically along this path, based on a reading of Gramsci that was heavily influenced by the situation and by the challenges it presented, considering that the importance of hegemony as a theme as well as political pluralism emerged as essential to democracy.[2]

The politico-cultural defeat of the PCd'I put the workers' movement and the 'Gramscian' party in a strategic dilemma, from which they were unable to get out. The turning point was the so-called 'national solidarity' government of 1978, when the minority Christian Democrat administration received Communist support, justified by the need to defend 'democracy' in the face of terrorism. From that moment on, the PCd'I stood defeated in the debate about democracy and socialism, and began declining until its extinction in 1991, exactly seven decades after its creation in 1921. The studies about Gramsci naturally resounded with the impact of the situation as well as the impact of the broader 'crisis of Marxism', which ultimately was identified with the 'crisis of ideologies'. At this point Gramsci became somewhat ostracised in Italy, even if the dissemination of his work among various countries (including Brazil) maintained a certain energy.

With the political and cultural defeat of the PCd'I and associated intellectuals, Gramsci stopped being seen as a theoretician of democracy as the transition to socialism in the advanced social formations peculiar to the West. Taking advantage of the interpretations of the 1970s, which had a politicist bias, liberal interpretations won the debate. The tendency now was to box Gramsci into the Italian cultural tradition, making him a 'classic' thinker, and in the best of cases emphasising his connections with Croce, Gobetti or Salvemini. Within

---

2   There is an important example of this interpretation in Brazil in Coutinho 1981. There are
    later, revised and extended editions of the book, as well as an English edition, adapted and
    updated: Coutinho 2012. Dias et al. 1996 brings a deliberately polemic response.

this context, in which the view of a 'mature' Gramsci open to social democracy or even liberalism tended to impose itself, there rose the figure of a liberal socialist philosopher like Noberto Bobbio, as well as others.[3]

Another reading, of a liberal Catholic inspiration well-represented by Augusto del Noce, pointed to the establishment of a connection between the thought of Gentile and Gramsci by means of actualism and the 'will to power' of Nietzschean inspiration, itself supposedly present already in the work of Marx. Thus there would be a sort of convergence between Gramsci and Mussolini, between communism and fascism, turning the Sardinian thinker into a 'totalitarian' theoretician. Here, we can see that Del Noce's intended critique of modernity, as well as his critique of Gentile, clears the way for the paradoxical approximation of Gramsci and fascism.[4]

In spite of his being relatively ocstracised, there was still a certain effort in Gramscian studies, yielding important works and research, which, incidentally, contributed to the present book. But the fact remains that especially after 1987 (the fiftieth anniversary of Gramsci's death), there has been an increasing tendency, which includes a considerable number of intellectuals connected with the PCd'I, to become more critical of the Russian Revolution and its historical developments, at times placing Gramsci on the side of liberalism, at times ignoring him, or even, at times, trying to see him as a victim of 'Stalinism' as much as a victim of fascism.

In an anti-Stalinist vein, Bukharin became ever more important (he was rehabilitated in the USSR in 1988, the fiftieth anniversary of his shooting) and so did the theoretical formulations of so-called 'Austro-Marxism'. The opening up of new archives fed a specific debate about Gramsci's personal trajectory, his family relations and his party relations, particularly with Togliatti and Grieco. Even though it is scientifically useful, this debate, because of the way in which it happened, contributed to the cultural 'depoliticisation' of the author of the *Notebooks*.[5]

After the failure of state socialism, the alleged exhaustion of the theme of revolution as a canon of explanation and historical teleology made sure that Gramsci could only remain relevant within a reformist orientation (or

---

3 Bobbio 1990. Through a great number of lectures and publications, Norberto Bobbio set the tone in the debate about democracy in political and academic milieux, both in Italy and Brazil, roughly identified with a liberal understanding of Gramsci.

4 Del Noce 1978.

5 Natoli and Pons 1990, probably the most representative text of the approach that attempts to connect interpersonal relations and large-scale political problems. A more recent take can be found in Nieddu 2004.

within the agenda of passive revolution) that gave preference to democratic institutions. Political action, in these terms, should be concerned with points of transition to the expansion and spread of democracy. The widely repeated discourse that predicted a world inclined to the spreading of peace, democracy and citizenship, after the end of the USSR and state socialism, in an effort to update them, eventually created a historical mystification as it posited a split between Lenin and Gramsci. Thus a virtually inverted image of Gramsci was created from the actual Gramsci.[6]

Even though work on Gramsci saw some dissemination, expansion and various diverse interpretations, which fed political and cultural studies concerned with specific issues, the fact remains that Gramsci was left virtually absent from Italy's political and cultural life. Starting in the 1990s, his work was studied by a relatively small group of intellectuals, from a philological perspective, so as to recover the intrinsic value of his theoretico-political elaboration. Such a study, not so much connected to party action, can occasionally recover, at least partially, the strength of Gramsci's ideas for transforming society.[7]

However, the fundamental element that has to be considered in order to explain this new 'imprisonment' of Gramsci is the strength and the effectiveness of the assault of capital, in the realms of production and culture, against the world of labour, its institutions and cultural representations. The 'deconstruction' of the working class and its politico-cultural movement achieved by the organic intellectuals of capital placed inside the organisation of production and the means of diffusion of information, generalising post-modern ideas, renders the questions posed by Gramsci meaningless and incomprehensible. In a world dominated by the fragmentation of subjects and in which any notion of the contradictory totality of the real makes no sense, it is not possible to invest-

---

6   Vacca 1998. This collection of texts by Giuseppe Vacca is an example of the tendency to see Gramsci as an early critic of 'Stalinism', as well as the tendency to interpret the theme of hegemony as something fundamentally related to the issue of consensus and subjectivity. Such an understanding of hegemony, extended to the field of international politics, brings this 'Gramscism' politically closer to liberal democracy and neo-contractualism, following Gorbachev's failed policy of appeasing capitalist imperialism. In Vianna 1997, pp. 28–30, we find a similar reading, in which the author clearly states that we are no longer living in the time of revolutions, at least as the *fiat* of historical development, since they only survive as a manifestation of the periphery. The heuristic decline of revolution, on the other hand, is connected to the alleged failure of work as an explanatory variable. In the same book we still find a tendency to project the theme of hegemony exclusively onto the level of superstructures and democratic institutions, onto an Americanism without Fordism.

7   In this aspect we must highlight the work being done by the International Gramsci Society group, such as Frosini and Liguori (eds.) 2003.

igate human emancipation from the alienation of labour as imposed by capital, looking towards an integral humanism.[8]

An actual rebirth of political theory and the philosophy of praxis as proposed by Gramsci would require the emergence of a new workers' movement, a new global movement of protest and antagonism to the universal control of capital. A movement, that is, which could pose the material reestablishment of communism in the twenty-first century – which still displays characteristics that are too uncertain from a practical and theoretical point of view.

We can only be sure that it is necessary to start with a radical critique of the present world bourgeois order and its peculiar features. A critique not only of the means of reproduction of capital, but also of the dominant politico-cultural forces based on the fragmentary perspective of post-modernism, which proposes completely separate struggles in the face of the coming barbarity, devoting its energies to environmental, ethnic or gender problems, without realising that it is exactly the generalisation of the proletarian question and of human work as abstract work that puts these contradictions in evidence, presenting them as a generic problem of humanity. Thus the question of human work and the recreation of the proletariat as a class is still relevant in the circumstances of twenty-first century capitalism, even if deprived of that peculiarist and identity-seeking tendency that prevailed in previous phases and that proved the main obstacle to a perspective of self-emancipation.[9]

The state of defeat into which the perspective of labour and the social theory originating in Marx have fallen, as well as the need for a new foundation of socialist praxis in order to face up to the barbarity now threatening to envelop humanity, require us to resume the study of the communist refoundation of the twentieth century. Even before the death of Engels in 1895, the impulse towards a radical critique of capital contained in Marx's work tended to become diluted, being overcome by innovative forms of high bourgeois culture such as positivism and neo-Kantianism. The intrusion of positivism and neo-Kantianism into the culture of the workers' movement, strongly illustrated by revisionism – among other things – subsumed the working class under bourgeois hegemony, in the form of reformism.[10]

---

8   Netto 2002, pp. 77–101. José Paulo Netto's remarks on the present situation of Lukács's work and the conditions proposed for its return apply very well to Gramsci.

9   On the theme of the permanence of the centrality of work for human sociability under present-day capitalism, see Antunes 1999.

10 It does not follow that the reformist trend of the workers' movement and the reformist intellectuals, especially in Germany, have not provided us with theoretical work of a high cultural standard. See Bertelli 2000.

The theoretical and practical refoundation of communism in the twentieth century, particularly with Lenin and Rosa Luxemburg, began with the recovery of Marx's materialist dialectics, the critique of capitalist imperialism, the role of the peasantry in the revolutionary process and the rupture with reformism. Even if there were disagreements – on imperialism, the party-form and workers' consciousness, reformism, the issue of land reform, nationalities, and the theoretical and organic scission – the fact remains that both these authors agreed on the actuality of the international socialist revolution, an element that essentially defines this aspect of Marxism and the workers' movement.

Gramsci (just like Lukács) belongs to the second stage of communist refoundation, distinguished by the defeat of the international socialist revolution, the beginning of socialist transition in the USSR – which faced a situation of backwardness and isolation – and confrontation with the assault of capital in the guise of fascism. This stage was marked by the vicissitudes of the theoretical and organic scission with reformism and by the political formula of the united front. The question of the particularisation of hegemony is posed precisely within this situation, when the national question becomes decisive for the strategy of international socialist revolution. The space of communist refoundation coincides with the space of the emergence of the international socialist revolution between 1917 and 1921, that is, within the territory of the Russian, German and Austro-Hungarian empires, as well as the Kingdom of Italy.[11]

The attempt to place Gramsci within the historical and cultural context indicated by the outlines of such a theoretical and practical movement, referred to in this text as communist refoundation, can help us escape from a false dilemma that has long been a part of the discussion between a 'Leninist' Gramsci and an 'indigenous' one, a supposed follower of the best democratic traditions of Italy and the liberal West. To understand the context of the refoundation and the multiplicity of sources dialectically used for a radical critique of the real, without any one-sidedness, is the best way of understanding Gramsci's place within this socio-historical context.

The following text will attempt to hold on to two related aspects of interpretation and exposition, the concrete-historical, and the theoretico-political, thus establishing the link between Gramsci's theoretico-practical work and the socio-historical context of the refoundation of communism. Once the link between the theoretical interpretation and the movement of the real has been established, we will attempt to read Gramsci through his own perspective and writings, without asking him to hold values and concepts which have little

---

11   Del Roio 1998.

to do with him. Neither do we intend to interpret Gramsci simply through the authors who influenced him and by his own readings. The emphasis in this study will be on the subjectivities active within well-determined concrete conditions, so that we may hope to contribute a few words on what was an important moment in the history of socialist political science. We must bear in mind, nonetheless, that emphasising subjectivity means privileging a part of the material world built by man, and not to commit the error of taking politicism or culturalism as our method.[12]

Our explicit goal is to show Gramsci's place within the context of the communist refoundation of the twentieth century, and this requires locating the foundations of his politico-cultural formation: the historical circumstances, the authors and the trends that had the greatest impact in his formation. We must bear in mind also that other possible influences may have been left aside, here, since we are dealing with a cultural environment – with its points of contact and conflicts – rather than with the determination of an intellectual and cultural genealogy. It is difficult and even undesirable clearly to distinguish between his 'national' and 'European' influences, considering the peculiar cosmopolitan tradition of Italian intellectual life and the internationalist perspective that fed the trend of communist refoundation.

Thus Benedetto Croce, according to Gramsci's reading, is an intellectual who links cosmopolitanism and the national terrain, following certain class interests. Sorel is a Normand French intellectual with a strong presence in Italy. Italy did not exist as a state in the times of important classical political scientists such as Machiavelli and Vico, but their thought and influence on the European context came from a particular 'national' standpoint. Labriola, in turn, was an author better-known among small socialist groups scattered through Europe, which would later contribute to the refoundation of communism, than among his own Italian peers. Similarly, there are strong indications that Gramsci's involvement with the trend of communist refoundation, while supported by his original stance against positivism and reformism, had its origins in the rebellious and revolutionary culture of Germany, particularly Rosa Luxemburg and Karl Korsch.

The actual meeting with Lenin and Bolshevism, which began in 1923, was decisive for Gramsci's passage to a superior theoretico-political synthesis of his own thought, something he needed in order to leave a subordinate situation

---

12   These methodological observations are suggested by Gramsci himself, and have been used
      by Losurdo 1997a, pp. 128–34; Baratta 2000, pp. 223–9; but also by Haupt 1978, pp. 3–37 and
      Agosti on Hobsbawm 1980, vol. 1, pp. 379–80.

inside the PCd'I, then led by Amadeo Bordiga, and, at the same time, to consider a strategy of revolutionary struggle for the specific Italian situation that was also relevant on the international scale. It was through this movement of thought that Gramsci joined the trend of communist refoundation, becoming precisely the most important element of its theoretico-practical deepening and development.

From Lenin comes the concern with translating the specificity of the Russian Revolution into the specificity of the Italian Revolution, in a strange dialectical movement that goes from the universal to various different particulars. Hence the need to develop the revolutionary party of the working class and to envisage the alliance between workers and peasants. Gramsci's path, though, leads to Marx by a paradox. This path was made easier because, in his theoretical conceptions, the factory and the world of workers remained central in theory and in practice, something he took from Sorel, Korsch and Luxemburg. Thus the path to Marx is paved with the permanent nexus between the process of factory production and working-class politics with the perspective of the socialist revolution.

The guiding thread that allows Gramsci to reach a new theoretical synthesis, pointing to higher levels, is the political formula of the united front. Even though the question had presented itself already in the Russian Revolution of 1905, it was in the beginning of 1921 that this political formula became central to the theoretical debates of the Communist International. What we will try to show here is precisely that Gramsci, while using this formula to reach a new theoretical synthesis of his own thought, was also its most effective exponent, in the very moment when the Comintern was going through a phase of theoretical regression.

The question presented to the trends of the left by the political formula of the united front, and particularly those trends informed by the historical experience of the socialist revolution in Russia, stretched throughout the whole of the twentieth century, in the most varied situations. Thus the discussion we propose here retains its theoretical and political relevance to the extent that the tasks indicated for the united front, that is, the unification of workers and the establishment of their hegemony over social life as a whole, are still unfinished, pointing in fact to a greater complexity and a greater number of theoretical and practical difficulties.[13]

---

13   Perry Anderson is among the authors who highlighted the continuity between the late
      Lenin and Gramsci in the *Prison Notebooks*, brought together by the concept of the united
      front. Thus one of the goals of the present study is precisely to observe how this continuity
      was created. See Anderson 1976, pp. 7–74.

The emphasis of this study, just like that of the author in question, it is worth repeating, will be laid on the political praxis, the peculiarities and the subjectivities present in certain concrete situations. The period in question starts in 1919, when the questions of the scission in socialist ranks and of the revolution had become more intense in Italy, with the experience of the factory councils and *L'Ordine Nuovo*, and lasts until Gramsci's arrest at the end of 1926, when the issue of communist refoundation and particularly that of the united front had become relatively mature for the leadership that was now taking shape.

In order to follow this trajectory, it is necessary to locate the origins and the dynamics of the problem of the cleavage affecting the theoretical trend of the communist refoundation within the context of the international socialist revolution, the defeat of which gave birth to the political formula of the united front. The Third Congress of the Comintern proved an important beacon for the examination of this problem, as the Congress promoted the meeting of the different peculiarities of Russia and Germany, the axis generating the political formula in question.

In connection with this problem, we discuss the politico-cultural foundations of Gramsci's thought, as well as its focus on the communist scission, consummated with the foundation of the PCd'I. After that, we discuss the problem of the extreme complexity of the consolidation of the communist scission in Italy, between a dispute with the leadership of the Communist International and the theoretical and practical challenge of facing fascism's offensive.

Stuck between the needs to defend party unity in order to face off fascism and to preserve the international link, without having the party move to the right or seeing a recursion of the scission, Gramsci saw in the political formula of the united front not only a remedy to a difficult problem, but also the possibility of a great theoretical leap towards the simultaneous consolidation of the scission and a confrontation with fascism.

The additional difficulty, something which could hardly have been fully understood at that precise moment, was exactly the theoretical regression of Bolshevism and the dispersion of the German Spartacists. However, as this phenomenon was taking place, Gramsci decisively entered into the trend of communist refoundation, looking for a new theoretical synthesis – drawing mainly from Lenin, but also from Trotsky and Bukharin. He applied himself to envisaging a new revolutionary party that would point towards a synthesis between Luxemburg's and Lenin's previous formulations, which had also been born from experience. Amidst the anti-fascist struggle, Gramsci developed a new conception, theoretically superior to those common in the Comintern, and applied himself to the formation of a new revolutionary leadership.

The theses of the Third Congress of the PCd'I suggested that the leadership had matured significantly in the way they perceived the national peculiarity of the alliance of workers and peasants. However, the ominous effects of the scission among the Bolshevik leadership, as well as the consolidation of fascism in Italy, created new divisions and difficulties, before which the intellectual and political abilities of Gramsci and the Communist leadership proved insufficient.

Prison and the *Prison Notebooks* led Gramsci to a new, particular stage, in which the relative autonomy of the theoretician must prevail. Detained by fascism and sentenced to a slow decay, Gramsci created a work of resistance and anti-fascist, anti-capitalist confrontation that intended to materialise his conviction 'that it is necessary to do something "für ewig", this last being a complicated and difficult concept of Goethe', as he wrote in a letter to his sister-in-law Tatiana Schucht. In that same letter, Gramsci announced his first outline for what would become the *Prison Notebooks*, announcing his intentions to study the public spirit of Italian intellectuals in the nineteenth century, the theme of comparative linguistics, Pirandello's theatre as an example of a change in audience taste, the feuilleton and popular literary taste. Gramsci thus went back to the concerns of his youth in the Facoltà di Lettere and his permanent work as a close follower and instigator of 'the creative spirit of the people'.[14]

In the *Prison Notebooks*, Gramsci deepened and developed the political formula of the united front as a strategy for the construction of hegemony and the transition to socialism from the analysis of particular situations within the context of world history, like a ray of light falling on a group of prisms. But the very theoretico-political content of this political formula is itself a struggle for hegemony, a conflict among different, moving subjectivities, which retains its political and historical relevance.[15]

The research behind this book was partially financed by FAPESP – Fundação de Amparo a Pesquisa do Estado de São Paulo [Foundation for the Support for Research of the State of São Paulo], which supported me during my stay in Italy in the second half of 1999 and also provided the indispensable help for the publication of the end result. I thank Enrica Collotti-Pischel for her welcome in the Facoltà di Scienze Politiche dell'Università degli Studi di Milano. I also wish to express my sincere thanks to Donatella De Benedetto, Giorgio Baratta and Guido Liguori, who, almost without being aware of it, have greatly contributed

---

14   Gramsci 1996a, pp. 54–7.
15   Baratta 2000, pp. 237–46.

to this work. Of great significance were the intellectual stimuli provided by Aldo Agosti and Domenico Losurdo, especially in their fruitful visits to UNESP. I also express my gratitude to Anna Maria Martinez Correa, José Antonio Segatto, Osvaldo Coggiola, Ricardo Antunes and Tullo Vigevani, the first to read and to comment on this work as public examiners for the habilitation in Political Theory at the Faculdade de Filosofia e Ciências da Universidade Estadual Paulista (Marília campus). Finally, I thank my peers at the Instituto Astrojildo Pereira and the research group 'Cultura e Política do Mundo do Trabalho' [Culture and Politics of the World of Labour], particularly my students, who provided me with an indispensable intellectual environment. The occasional virtues of this work must be shared with all of them, while the weaknesses must naturally be ascribed to the undersigned.

CHAPTER 1

War, Revolution and the Communist Scission in Gramsci

1   Communist Scission and Communist Refoundation in Lenin and Rosa Luxemburg

In the first months of 1920, Lenin had already realised that the international socialist revolution was losing momentum and the urge for the dissemination of the socialist revolution affirmed in 1919 – the year of the foundation of the Communist International – should be replaced by emphasis on the need to preserve the Russian origins of the revolutionary process and the enlistment of the Western working class through the establishment of communist mass parties. In the short work *Left-Wing Communism, an Infantile Disorder*, written in April and May of 1920, Lenin explains that the application of fundamental principles of the socialist revolution, the dictatorship of the proletariat and soviet power 'demands not the elimination of variety or the suppression of national distinctions', because 'to seek out, investigate, predict, and grasp that which is nationally specific and nationally distinctive, in the concrete manner in which each country should tackle a single international task' would be the communists' task.

'Of course, there can be no question of placing conditions in Russia on a par with conditions in Western Europe', wrote Lenin, already seeking the aforementioned national distinctions and trying to point out a few fundamental differences between the Russian East and the West. Lenin admits that 'it was easy for Russia, in the specific and historically unique situation of 1917, to start the socialist revolution, but it will be more difficult for Russia than for the European countries to continue the revolution and bring it to its consummation'.

Lenin remarks that the issue of the scission had been fundamentally solved by the Bolsheviks when they began their fight against Menshevik reformism and the petit-bourgeois 'leftism' of the anarchists and Social Revolutionaries. Even the 'leftist' outbursts inside the Bolshevik party were met with a firm hand, says Lenin, particularly because the party's steely discipline had been tempered by clandestine struggle.[1]

---

1   Lenin apparently underestimated the strength 'left-wing communism' had even in the Russia of the soviets, where theoretical conceptions influenced the economic-political orientation in the period where forces were gathered to defend the revolution.

In the West, the communist refoundation took a long time to begin tackling the issue of the scission, after the imperialist war was underway, so the complexity of the problem in this case was far greater. Besides the necessary hurry to solve the dilemma, one must take into account the difficulty of facing a deep-rooted reformism in the unions and workers' parties used to parliamentary disputes and lacking a clandestine structure. Communist participation in unions and parliament as a revolutionary minority was thus indispensable for the consummation of the scission with reformism and with 'leftism', so that the working class and the proletarian masses would be able to identify with the party.

Considering the posture of reformism regarding the imperialist war and its influence on the masses, Lenin believed that the scission with this trend should come before, in time as well as in importance, the scission with 'leftism', even though the historico-political moment may require compromises with them.[2] Yet, while Lenin decidedly fought the 'leftism' that was part of German communism, the need to hasten an already late scission led him critically to support the 'leftism' of Italian socialism.

Germany already had a communist party, which stood a great chance of absorbing a significant share of the USPD, the Independent Social Democratic Party of Germany, and thus becoming a mass party at a time when the 'leftist' communist tendency was to break the existing party. Lenin's attitude was to support the merging of the KPD, the Communist Party of Germany, with the left wing of the USPD, broadening communist influence and enlarging the gap with the reformists, so that the 'leftists' would be isolated.

In Italy, the scission was not yet consummated and there was a tangible possibility that it would draw most of the PSI (the Italian Socialist Party) to the Comintern. For Lenin, this meant supporting the fraction that most strongly supported splitting with the reformists and joining the Comintern, that is, Amadeo Bordiga's 'leftist' trend, which had been somewhat organised since the end of 1918. Italian socialism or maximalism, the majority trend, made statements favouring the Russian Revolution and the Comintern, but it also defended the unity of the PSI, and this included keeping the reformists within the party.

The small, relatively obscure *L'Ordine Nuovo* group, while it aligned itself with the maximalists in the internal disputes of the PSI, tended to identify itself with revolutionary syndicalism and 'spontaneism', not only because of the

---

2 Lenin mentions the example of the commitment to the agricultural programme of the Russian Revolution, when the Bolsheviks supported the Social Revolutionaries' proposal, but he is not as explicit as regards giving support to 'leftism' against reformism in Italy.

enthusiasm it aroused in Georges Sorel in France, but also because the experience of workers' self-government in Turin referred to the forms of organisation of the IWW – Industrial Workers of the World – the shop-stewards in England and the USA, and the Russian and German councils.[3]

Even though Lenin considered 'leftism' absent from Russia, he highlights firm points in the theory of socialist transition and proletarian dictatorship that run counter to some Bolsheviks' possible expectations that the transition should be an accelerated process, and also anticipates the political formulation that would lead to the New Economic Policy (NEP) about a year later.[4] Lenin argues that the dictatorship of the proletariat constitutes a relentless struggle against the bourgeoisie, a stronger enemy with international ties, whose power, however, also lies 'in the force of habit, in the strength of small-scale production', which 'engenders capitalism and the bourgeoisie continuously'.

During the transitional period, 'the abolition of classes means not merely ousting the landowners and the capitalists – that is something we accomplished with comparative ease; it also means abolishing the small commodity producers, and they cannot be ousted, or crushed; we must learn to live with them. They can (and must) be transformed and re-educated only by means of very prolonged, slow, and cautious organisational work'. Or, in short, 'the dictatorship of the proletariat means a persistent struggle – bloody and bloodless, violent and peaceful, military and economic, educational and administrative – against the forces and traditions of the old society. The force of habit in millions and tens of millions is a most formidable force'.

---

3 Fiori 1995, pp. 143–4.

4 As the beginning of war took part of the Bolsheviks to exile in Switzerland, the 'left-wing communism' of the 'group of Baugy', formed by Bukharin, Radek, Piatakov and others, came into being. They believed the socialist revolution had actually happened in Russia, that the war should be transformed into a war of revolutionary offensive and that any socio-economic measures should be immediately socialist. Lenin belonged to the party's 'centre' and agreed with the understanding that the revolution was actually socialist, but he also thought revolutionary Russia should retreat from the war, using this argument to appease the 'left' when the Treaty of Brest-Litovsk was signed. The situation of emergency that arose from civil war and imperialist intervention gave more weight to the opinion of the 'left' regarding the measures taken. In 1921, when the NEP began, Lenin's position regarding socialist transition once again prevailed, if only for some time, as his death led to a new dispute. It must be highlighted that important characters in this historical plot, which only reached its conclusion in 1929, changed positions more than once. Left-wing communism in Russia has a few similarities with Western left-wing communism, but they must not be confused. See Hájek 1975, pp. 359–75.

Many economic and legal institutions engendered in the age of the bourgeoisie are preserved during the first steps of the socialist transition, particularly because 'after the first socialist revolution of the proletariat, and the overthrow of the bourgeoisie in some country, the proletariat of that country remains for a long time weaker than the bourgeoisie', owing not just to the bourgeoisie's international ties, but also to its ability to rise again out of small mercantile production, with which it is nevertheless necessary to compromise in the first stages of socialist transition.

Thus at the same time Lenin insists on a theoretico-political scission as a foundation for the communist movement, contributing to division amongst the socio-political forces of the working class, he also strongly argues for the need to ally with the small mercantile producers. Such an alliance made victory possible for the revolution in Russia, but also necessarily led to the NEP, disregarding the commitment to 'left-wing' communism made during the confrontation with imperialism and its Russian allies.

These observations by Lenin were relevant to the greater part of Western communism, and at least provided a partial explanation for the defeat of the socialist revolution. When Hungary, for instance, witnessed the establishment of a council republic, Hungarian communists did not give the issue of the scission due consideration, and so agreed to merge with the social democrats, and did not become aware of the need to associate with the small agricultural mercantile producers, thus losing the support of the peasantry, which allied itself to the victorious feudal-bourgeois counter-revolution. 'Leftism' in Austria led the communists to political isolation, and had already brought the defeat of the German Revolution. This is how the prevailing of 'leftism' contributed to the defeat of the international socialist revolution within the very space of communist refoundation.[5]

---

5 Left-wing communism may be seen as a diverse political trend placed between the communist refoundation (which consisted of Bolshevism and Spartakism) and revolutionary unionism. It generally defended the existence of a vanguard party followed by the masses at the moment of revolutionary outbreak, organisation by councils or revolutionary unions, and a radical critique of bourgeois parliamentarianism, while believing that revolution in the West would take longer and be more difficult to accomplish because of its peculiarity. Its greatest theoreticians were Anton Pannekoek, Hermann Gorter and Gyorgy Lukács. The first two left the communist movement and Lukács joined the trend here called communist refoundation. The name of Karl Korsch must be remembered as well. He began as a member of the USPD and gradually moved to the left of the communist movement, until he was expelled from the KPD in 1927. Left-wing communism in the 1920s was more distinctively practical, lacking sophisticated theoreticians.

The person who best understood Germany's singularity within the context of the international socialist revolution was Rosa Luxemburg. As early as 1905, it was obvious to her that there was a close link between the revolutionary processes in Germany and Russia (as well as Poland), as the political revolutionary subject was identical in both countries, where the proletariat was immediately opposed to the bourgeois order, even if the Russian Revolution had been formally bourgeois in its nature.[6]

Luxemburg's theoretical perspective ascribed great importance to the theme of the self-activity of the masses and the creation of their self-government, so that she saw the critical consciousness and the revolutionary party itself as a product of this activity and not as an ever-necessary instrument to centralise and coordinate the struggle of the working class. For Luxemburg, social-democratic political action 'arises historically from basic class struggle' and 'social democracy is not actually connected to the organisation of the working class, even though it is the working class's specific movement'.[7]

The outbreak of war in 1914 was also characterised as imperialist by Rosa Luxemburg, a product of the contradictions among the great powers in their fight for the world market. Against the military barbarity proposed by imperialism stood the weight of the international socialist revolution, but the Socialist International largely decided to accept the thesis of the European bourgeoisies that the war was about 'national defence'.

---

6 Luxemburg 1976, pp. 348–9.

7 Luxemburg 1976, pp. 212–13. The terms of the dispute about the origins of the politico-revolutionary consciousness of the working class are very well known, even if too often simplified. The dispute happened in the early twentieth century, when Lenin (in a sense following in the footsteps of Kautsky) understood that the mere opposition between capital and labour in the productive process would limit the consciousness of the working class to a corporate-unionist dimension. Only the dimension of the contradictory social and state totality, with its resulting contact with other social strata, establishing alliances and defining political goals, could feed the revolutionary consciousness. Thus we find in Lenin an overestimation of the sphere of state politics and also the role of revolutionary intellectuals as bearers of the consciousness of the historical interests of the working class, with a possible inclination towards idealism. See on this Gerratana 1981, pp. 163–92, and, more recently, Mordenti 2003, pp. 193–205. Rosa herself understood revolutionary political consciousness as already present, even if in rudimentary form, at the core of capitalist contradiction, and believed the accumulation of struggles would increase critical consciousness and the organisation of the working class, which would have the socialist movement and revolutionary Marxism as an internal, constituting element, and not something external to the very social relations of production of capital. It is necessary to consider the subsequent converging distortions, coming from both Lenin and Luxemburg, but we shall see how Gramsci seeks to overcome the antinomy present in the dispute.

The explanation for this political attitude can be found in the predomin-ance of reformism within social democracy, a reformism that originated in the gap between the everyday life of the masses under the order of capital and the historical goal of socialist fulfilment. The material gains and the organisational strengthening of the workers' movement within bourgeois institutions encour-aged the union bureaucracy to superimpose itself over the workers' party, and the cleavage between economic and political struggle, in full agreement with the sociability engendered around the accumulation of capital. In contrast, only a mass struggle enveloped in socialist theory is able to synthesise these dimensions and set a revolutionary process in motion.

While the defeat of the Socialist International led Lenin to urge the founda-tion of a new International, Luxemburg expected its recreation from within the very process of self-criticism and revolutionary struggle against the war. Before being arrested for denouncing the war, Luxemburg helped establish the small group that became known as The International, owing to a publication with the same name that lasted for only one issue. This edition, published in Febru-ary 1915, included an article by Luxemburg, urging the reestablishment of the International on revolutionary foundations. Following this, she was soon taken to prison, where she wrote *The Crisis of German Social Democracy*, an essay that became known as the 'Junius Pamphlet' because of the pseudonym she used. It was published one year later, in 1916, and it urged the creation of a 'new Interna-tional', a phrase that contains some ambiguity, as it discusses neither the form nor the timing of the construction of this new entity.

The 'Junius Pamphlet' recounts the whole struggle of the Second Interna-tional against the risks of imperialist war until the unmistakable capitulation of August 1914, following the escalation of conflicts in world politics. It shows how German social democracy claimed to enthusiastically support the German war against Russian Tsarism in the name of a Western civilisation threatened by Eastern barbarity, and that this is consistent with the position of Marx and Engels, who saw the Russian régime as the stronghold of European feudal reac-tion. Luxemburg, however, believed the situation to have been inverted since the end of the nineteenth century and particularly after the Russian Revolution of 1905, when 'Russian support against the German revolution was replaced by German support against the Russian revolution'[8] and when 'it is the European reaction, the Prussian-feudal reaction first and foremost, that now constitutes the stronghold of Russian absolutism'.[9]

---

8   Luxemburg 1976, p. 497.
9   Luxemburg 1976, p. 498.

Even though the social-democratic majority decided to halt class struggle in the name of 'national defence', hoping later to resume exactly where it had left off, Rosa Luxemburg insisted that 'in the present war, a class-conscious proletariat cannot identify its cause with either belligerent side',[10] considering that the real question was 'the proletarian masses' ability to fight in the struggle against imperialism'.[11] With the purpose of establishing guidelines for the action of The International group, which soon would become the Spartacus League, Rosa Luxemburg added a postscript to her pamphlet explaining a few principles, arguing for instance that the Second International's support for the war led to its collapse, recognising the ruling classes had become stronger and assuming the thesis of the impossibility of national wars in the age of imperialism. The struggles for peace, for the international proletarian revolution and against imperialism are thus fused into a single action.

The main tool of action would be the creation of a 'new International for the workers, one that guides and unites revolutionary class struggles against imperialism in every country'.[12] Such a new International should be centralised and have authority over the policies of its national sections, but the immediate task would be 'the spiritual emancipation of the proletariat from the rule of the bourgeoisie, as expressed by the influx of nationalist ideology', since 'the proletariat's fatherland is the Socialist International, everything else must be subordinated to its defence'.[13]

Lenin refutes or points out the insufficiencies of some of the theses proposed by Rosa Luxemburg, beginning with the statement that a national war in the age of imperialism would be impossible. Such a war could happen (and, indeed, it did) in the wars of liberation of the peoples subjected to imperialism, in the collapse of European empires (Austria-Hungary and Russia) or even in the case of a greater country subjugated as the result of a war in progress. Lenin also disagreed about the possibility of a war of national defence different from a war that defended a socialist state subject to imperialist harassment, as Luxemburg believed an advanced democratic republic deserved to be defended.

Concretely, however, the nodal point separating two of the most important theoreticians of the communist refoundation at this moment was the issue of the scission. Whether Rosa Luxemburg intended to avoid disagreements with the political group to which she belonged or had a peculiar reading of the German situation, the fact remains that she made no explicit reference to the

---

10   Luxemburg 1976, p. 540.
11   Luxemburg 1976, p. 541.
12   Luxemburg 1976, p. 550.
13   Luxemburg 1976, p. 551.

need to split with reformism and with the leadership that took the workers' party to that situation. According to Lenin's critique, she thus concealed the link between 'social-chauvinism' and 'opportunism', the nationalist stance of social democracy and reformism. For Lenin, 'this is wrong from the standpoint of theory, for it is impossible to explain the "betrayal" without linking it up with opportunism as a trend with a long history, the history of the whole Second International'. Lenin still remarks that this stance may have been a step backward with regard to the article of Otto Rühle, the future 'leftist' leader of the KPD who held the division of the SPD to be inevitable.[14]

The reason for the disagreements between Lenin and Rosa Luxemburg can perhaps be found in the specificity of the countries in which their respective revolutionary activities were focused, going beyond strictly theoretical questions. Maintaining the impossibility of national wars or the presence of national bourgeoisies among subjugated peoples arose from a certain understanding of imperialism, which by then would have already globalised the accumulation of capital, amidst deep social and military tensions. For Luxemburg, 'Imperialism is the political expression of the accumulation of capital in its competitive struggle for what remains still open of the non-capitalist environment'.[15]

For the first time, the preponderance of reformism within the workers' socialist movement was seen by Luxemburg as the result of a conflict inherent to a class living within the bourgeois order at the same time that it aimed at building a new order, and thus what we have is a basically politico-ideological phenomenon. Lenin, instead, saw reformism as the result of a social scission within the working class, giving birth to a specific ideology of the 'labour aristocracy'. Such a scission led to the neglect of the interests of the proletarian masses and had as its counterpart differentiation within the bourgeoisie, which created the financial imperialist oligarchy.

From this analytical disagreement arose a disagreement in political tactics, especially concerning the policy of alliances. To Luxemburg, the unity of the working class was a vital element for the victory of the revolutionary process, and to her the fight against reformism should happen within a united socialist movement, which included the alliance with the agricultural proletariat as well. Thus the alliance with reformist sectors was more important than the

---

14   At this point, Lenin was closer to the 'internationalist communist' group, of which Otto
      Rühle was part, than Rosa Luxemburg's International (and therefore the Spartacists),
      owing precisely to the *scission*.

15   Luxemburg 2003, p. 426.

alliance with the peasantry, because in Germany (and in Central and Eastern Europe generally) this social stratum, unlike its Russian counterpart, was strongly connected to the notion of private property, and was only weakly politicised. It is known that, for Lenin, the alliance with the peasantry was essential for the victory of the revolution, while the 'labour aristocracy' with its union and party leaders should be regarded even as enemies of the proletariat.

For Luxemburg, the revolutionary party is the product of a theory that includes the workers' movement, unifying its everyday struggle against capital with its historical goal of realising socialism, and so the politico-ideological fight against reformism is at one with the mobilisation of the masses and the construction of the party. Given the complexity of the German social form, the timing of the revolution would be slower than that of the Russian East, and would go through many transitional phases and more differentiated stages. So we understand Luxemburg's resistance to the theme of the *scission*. For Lenin, on the other hand, the scission, understood in all its socio-political and organic-ideological complexity, was essential to the communist refoundation, such that 'a very great defect in revolutionary Marxism in Germany as a whole is its lack of a compact illegal organisation that would systematically pursue its line and educate the masses in the spirit of the new tasks; such an organisation would also have to take a definite stand towards opportunism and Kautskyism'.

It is well-known that upon leaving prison at the end of 1918, when the war had finished and the German Revolution was in progress, Rosa Luxemburg acquiesced as she realised that the scission and the foundation of a communist party were inevitable. However, contrasting with her 'leftist' companions, such as Otto Rühle, she continued to insist that the pace of the international socialist revolution in Germany should be dictated by the need to conquer the majority of the working class and to create a new party, and it would be difficult to establish a deadline for that.

Factory councils and workers' and soldiers' councils should shape the strategy for the anti-capitalist struggle and serve as the basis upon which a new direction for social life would be organised. Mass strikes, besides highlighting the centrality of the factory, would be the proletariat's immediate means of fighting the bosses, the fundamental moment of the revolution, the outer form of the struggle for socialism, since

> the struggle for socialism can only be accomplished by the masses, in a physical confrontation with capitalism, in every company, setting every worker against their boss. This is the only way to have a socialist revolu-

tion. ... Socialism must be made by the masses, by every proletarian. Where they are tied to the chain of capital, the chain of capital must be broken.[16]

The ongoing revolution's immediate task would be to 'extend the system of workers' and soldiers' councils, but also to include agricultural workers and small peasants in this system', so that they would be mobilised against the landowning peasants, the likely mass basis of the counter-revolution. The role of the workers' councils, as an institution of revolutionary power, would be 'to undermine the foundations of the bourgeois state, no longer separating but rather uniting the public legislative and administrative powers and handing them to workers and soldiers'. The revolution would take place through the dissemination and continuous strengthening of the councils and their ability to take on production and administration roles, so that 'the conquest of power would not happen at once, but gradually, by driving a wedge into the bourgeois State until all positions are taken and controlled', before reaching the point of 'the workers' councils possessing all State power'.[17]

In Rosa Luxemburg's revolutionary strategy, therefore, the workers' and soldiers' councils would gradually extend until they formed an anti-state that would absorb the roles of managing the production process and public affairs. In a process of more or less extensive duration, it would be possible to observe the emptying-out of the bourgeois state, as well as of the social-reformist union and party: institutions created by the working class but absorbed by capitalist rule. Luxemburg realised that in the course of the revolutionary process in Germany, to a certain extent 'the issue of the struggle for emancipation is identical with the fight against unions', because 'official unions have proved to be an organisation of the bourgeois State and the capitalist ruling class' and should be replaced by 'the workers' and soldiers' councils as bearers of all political and economic needs and organs of power of the working class'. According to this view, the taking of state power would be nothing but the final act of the revolutionary process.

However, the political defeat of Rosa Luxemburg by the views of 'leftism' in the very moment of the foundation of the KPD, views which predicted imminent mass insurrection and seizing power, led to the initial defeat of the German Revolution and to her own assassination. Resistance to the scission was also to be seen in the justification for the abstention of the German delegation in

---

16   Luxemburg 1976, p. 622.

17   Luxemburg 1976, p. 629.

the foundation congress of the Communist International, which took place in March 1919 and was dedicated precisely to the memory of Rosa Luxemburg and Karl Liebknecht, executed in January of the same year. The German MP Eberlein argued that the new International should begin after at least a few communist parties had been consolidated among the masses in some of the more important imperialist countries. In other words, there remained not only resistance to the scission, but also the view that it should happen only under the influx of the mass movement itself.

Rosa Luxemburg's significant political intervention in the foundation congress of the KPD, with its rich theoretical and practical implications, was resumed in a certain way a few months later by the experience of the factory councils in Northern Italy, when Antonio Gramsci and the *L'Ordine Nuovo* group played out the last scene of the international socialist revolution based on the workers' councils. Rosa Luxemburg also presents us with indispensable elements for the understanding that Gramsci would later bring to the political formula of the united front and for a long-term revolutionary strategy.

2   Liberalism, Revisionism and the Problem of the Scission (or Cleavage) in Gramsci

It is easy to observe a few similarities between Rosa Luxemburg, the most important character in the communist refoundation of the twentieth century in Central-Eastern Europe, and the stances and attitudes of Antonio Gramsci, such as their opposition to reformism and to institutionalism, and faith in self-activity and in the capacity of the working class for self-government, the significance of the factory in the struggle against capital, the emphasis on autonomy and independence regarding capital, as well as resistance against the organic scission of the workers' party. Rosa Luxemburg's and the Spartacists' formulations in defence of the workers' councils [*Arbeiter Rät*] as means to control production and seeds of a new social order had a great impact on Gramsci's reflections, and so did the whole debate, diverse as it was, about the councils.[18] Concerning the issue of the scission, the greatest theoretician of the second stage of the communist refoundation was defeated by the 'leftist' trend of the Italian revolutionary movement, which had Amadeo Bordiga as one of its noteworthy leaders.[19]

---

18   Spriano 1971, p. 59 ff.

19   Later, when Gramsci overcame his momentary alliance with Bordiga and began to formulate a theory of the revolutionary political party, the echoes of the organisational conception of Rosa Luxemburg continued to be felt, even if not explicitly, because after

The influence of Rosa Luxemburg on György Lukács's conversion to communism is more widely known, even though his initial views, just like Gramsci's, were in tune with the 'leftism' so common in Western Europe. So it does not seem absurd to suggest that Gramsci, just like Lukács, may have been significantly influenced by the theoretico-political ideas of that great revolutionary activist, right after her death, at the very moment in which he pondered his own path, in the face of the Russian Revolution.[20]

Surely the theoretical elaborations of the Spartacists, as well as the Hungarian experience, had an influence on the Italian factory councils movement, especially insofar as it was inspired by the initiative and self-determination of the masses, in its opposition to measures born out of the consensus between the state and union bureaucracy, and the importance given to the control of production as the core of the struggle against capital. The Spartacist position, however, was in the minority in the debate on the councils and their role in the state in Germany and Austria. The social-democratic position prevailed, seeing the councils as supplementary organs of the economic mechanism.

---

the 'German October' (1923) and the Fifth Congress of the Comintern (1924) the Polish revolutionary's name was eclipsed by the theoretical regression experienced by communist organisations.

20   After the Hungarian revolution's defeat, Lukács established himself in Vienna, dedicating himself to *Kommunismus*, the weekly paper of the Communist International, which discussed issues concerning Central Europe and the Balkans. Lukács's leftism had its core in a refusal of compromises and mediations that implied ethical concessions. It can be seen that his leftism underwent an inflexion already in the last essays comprised in *History and Class Consciousness*, written in 1922 and published the following year. The defeat in the KPU's internal dispute as well as the defeat of the international socialist revolution, which attacked the theoretical basis of leftist communism, put Lukács in a slow path towards Lenin's conceptions and the united front policy. Dividing himself between Vienna and Berlin and joining the trend of communist refoundation between the end of 1923 and 1924, Lukács, just like Gramsci, found himself amidst the theoretical regression that affected the movement after 1924. Landler's and Lukács's position within the KPU, first arguing for communist participation in social-democratic unions and later contributing to the formation of a left social-democratic party, show how the united front, in his view, should be engendered under the name of the 'democratic republic' instead of 'proletarian dictatorship'. Lukács became one of the most fruitful theoreticians of the political formula of the united front in his 'Theses on the political situation in Hungary and the tasks of the KPU' of 1928–9. In his study of the *Young Hegel and the Problems of Capitalist Society*, concluded in 1938 in the USSR, Lukács presents the foundations of the political formula of the 'democratic dictatorship', as a moment in the subaltern classes' struggle for power and defending Hegel as a possible emancipatory horizon within the bourgeois order, in contrast with the feudal world. See Konder 1980.

Gramsci's view on the centrality of the factory and the scission regarding the political state of capital was shared by Karl Korsch, whose ideas were influenced by revolutionary syndicalism. Gramsci, however, already believed that it was out of the productive process that a new policy would be born, a policy that would be revolutionary and proletarian, that should be socialised with the purpose of undermining the private order of capital and generating a new order and a workers' state.[21]

It is unquestionable that the configuration of Gramsci's world view, besides having received the impact of his social and cultural background, especially Salvemini's meridionalism, was a product of apparently diverging influences. Gramsci's whole trajectory, from its very beginning, collided with neo-Kantian or positivist high bourgeois culture, which exerted its hegemony over the workers' and socialist movement, and with the anti-modern Catholic ecclesiastic tradition.

Gramsci started with the problems posed by the 'crisis of Marxism' at the turn of the twentieth century and the 'revisionist' attempts that recovered analytically as well as politically the scission – typical of the liberal-bourgeois world – between the economic and the political and between public and private. Having discarded Bernstein for his connections with neo-Kantianism and reformism, Gramsci's reference point was the debate on Marx, which involved intellectuals such as Benedetto Croce, Giovanni Gentile and Rodolfo Mandolfo. Benedetto Croce's understanding of Marxism, which went back to Hegel and the problem of subjectivity, was very important. From Croce, he took the view of modernity as the 'religion of freedom' against the attitude of Catholic clergy, and also saw in historicist dialectics an instrument in the struggle against the many forms of positivist naturalism spread throughout Italy, the obstacles to the fulfilment of the bourgeois and modern revolution in that country. Thus Gramsci began as part of the liberal-democratic field, among the followers of the most advanced bourgeois culture of the beginning of the twentieth century.[22]

Gramsci was however directly influenced by the working-class culture of Turin, which objectively placed him in a different and even opposite point of view of social life. Thus Gramsci's long and complex parting with Croce began during the war starting in 1914, already with a new vanishing point, and probably extended up until 1923, when Croce published *Nuova Politica Liberale*,

---

21   On Gramsci's relation with Rosa Luxemburg and mainly with Korsch, see Dubla 1986, pp. 75–81.

22   Losurdo 1997a, pp. 17–34.

a magazine establishing a link between liberalism and fascism. Croce thus acted as a theoretician of the 'passive revolution' configured by the new régime, while Gramsci, who was in contact with Lenin, converged with the trend of communist refoundation.

Not only Croce, but also Giovanni Gentile and Gaetano Salvemini, as well as other champions of liberal culture, tried to see virtues in the great massacre that was now beginning, whereas Gramsci inclined towards an ever stronger opposition against the war. Different understandings of the meaning of the Bolsheviks' rise to power widened the gap between Gramsci and the liberals, even though he remained within the horizons of liberalism and the great French Revolution of the end of the eighteenth century. Disagreements about the meaning of historical materialism contributed to Gramsci's parting more and more with Croce, but the decisive point was their respective stances with regard to the proletarian world.[23]

It was initially through Croce that Gramsci absorbed the views of Georges Sorel.[24] Sorel can also be seen by the Left as a 'revisionist' author, to the extent that he opposed the socialist strategy of gradually taking over the institutional political space – particularly in the liberal parliament – but it was through him that Gramsci was able to see the world of factory work as a reality in itself, separate from the alienated sphere of the world of capital. For Sorel, the rupture established in the modern world between direct producers and owners is maintained by the existence of a political and cultural dimension consolidated by the intellectuals and political agents of the ruling class.

Such a rupture can only cease to exist if the social myth of the general strike becomes widespread, beginning with producers' common sense, fed by practical science, which, in its turn, would be the only way to set the proletariat against state and capital, both preserving and developing the producers' morale. Without losing sight of the relevant differences between Sorel and Luxemburg, Gramsci took from them an appreciation of spontaneity and mass strikes, workers' self-organisation and opposition to any form of state socialism.[25]

Whereas for Rosa Luxemburg the realisation of the political mass strike is indispensable for unleashing the revolutionary process, for Sorel it is irrelevant

---

23   Losurdo 1997a, pp. 35–74. It is also very useful to read Consiglio and Frosini 1997, pp. XXV–LVI.

24   On Gramsci's relation with Sorel, see Badaloni 1975, pp. 30–76; Paggi 1984, pp. 308–19; Gervasoni, 1998, pp. 165–79; Medici 2000, pp. 127–45.

25   The theoretical conception of state socialism was outlined by Robert Owen in England and by Ferdinand Lassalle in Germany. On the eve of the 1914 war, it was once again endorsed by sections of social democracy.

whether a general strike is viable at all. For him, the important thing is that the myth entails, in the form of drama and images, the irreducible conflict against the social order, so that 'the whole issue amounts to knowing whether a general strike contains all that the socialist doctrine expects of the revolutionary proletariat'.[26] The new social order would be managed by the producers' morality, creating a new bloc guided by a novel ethical dimension. A moral reformation feeding and widening the 'spirit of cleavage' is a condition for the masses to fall in love with and spread the social myth of the general strike.

Gramsci starts from Sorel in this critique of Jacobinism, understood as a separation between leaders and followers, implying an ever-present emphasis on the self-education and self-organisation of the masses and a critique of the preponderance of intellectuals, always as a means to preserve the 'spirit of cleavage' of the proletariat with regard to the social order. However, there was always one decisive difference between Sorel and Gramsci, and which served as the basis of Gramsci's political science: the notion that politics permeated the production process, considering that the factory represented a crucial element in the dispute for political and social power – that is to say, for hegemony. Thus 'economics' is and always was 'political'. Hence Gramsci's stance against all the forms of politicism so typical of the Italian socialist tradition, and his insistence that the proletariat should organise itself according to production units, considered 'a normal reflection of the class struggle in the most intensely capitalist countries'.[27]

Even when Gramsci adhered to the organic scission of the workers' and socialist movement, his purpose was to guarantee the 'spirit of cleavage' and the autonomy of the working class from the state and capital. Similarly, his whole thought on the revolutionary political party and the formation of a new stratum of intellectuals maintained this condition, without which there would be a reversal towards politicist reformism. As we know, in the *Prison Notebooks* Gramsci began redefining concepts from Sorel, such as 'common sense', 'moral and intellectual reform' and 'historic bloc', all the while maintaining an original difference in his thought.

Sorel's pessimistic view may also have been among the reasons for Gramsci having been partially affected by the historicist perspective of Machiavelli and Vico, whose works investigated periods of historical decline, whereas positivist evolutionism and neo-Kantianism believe in the indefinite progress of the social life of mankind. The intertwining of Sorel and Machiavelli can be

---

26   Sorel 1998.
27   Gramsci 1999a, p. 142.

observed in the idea which they share of constructing a 'new order'. Gramsci, while preserving and redefining Sorel's 'spirit of cleavage', also draws from Machiavelli the perspective of the foundation of a new state.[28]

And as concerns the accusations of 'revolutionary syndicalism' cast against the factory councils movement, Gramsci recalls with regard to Sorel's work that:

> surely we are far from accepting the whole of it. We do not accept the unionist theory, in the way it was presented by apprentices and appliers, and in the way it perhaps did not even exist in the mind of the master, who nevertheless apparently consented to it at some point. We have no sympathy for those unchecked habits of growing mental laziness that have been introduced in our country on behalf of theoretical socialism.[29]

In Gramsci's thought, there is a clear dissociation between Sorel's work and his flexible mind – in contrast with his so-called followers in Italy – and at the same time there is an implicit acknowledgement of Sorel's influence in his intellectual formation. On Sorel, Gramsci also says that:

> At his best, he seems to preserve in himself something of the virtues of his two masters: Marx's sharp reasoning, and Proudhon's emotional and plebeian eloquence. And he did not enclose himself within any formulas, keeping that which was vital and new in his doctrine, i.e., the affirmation of the requirement that the proletarian motion express itself in its own forms, that it bring its own institutions to life. Today he is able to follow, not only with his eyes replete with intelligence, but also with his fully understanding soul, the accomplishing movement begun by Russian workers and peasants, and he may even call 'companions' those Italian socialists who wish to follow that example.[30]

It is this manner of posing the question that allows Gramsci to invest in an approximation between Sorel and Lenin, in the process of constructing his own understanding of the real, within the context of the international socialist revolution and the experience of the Turin factory councils. Sorel himself saw the experience of the councils as a whole as something close to the theories he had been developing. Later, the persistence of Sorel's influence in Gramsci's

---

28   Medici 2000, pp. 127–45. It is worth noting that in this book Rita Medici argues that Rodolfo Mandolfo was an important influence in Gramsci's theoretical and intellectual formation.

29   Gramsci 1973, pp. 31–2.

30   Ibid.

political science would become manifest in his understanding of the political formula of the united front. Actually, this whole discussion can only be satisfactorily understood if we take into consideration the variety of ideological forces that were attracted by the Revolution in Russia and converged with communism. Only thus can we understand that Gramsci's encounter with Lenin happened through the partial mediation of the differentiated area of leftist Western communism.

Another author who contributed to Gramsci's formation as a theoretician and to the definition of his singularity in the communist refoundation was Antonio Labriola, whose intellectual formation, just like Croce's, had its roots in the Neapolitan Hegelianism of the Spaventa brothers.[31] In the 1890s, an intense exchange of letters between Labriola and Engels brought the former closer to the 'doctrine of critical communism'.[32] As he adhered to historical materialism, Labriola broke not only with the tradition of the Spaventa brothers, but also with their intellectual disciples, who went deeper in their 'revision' of Marx's work. It must be noted that Labriola's encounter with the thought of Engels and Marx happened precisely when the 'crisis of Marxism' and the debate on 'revisionism' exploded, making Labriola a thinker who ran counter to his time.

Separate from the outset from the movement that wished to create the Italian Socialist Party – which was led by a certain type of petit bourgeoisie that he despised, and which had an ideological view engulfed by positivist-stamped reformism – Labriola saw Benedetto Croce and Georges Sorel gradually distance themselves from him. While Croce decided to start over from his Spaventa uncles' Hegelianism in a wholly original way, Sorel began a reflection that associated Marx and Proudhon. Labriola's intellectual and political isolation in Italy was partially compensated by a significant reception of his work among the anti-revisionist current of Europe, particularly in Russia – including Lenin himself.

Through Labriola and his dialogue with Engels on the one hand, and through Bolshevism on the other, Gramsci arrived at Marx and critical communism, re-elaborating the whole production of the 'revisionists' who were involved in the 'crisis of Marxism' at the turn of the century and who had so much contrib-

31   Brothers Bertrando and Silvio Spaventa founded a Philosophy School in Naples in 1846, which began the dissemination in Italy of German idealist philosophy, especially Hegel. The brothers played an important role in Italian public and intellectual life. When Bertrando Spaventa transferred to Turin, he began working for the dissemination of Italian thought throughout Europe. See Losurdo 1997b.

32   Labriola 1977, p. 35.

uted to his own intellectual formation. In his opposition to the 'economism' of Achille Loria, Gramsci, together with Engels and Croce, invoked the name of Labriola as an exponent of dialectical thought.[33]

At this point, it can be observed that, before approaching Lenin's work with greater attention and establishing a new encounter with Marx's work, within a new perspective, Gramsci had absorbed many contributions from the culture of anti-capitalist struggle engendered in the West, especially in France and Germany, and always remained at a distance from reformist and positivist socialism. Besides, his deep insertion in the Italian cultural tradition, with a peculiar cosmopolitan tendency, as well as his origins in the subaltern classes of Italy, both in Sardinia and Piedmont, provided him with the essential elements for exploring the route that would lead to critical communism.[34]

This was how Gramsci, armed with an idealist dialectic and the 'spirit of cleavage' of the producer from the world of institutional politics, intervened in the concrete issue of the organic *scission* of the workers' and socialist movement in Italy, particularly complex because the PSI had a peculiar position within the political spectrum of the Socialist International and especially because it did not support the war. The prevalence of the maximalist trend within the party since 1912 had made it possible for Italian socialists to keep a 'neutral' stance on the war and also stand in open sympathy with the socialist revolution that had begun in Russia. The participation of the socialists in the internationalist meeting at Zimmerwald in September 1915 had already placed the PSI on the side of opposition to war and support for the socialist revolution. The Fifteenth Congress of the PSI, which took place in Rome in September 1918, witnessed the victory of the maximalists who supported the Russian Revolution and also peace and revolution for Italy.

The victorious current had Gramsci's unwavering support. However, he did not cease to draw attention to the fact that the construction of a working-class party was only beginning, as it would 'need to destroy the collaborationist and reformist spirit; it needs to mark out with accuracy and precision what it is we understand by "the state", and how, in the attitudes that best fit the party, there is nothing in contrast with Marxist doctrine'.[35]

This meant the path for creating a socialist state not from liberal institutions, but from 'a systematic development of professional organisations and local entities, which the proletariat was able to generate within the individualist

---

33   Badaloni 1975, pp. 3–55; Losurdo 1997a, pp. 17–34.
34   In order to follow Gramsci's intellectual and political trajectory in the decade in which he lived and fought in Turin, it is very useful to look up D'Orsi 2004, Olmo 1998 and Dias 2000.
35   Gramsci 1973, p. 215.

régime'.[36] It is easy to see that for Gramsci, the proletarian state could not be born from some sort of democratic advance within the liberal-bourgeois institutions, but only from the social institutions generated by self-organisation in the sphere of labour, aiming at its own liberation. Once again, it is possible to observe the similarity with Rosa Luxemburg's thought.

The leadership of the PSI decided to join the Communist International as soon as it was founded, a decision later confirmed by the Fifteenth Congress of the party, which took place in Bologna in September 1919. The maximalist majority agreed with the Bolsheviks only on the higher goal – the perspective of the realisation of socialism – but remained on the side of reformism concerning their theoretical view of the socialist revolution, especially the role that should be played by subjectivity. The reformists themselves saw in maximalism a mythological contamination sprung from the events in Russia. They believed that the revolution would fail in Russia and that in Italy the maximalists would be responsible for making the working class stray from the only practicable path, that of social and democratic reforms accomplished in the hard struggle of everyday life.

By the end of 1918, Amadeo Bordiga in Naples had begun organising a new tendency within the PSI, which would be radically critical of capital. With the purpose of opposing reformism and maximalism, Bordiga recuperated certain formulations from Marx on the inevitability of the capitalist crisis and the socialist revolution, taking from Bolshevism the idea of the vanguard party. The Neapolitan revolutionary insisted on a total scission with bourgeois institutions: this in itself led to proposing a scission with reformism and its maximalist variant, since it considered this theoretico-political trend a requirement of the bourgeois order for its own reproduction.

So it was that, as early as the Bologna Congress, Bordiga came up with an autonomous political proposal on behalf of a group that was fundamentally only present in Naples. Soon after the Congress, the weekly *Il Soviet* saw the 'abstentionist' communist fraction gathering around it, a tendency which would soon attempt to establish a link with the Comintern and which was enthusiastically received by young socialists.[37]

On the other hand, in Turin, Antonio Gramsci, Palmiro Togliatti, Umberto Terracini and Angelo Tasca were launching the periodical *L'Ordine Nuovo*. Its first issue came out on 1 May 1919, and gave birth to a new trend in the *scission*. Having a cultural basis that was very different from that which permeated

Italian socialism, but which was precisely that which would give substance to the *scission* and communist refoundation, at the outset this small group remained attached to maximalism not only in party politics but also in its overt concern with the higher goal and the outlines of the future socialist state.

A significant about-face would take place in June, when Gramsci's editorial 'Workers' Democracy' was published in the paper's seventh issue, posing the following question: 'How can the present be welded to the future, so that while satisfying the urgent necessities of the one we may work effectively to create and "anticipate" the other?' Gramsci reaffirmed his overt stance that the revolutionary state is born precisely from the antagonistic activity of the workers in the face of capital, and started from the idea that

> The socialist State already exists potentially in the institutions of social life characteristic of the exploited working class. To link these institutions, co-ordinating and ordering them into a highly centralised hierarchy of competences and powers, while respecting the necessary autonomy and articulation of each, is to create a genuine workers' democracy here and now – a workers' democracy in effective and active opposition to the bourgeois State, and prepared to replace it here and now in all its essential functions of administering and controlling the national heritage.[38]

Though he recognised the roles of the socialist party and the unions, Gramsci believed that 'the workshop with its internal commissions, the socialist clubs, the peasant communities – these are the centres of proletarian life we should be working in directly', because 'whoever wills the end, must will the means. The dictatorship of the proletariat represents the establishment of a new, proletarian State, which channels the institutional experiences of the oppressed class and transforms the social activity of the working class and peasantry into a widespread and powerfully organised system'.[39]

It is possible to notice in the excerpt both the echoes of Rosa Luxemburg's elaborations and the seeds of Gramsci's prison reflections, when he hypothesised on the gestation of a civil society that organises the workers' hegemony against capital's state and gives birth to a new state. Once the potentials of the factory councils had been understood, *L'Ordine Nuovo* emerged as a pole of attraction and expansion for the movement when it was just beginning. Making analogies with the English shop-stewards, the German *Räte* and

---

38   Gramsci 1999a, pp. 107–8.

39   Gramsci 1999a, pp. 109, 112.

above all with the Russian *soviets*, the movement joined the ongoing process of the international socialist revolution.

For Gramsci, the factory council is the nucleus of the new social order, but its political expansion demands a radical reform of the trade union (and the party). Trade unions must cease to be mere social institutions of bourgeois democracy and 'emerge from the very place of production, with capillary sources, so that they become the spontaneous, higher expression of workers'.[40]

Gramsci's reflection begins with the productive process as the field of political action, and also from the foundations of capitalist production, contemplating the dissolution of the power of capital by means of the workers' control. Indeed, for Gramsci, 'revolutionary organizations (political parties and trade unions) arise in the sphere of political liberty and bourgeois democracy, as affirmations and developments of liberty and democracy in general, and where relations of citizen to citizen still exist. The revolutionary process takes place in the sphere of production, in the factory, where the relations are those of oppressor to oppressed, exploiter to exploited, where freedom for the worker does not exist, and democracy does not exist'.[41]

Therefore, he wrote, still discussing the factory councils:

> The party and trade unions should not project themselves as tutors or as ready-made superstructures for this new institution, in which the historical process of the revolution takes a controllable historical form. They should project themselves as the conscious agents of its liberation from the restrictive forces concentrated in the bourgeois State. They should set themselves the task of organising the general (political) external conditions that will allow the revolutionary process to move at maximum speed, and the liberated productive forces to find their maximum expansion.[42]

The reason for all this is that the productive process of capital is where the workers' conscience and solidarity emerge, and it is in the self-management of production that the emancipation of work can be found. There is, here, a new reading of Sorel and a leaning towards Rosa Luxemburg and maybe Korsch as well, insofar as the productive process must not be the realm of absolute separation from politics and the state; instead, it would have to be

---

40   Spriano 1971, p. 174.
41   Gramsci 1999a, pp. 363–4.
42   Gramsci 1999a, pp. 367–8.

politicised such that it could become the basis for a general reorganisation of social relations and the institutions of a new state. Thus we have the complete opposite of reformism.

The fast growth of the factory councils sparked different interpretations within the PSI itself: the reformists compared the movement in the Turin factories to a new form of anarcho-syndicalism; the political and union leadership of the party did not accept the participation of the whole of the proletarian mass in the movement, including workers not affiliated with the party or the union; Bordiga's leftist communists believed that the movement paid too little attention to the issue of the revolutionary party and the taking of state power, conforming to their Sorelian inspiration.

While the group of 'abstentionist communists' had since February 1920 preached the need for a *scission* and the creation of the revolutionary party, the emphasis given to the social institutions of the working class as the core of the new state as well as the scope of the international socialist revolution led the communist group of *L'Ordine Nuovo* to treat this important issue as something smaller, thus allowing itself to be enveloped by the maximalism prevailing within the PSI. However, when they needed the party's and the trade union organisations' active support in order to face down the bosses' offensive, this support was denied them.

The bosses' attempt to restrict the action of the factory councils found an answer in 1920 in a general strike in the whole of the Piedmont, including various different categories of workers. While the state called on the army to secure order, the General Confederation of Labour (CGL) opposed the movement. The meeting of the general leadership of the PSI, originally scheduled for Turin, was transferred to Milan, adding to the opposition to the strike started by the factory councils. Every trend in the party presented arguments opposing the strike and the perspectives it brought.

The isolation brought defeat to the *L'Ordine Nuovo* group and the factory councils movement. Their existence was recognised, albeit within parameters established by capital, without achieving their desired goal of workers' control of production. The underestimation of the issue of the *scission* was exacting its toll, and the CGL had to find a way that offered continuity to the effort to come to terms with medium capital. However, it was not sufficiently clear to the socialists at the time that big capital had decided to take the offensive not only against the world of labour, but against the liberal institutions themselves, these latter having proved unable to preserve their class interests. So it was necessary to use the discontent of the small bourgeoisie and the war veterans, amidst an atmosphere of social crisis, to deal with a new situation and thus keep up the momentum.

Gramsci had prepared a document, presented during the meeting of the National Council of the PSI, a little before the general strike in April, named 'Renewing the Socialist Party', later published in *L'Ordine Nuovo* of 8 May. It described the situation and took a significant step towards the scission. It pointed to the existence of a revolutionary situation in the country: there was an expanding social subjectivity, in which 'industrial and agricultural workers throughout Italy are irresistibly set upon raising the question of the ownership of the means of production in an explicit and violent form'. On the other hand, 'the industrialists and landowners have achieved a maximum of class discipline and power', while the bourgeois state had created a body of armed mercenaries (meaning the Royal Guard) and resorted to terrorism.[43]

Thus, 'the present phase of the class struggle in Italy is the phase that precedes: either the conquest of political power on the part of the revolutionary proletariat and the transition to new modes of production and distribution that will set the stage for a recovery in productivity – or a tremendous reaction on the part of the propertied classes and governing caste'.[44]

He added, 'no violence will be spared in subjecting the industrial and agricultural proletariat to servile labour: there will be a bid to smash once and for all the working class's organ of political struggle (the Socialist Party) and to incorporate its organs of economic resistance (the trade unions and co-operatives) into the machinery of the bourgeois State'.[45]

It was precisely with the purpose of preventing the realisation of such a prescient anticipation of later fascism that Gramsci directed a true and proper accusation against the leadership of the PSI, with all its contradictions and inconsistencies. The PSI had not proven able to rally the workers' and peasants' forces because it did not seize the moment for the international socialist revolution of which Italy was a part, remaining a parliamentarian party acting within bourgeois liberal democracy, absent from the international politics of the workers' movement. Joining the Comintern had not had the necessary theoretical and practical consequences – the polemics with reformism had not even started yet. Besides, 'while the Party's revolutionary majority has found no mouthpiece for its thoughts or executor of its intentions in the Party's leadership or press, the opportunist elements for their part have been powerfully organised and have exploited the Party's prestige and authority to consolidate their positions in Parliament and the trade unions'.[46]

---

43   Gramsci 1999a, p. 273.
44   Gramsci 1999a, p. 274.
45   Ibid.
46   Gramsci 1999a, p. 276.

On the threshold of the scission, Gramsci stated that the core of the political issue lay wholly in actually transforming the PSI and making it, both organically and ideologically, a communist party. This would mean excluding the reformists and adopting a revolutionary programme and a revolutionary practice, or else 'the working class will instinctively move to form another party', or even perhaps move to anarchist positions, notoriously opposed to party organisations. Whether by means of a profound renewal in the PSI or a scission, a new organism would be created – the revolutionary party which the Italian working class needed at that moment, 'a homogeneous, cohesive party, with a doctrine and tactics of its own, and a rigid and implacable discipline', the only one able to find solutions to the problems presented by reality, and 'to organise the setting-up of factory councils to exercise control over industrial and agricultural production', and 'to conquer the unions, the Chambers of Labour and the General Confederation of Labour in an organic fashion'.[47]

The defeat of the April general strike as well as the rejection of the document which Gramsci had prepared for the meeting of the General Council of the PSI brought even greater fragmentation to the more leftist socialist tendencies. Gramsci apparently chose to act in the two ways that presented possible paths of development for the PSI. In May, he participated as an observer in the convention of the abstentionist communist fraction, where his proposal for the formation of a nationwide communist fraction that did not take abstentionism as a matter of principle was rebuffed. Gramsci believed that this could be the way to rally the scattered communist forces and create a strong renovating trend within the party, one which if defeated could walk towards an organic *scission* that appealed to a significant portion of the proletariat.

However, even within the small *L'Ordine Nuovo* group, various and serious disagreements were arising among the founding nucleus. While Gramsci argued with Tasca in favour of the factory councils, Terracini and Togliatti aligned themselves with the party leadership, and were followed in this by other revolutionary communists. The director of *L'Ordine Nuovo* found himself isolated in his project of renewal, being followed only by a group of workers. Within the vast representation of the workers' and socialist movement at the Second Congress of the Comintern, among union leaders, congressmen and party leaders, Gramsci's isolation was made even more conspicuous.

Serrati was the best-known Italian within the Comintern, and also he who inspired the greatest confidence. Together with Graziadei and Bombacci, he was one of the official delegates to the Congress, which also indicated the mar-

---

47   Gramsci 1999a, pp. 276–80.

ginal position of Bordiga, who failed to create a leftist, abstentionist and more homogeneous communist trend in the international arena. The Italian delegation was heavily criticised and urged to break with the reformists. There was surprise when Lenin praised Gramsci's document: 'Concerning the Socialist Party of Italy. The Second Congress of the Third International considers that the criticism of that party and practical proposals submitted to the National Council of the Socialist Party of Italy in the name of the party's Turin section, as set forth in *L'Ordine Nuovo* of 8 May 1920, are in the main correct and are fully in keeping with the fundamental principles of the Third International'.[48]

Here we can already glance at the foundations for Gramsci's future strategy for rising to the PCd'I leadership: given his isolation within the party, he had to emphasise strongly the international politics of communism, making the national question dependent upon the international context. It was this perspective that allowed Gramsci to see in fascism the international dimension of a phenomenon with Italian roots and to propose a revolutionary strategy for Italy, without ever losing from sight the international nature of the socialist revolution.

The document published by the Comintern on the Italian question after its Second Congress followed Gramsci's views, by and large. It displayed great hope in the Italian revolution, even if it acknowledged that 'it is visible to all that the Italian bourgeoisie is not as impotent as it was a year ago'. The Comintern insisted that 'in Italy, all the basic conditions for a great victorious proletarian revolution that embraces the whole of the people are now present' at the very moment when the flame that kindled the international socialist revolution was being extinguished.[49]

In Italy as well as in other places, the organisation of revolutionary subjectivity was at the heart of the matter, considering that 'the long indecision' of the Socialist Party pointed to its inability to become the body that could lead and unify the movement. This was due to the actions of the 'reformists and liberal-bourgeois elements' present in the party ranks and especially so in its parliamentary representation and the union leadership – and they had to be pushed away. Hence the priority given to 'purifying the party of its reformist elements, and making the party collaborate with the best proletarian part

---

48   Gramsci 1999a, p. 445.

49   'Lettera del Comitato esecutivo al Comitato centrale e a tutti i membri del Partito socialista italiano. Die Kommunistische Internationale, 13, 1920'. Quoted in Agosti 1974, vol. 1, pp. 315–20.

of the syndicalists and anarchists in the revolutionary struggle', which acknowledged the relative strengthening of these trends, as well as the fact that 'the
party must pay the strongest attention to the important movement of the factory councils'.[50]

The Italian working class, as if listening to the revolutionary expectations of
the Comintern, reacted radically to the bosses' provocation of locking out the
factories of Milan in late August, thus sealing the failure of the negotiations
between capital and labour, which had been going on since June. The FIOM
(the Italian Federation of Metalworkers) then decided to take over the factories, beginning 1 September. The claim being made by Gramsci and *L'Ordine
Nuovo* came to life in the form of workers' self-management and the transfer
of authority, becoming a revolutionary movement opposed not only to capitalism and the state, but also the reformism entrenched in the unions and the
Socialist Party.

It was precisely those social institutions of the working class which lived
within the liberal state that acted to prevent the factory occupations movement, organised in councils, from spreading and creating a truly revolutionary
situation. First of all, there was the attempt to prevent the Federation of Manual
Workers, strong in the Emilia-Romagna region, from joining the movement.
Soon after, under strong pressure from the CGL, the PSI made an agreement
with Giolitti's liberal government on the issue of wages and a future form of
controlling production. As it at least apparently answered some of the original
demands of the workers, the alliance between the reformist trend in the PSI
and CGL and the liberal government emptied out the movement and made the
scission inevitable, given the inability of the socialists to take the working class
out of its subaltern situation.

Gramsci, following a trajectory similar to that of Rosa Luxemburg, had first
insisted on defending a necessary 'renewal of the socialist party' as a means
to empower the workers' movement, preserving its unity as much as possible.
However, as he saw the connection between the liberal-bourgeois state and the
workers' own union and party institutions, he realised that this route would
be impossible and began to emphasise the centrality and importance for the
working class of autonomous and antagonistic organisation. The reason for
this changed attitude towards the scission was presented by Gramsci, and not
without some irony, in the statement that, as members of the *L'Ordine Nuovo*

---

50   'Lettera del Comitato esecutivo al Comitato centrale e a tutti i membri del Partito socialista
        italiano. Die Kommunistische Internationale, 13, 1920'. Quoted in Agosti 1974, vol. 1, pp. 315–
        20.

group, 'we simply made the mistake of believing that only the masses can achieve the communist revolution, and that neither a party secretary nor a president of the republic can achieve it by issuing decrees. Apparently this was also the opinion of Karl Marx and Rosa Luxemburg, and is Lenin's opinion'.[51]

As the movement started to decline, the Comintern made a belated appeal for extending the occupation of the factories 'until general insurrection', and for that 'the socialist party must become communist in the fullest sense of the word, i.e., a party that leads and guides the insurrection'.[52] The defeat and the disappointment that ensued made the Comintern demand urgency in evaluating and implementing the scission. So the PSI leadership went on to discuss the twenty-one conditions for being part of the Comintern, which were approved on 1 October. The approval of the scission on principle had a very small impact, as the decision would still have to be actually taken in the next party congress.

3   The Organic Scission of the Workers' Movement and the
       Foundation of the Communist Party in Italy

Three main trends arose as the congress of the PSI, to be held in Livorno, approached. Amazing as it may seem, none of them, not even the reformist 'socialist concentration', proposed breaking with the Comintern and Soviet Russia. The maximalist trend, in the majority, took the name of 'unitarian communist', defined as 'centrist' by the 'pure communist' fraction. The latter was officially established in Milan, during a conference on 15 October, which brought together representatives from all the groups that had unconditionally accepted the twenty-one points established by the Second Congress of the Comintern.

In a conference marked by concessions from every side, a manifesto was written. It was signed by Nicola Bombacci, Amadeo Bordiga, Bruno Fortichiari, Antonio Gramsci, Francesco Misiano, Luigi Polano and Umberto Terracini, and was to be spread among all socialist militants. The 'abstentionists' laid aside their principle of not taking part in elections based on liberal institutions, but there was no reference to the factory councils. The document aims, rather, at broadening support within the mass of party affiliates, emphasising the need

---

51   Gramsci 1999a, p. 485.
52   'Apello del Comitato escutivo al proletariato italiano' (September 22, 1920). *Die Kommun-istichje Internationale*, 14, 1921. Quoted in Agosti 1974, vol. 1., pp. 321–2.

to plan the decisions taken in the previous congress and update its programme, adjusted in line with the indications given by the Comintern's Second Congress and the evolution of the Italian socio-political process.[53]

For a moment, it seemed the tactics of 'renewal' as proposed by Gramsci would prevail. In those days, Gramsci identified the city of Turin as 'the seat of clear-headed political thought that threatens to win over the majority of the Italian Socialist Party and transform the Party from an organ prolonging the capitalist death-agony into an organ of struggle and revolutionary reconstruction'.[54]

In the convention held prior to the congress which the communist fraction held in Imola on 28 and 29 November, the diversity of experiences and constitutive tendencies actually made consensus even more difficult. Even though it is indisputable that the hegemony of the process fell with the *Il Soviet* group – the first to defend the *scission* and the only one organised nationally – other minor or local tendencies played a significant role in coming together with the *L'Ordine Nuovo* group from Turin, which had weight since it had led the workers' movement during the experience of the factory councils. Not only those which came from the 'abstentionist' trend from Turin, such as Giovanni Parodi, but also the Milan group, with figures such as Fortichiari and Repossi, and the maximalist leftist group of Bombacci, Gennari and Misiano were instrumental for making the new forthcoming party viable. Add to this the participation of the socialist youth, who joined the new communist tendency *en masse.*

Evaluating what had changed for the *L'Ordine Nuovo* group, a few days later Gramsci wrote that 'even after creating the communist fraction, which, when it becomes a party, has the historic mission of organising the revolutionary energies able to lead the Italian working class to victory and establish the workers' State, the particular task of our magazine and that of the groups of comrades who follow its activity with attention and sympathy will not be over'.[55]

Gramsci had finally agreed to the scission as proposed by the *Il Soviet* group, but *L'Ordine Nuovo* still faced the task of educating communist militants and forming the elements necessary for the construction of the new state, as well as contributing to the vast work of moral reform of the working masses. Thus he understood that 'the creation of the communist Party establishes the conditions for the intensification of our own work', since 'we will be able to dedicate

---

53   'Il programma di Milano'. Quoted in Manes 1996, pp. 21–8.

54   Gramsci 1999a, p. 487.

55   Gramsci 1973, pp. 171–2.

ourselves entirely to positive work, to enlarging our programme of renovation and organisation, awakening minds and wills'.[56]

The Comintern and Lenin himself pressed for the scission and harshened the tone of the dispute with Serrati, who intended to adapt the fulfilment of the twenty-one conditions to the Italian situation and thus to preserve part of the organisational apparatus held by the reformists. It is possible that the Comintern's stance on the Italian workers' movement had stimulated in Gramsci a greater commitment to the scission, in the way it was now being outlined: with a cut far further to the left than the cut made in other countries since the Second Congress of the Comintern. In a polemic with Serrati and the trend called 'unitarian', which was blamed for the crisis and the fragmentation of the party, Gramsci said that 'the Party has to be rebuilt, and henceforth the communist fraction must be considered and esteemed as a party in its own right, as the solid framework of the Italian Communist Party'.[57]

As the exact moment of the consummation of the organic *scission* of the Italian socialist movement approached, Gramsci anticipated not only the theoretical foundations of that *scission*, but also some of the elements in the script he would follow for formulating the idea of a united front and all his political science from the prison years. Gramsci begins by assuming that

> The working class is both a national and an international class. It must place itself at the head of the working people struggling to emancipate themselves from the yoke of industrial and financial capitalism on both a national and international scale. The national task of the working class is determined by the process of development of Italian capitalism and its official expression, the bourgeois State.[58]

Gramsci contemplates the specificity of Italian capitalism in the process of subjection of the countryside by the industrial cities and of the Southern and Central regions of the country by the North, thus creating 'the central problem of Italian national life, the Southern question', so that 'the workers' emancipation can be secured only through an alliance between the industrial workers of the North and the poor peasants of the South – an alliance designed to smash the bourgeois State'.[59]

---

56   Ibid.
57   Gramsci 1999a, p. 501.
58   Gramsci 1999a, p. 515.
59   Gramsci 1999a, p. 517.

This is why the necessary contents of the scission were expressed in the fact that 'the revolutionary working class will break with those degenerate socialist currents that have decayed into State parasitism. It will break with those currents that sought to exploit the position of superiority enjoyed by the North over the South in order to create labour aristocracies ...'[60]

For Gramsci, though, besides solving an historical and social question with a territorial expression, 'the Italian workers' revolution and the participation of the Italian working people in world affairs can come about only in the context of the world revolution', implying that 'the Italian working class knows that the condition for its own self-emancipation ... is the existence of a system of world revolutionary forces all conspiring to the same end'. The immense value Gramsci sees in the Communist International came from his clear perception that particular processes always happen within the context of the history of the human species, whose tendency is to unify under communism. This is why Gramsci saw the Executive Commission of the Comintern as 'the seeds of a world workers' government'.[61]

Gramsci, however, insisted on the link between production and revolution, 'economics' and 'politics', in which the perspective of unifying industrial and agricultural, manual and intellectual labour, should attack the very foundations of capitalist production. From the transference of the factory production process to workers' control, it would be possible to reorganise the social relations of production and create the conditions necessary for building a new state, under the banner of the world of labour as a whole. This is why 'for the communists, tackling the problem of control means tackling the greatest problem of the present historical period; it means tackling the problem of workers' power over the means of production, and hence that of conquering State power'.[62]

The ECCI sent a letter to the opening of the Seventeenth Congress of the PSI, in which it directly stated its position that 'the Italian communist fraction, which recently held a convention in Imola, is the only one to have put the matter in precise terms. Those who wish to remain faithful to the Communist international must support this fraction'.[63]

---

60   Gramsci 1999a, pp. 516–17. There is a clear mistake in affirming that Gramsci realises the importance of the Southern question and the worker-peasant alliance only after breaking up with Bordiga at the end of 1923.

61   Gramsci 1999a, pp. 517–18.

62   Gramsci 1999b, p. 47.

63   'Indirizzo di saluto del Comitato esecutivo al congresso del partito socialista italiano a Livorno'. *Die Kommunistische Internationale*, n. 16, 1920. Quoted in Agosti 1974, vol. 1, pp. 328–9.

Aside from the three main trends, the Congress also heard the words of an 'intransigently revolutionary' current, which later joined the 'unitarians' and a group that had decided to work against the scission between the 'pure' and 'unitarian' communists, including people such as Marabini and Graziadei and that, considering its failure to achieve its mission, chose to follow the path of the 'pure' communist fraction. On the side of the 'pure' communists were Umberto Terracini and Amadeo Bordiga, who worked to attract the largest possible number of communists, basing themselves on the decisions from the Bologna Congress and the indications of the Comintern's Second Congress, targeting their criticism on social-democratic reformism and Serrati's 'centrism'.

In contrast with France and Germany, where the 'centrist' socialist fractions had recently formally joined the communist parties and the Comintern – only to leave soon afterwards –, in Italy the *scission* would happen along far more leftist lines, frustrating the expectations which some nurtured of bringing the majority of the organised working class to the party. The support that the German Comintern delegate Paul Levi gave to Serrati helped fuel the polemics for a longer period, and the PSI to continue as part of the Comintern for a little more time. The fact is, though, that the communist fraction organised in Imola did not extend its support base much further, its motion acieving one third of the votes.

It was enough, however, for the Communist Party of Italy to be founded on 21 January 1921, in a separate congress held at the San Marco Theatre in Livorno. Amadeo Bordiga was its main leader, while Antonio Gramsci was only a deputy of the Executive Commission. This is clear evidence that the *L'Ordine Nuovo* group, at the moment of the organic scission of the socialist workers' movement, preferred to submit to the theoretical and political leadership of Bordiga, who was very different from Gramsci in his views on national and international issues, especially on the 'southern question'.

The Comintern, in turn, in spite of its order that the socialists be expelled, did not lose hope of attracting at least part of the 'centrists' at a later point, just as had happened in Germany to a certain extent; meanwhile, the PSI chose to preserve its ties with the Moscow-based organisation and appealed for reconsideration. Thus for some time the Comintern had two political organisations in Italy, though it was clear that the PCd'I came from leftist communism.

The foundation of the PCd'I happened at a moment when the process of the defeat of the workers' movement by the offensive of capital could already be felt, when economic crisis had already brought unemployment and pressure on wages, and the political crisis of the ruling power bloc and liberal ideology sought a solution by unleashing the process of fascism. Even though fascism had arisen in the cities, fascist violence began in rural areas before soon spreading into Italy's urban centres, targeting the workers' organisations and their leaders. Communists as well as socialists saw in fascism an instrument of ruling-class reactionary violence, in a desperate action to prevent what appeared to be the decline of their rule.

A number of elements pointing to the defeat of the international socialist revolution rained down in March 1921, exactly four years after its beginning in Petrograd. The end of the revolution and the necessary strategic reorientation made Russia once again resign itself to being a different revolutionary East, which had to face the imperialist West, where capital had taken the initiative and was mounting an offensive against the world of labour, thus affecting the array of decisions that had to be taken by Bolsheviks and communists around the world.

A disadvantageous agreement with Poland sealed the end of civil war and imperialist intervention against Soviet Russia. Forced to make territorial concessions, Russia found itself looking at a scenario of limitless social-economic devastation, provoking peasant revolts in certain areas. Penalised during the war to defend the revolution by the compulsory consignment of the harvest to the new state arising from the ashes of the former Tsarist empire, the peasants threatened to break the social alliance that had ensured the revolutionary victory of October 1917. The rising at the Kronstadt naval base, which had played one of the most important roles in the epic of the revolution, was just another sign that deprivation and the lack of organisation in the productive process could finish the task of destroying the transformation effort, a task that even the imperialist guns had proven unable to complete. The Tenth Congress of the RKP(B) – Communist Party of Russia (Bolshevik) – had to face all these problems, pointing as they did to the strategic turn which the communist movement would have to make in Russia, the West and other parts of the world.

After the unleashing of the socialist revolution in the most backward among the imperialist countries and its subsequent, albeit momentary, spread towards the West – whose turning point was the failure of the international political strike of 1919 – there was a simultaneous withdrawal to the Russian centre and expansion towards the periphery of capitalism. Thus, a greater opening for the emancipation struggles of the peoples of the East under imperialism took centre stage. In Turkey, Persia, India and China, the anti-imperialist movement received fresh impulse, even though bourgeois hegemony had surfaced.

The complete failure of the proletarian insurrection attempted by the KPD – Communist Party of Germany – in the so-called 'March Action', indicated the melancholic end of the strategy of mounting a general strike and armed insurrection against the bourgeois state, in that historic phase when capital was reorganising itself after having fallen into widespread imperialist war and having had to face off the socialist revolution. Even though the repression of the workers' movement was significant in liberal-imperialist states, considering the fact that trade unionism had been framed within the terms of restructuring production, the offensive by capital and the ruling classes was more virulent in those countries which had glimpsed the possibility of socialist revolution. The sequence of the weakest links in the imperialist chain was composed by those countries situated precisely within the space of 'passive' or failed bourgeois revolutions as well as that of communist refoundation, comprising Russia, Germany, Austria-Hungary and Italy.

In Germany, in spite of the defeat, the workers' movement preserved its vitality for a few years still, enough to occupy places in government and hound the bourgeois order, thus keeping alive the flame of socialist revolution. The rise of new states born out of the disintegration of the Austro-Hungarian Empire, or separated from the old Tsarist Empire, brought a national-bourgeois revolution of a restorationist nature. Seeing the concomitant emergence of the socialist revolution, the bourgeoisies found themselves forced into a compromise with the traditional ruling classes. The result in most cases was the emergence of liberal political institutions intertwined with powers proper to the old feudal absolutism.

The fact that this rosary of new states bordering Soviet Russia had established ties with imperialism set the trend for reactionary régimes to seek their legitimacy in anti-Bolshevism, nationalism and religion. Conservative and oligarchic social forces prevailed from the end of 1920 throughout the whole of Eastern and Danubian Europe.[64]

Even once the revolutionary impulse in Italy had been defeated, the crisis of the monarchic liberal state did not subside. It was followed by the intense activity of the fascist action squads, which, boosted by the landowners, unleashed a violent campaign against the social institutions of the workers' movement, attacking the Chambers of Labour, the cooperatives, the peasant leagues, and libraries, all with the support of the state's repressive apparatus. The destructive work of fascism extended from the region of Emilia in 1920 to the whole north and centre of the country, putting the union and party organisations of the

---

64   In the following years, the countries that detached themselves from Russia (Finland, Estonia, Latvia, Lithuania and Poland) or that arose from the disintegration of Austria-Hungary (Austria, Hungary, Czechoslovakia and Yugoslavia) tended to become imperialist and fascist areas of influence, because their territorial fragmentation made it easier for German and Italian expansion to resume. Czechoslovakia was a remarkable exception, as it was able to preserve at a great cost its liberal democracy until 1938, when it was occupied by Nazi Germany.

working class on the defensive and spreading wherever there were proletarian organisations. By April of the following year, it had reached mass proportions.

Concerned with organising its forces and putting itself forward as the new vanguard of the working class against capital's offensive – which was now using the battering ram of fascist 'squadrism' – the recently created PCd'I (Communist Party of Italy), tried to keep alive the hope and the faith in the inevitability of the socialist revolution. Notwithstanding the defeat of the international socialist revolution, including (and especially) in Italy, the communists preferred to see in fascism a mere instrument of bourgeois and governmental reaction, a sign of the weakness of the property owners' rule, and not the beginning of an offensive destined to reconstitute the dominant power bloc and alter the profile of the working class itself.

Rather, they expected the fascist wave to pass and leave in its place a coalition government similar to that of Germany, composed by the liberal element of the bourgeoisie and social democracy, a solution that would place the working class under the influence of the communist vanguard. In this interpretation, we can already see the nexus between fascism and social democracy as possibilities for the reconstitution of bourgeois rule.

Gramsci's writings in the daily *L'Ordine Nuovo*, though limited by party discipline, point to a certain self-criticism regarding the moment of the *scission* that created the Communist Party, and also to a clear perception that the moment of fascist reaction would be more profound and widespread and would last longer than most socialists and communists thought. Feeling the defeat of the Italian workers' movement, Gramsci laments that 'the Livorno split should have come about at least a year earlier, for the communists to have had the time to give the working class the organisation required by the revolutionary period in which it is living'.[65]

Thus Gramsci notes, as he many times would do again, that the delay in splitting with reformism and the absence of a revolutionary workers' party caused irreparable damage to the workers' struggle, not only in the moment of offensive, but also when it needed a defence against fascist attack. He had not lost, however, his subjective confidence in the victory of the working class and in the socialist revolution, insisting on the strategic conception that oriented the *scission* and the communist refoundation during the War.

Gramsci knew from the outset that fascism arose as an international phenomenon and not as something specific to Italy, a view that became commonplace in the following years. For him, this phenomenon meant 'the attempt

---

65   Gramsci 1999b, p. 64.

to resolve the problems of production and exchange with machine-guns and pistol-shots' – an attempt made by the small and middle bourgeoisie, 'and this stratum feeds fascism, provides fascism with its troops'.[66]

Italy, however, was not even the forerunner country of fascism, considering that the organisation of the small and middle bourgeoisie in armed groups had begun in Spain since 1918, even if it was 'an exemplary case', as 'it represents a phase through which all the countries of Western Europe will pass, if economic conditions continue as they are today, with the same tendencies as at present'.[67] Gramsci warned that the situation was only the beginning of something worse, but that, already at that point, 'the proletariat learns by experience what dictatorship by an exploiting and oppressing class means', and also 'observes what are the roles of State and government in a dictatorship'.[68]

Without ever separating his lucid analysis of the movement of the real – even if describing situations of extreme difficulty – from proclaiming the historic goal of the socialist revolution and the foundation of a proletarian state, Gramsci expressed his tranquility and serenity arising from his confidence in a solid theoretical basis: 'We are calm, because we have a compass, because we have a faith. Even if we are deep in the most sombre and atrocious situation, we believe in the development of the good forces of the working people, we are certain that this people will triumph over any loss of spirits, over any dark barbarism. Our conception of the world can be summed up in the profound conviction that evil shall never prevail'.[69]

Besides having such an unshakeable faith in the victory of the proletariat, Gramsci, following the example of the greater part of Western communists, seemed to insist – not without contradicting his intuitions as to the nature of fascism – on the strategic conception of the socialist revolution prevalent during the first phase of communist refoundation, particularly Lenin's, soon after the beginning of the imperialist war. Gramsci suggests a relation between the domestic revolts which Soviet power faced, especially in Kronstadt, and the occupation of certain industrial centres in Germany by the imperialist forces who had won the War. The destruction of the socialist revolution in Russia and the subjection of Germany through the diminishing of its productive capacity would only confirm the reconstitution of the imperialist powers of the Western liberal states, neutralising proletarian antagonism from within these states themselves.

---

66   Gramsci 1999b, p. 61.
67   Gramsci 1999b, p. 62.
68   Gramsci 1974, p. 114.
69   Gramsci 1974, p. 98.

Germany would become the weak link in the imperialist chain if Soviet power could be secured in Russia, because 'finally in Germany the choice imposes itself, on the one hand there is the power of the capitalists, which cannot secure the country's independence, and the power of the workers, which can ally itself with Russia and a tremendous federation of proletarian States, which would be decisive for the world revolution and the emancipation of all classes and all oppressed peoples'.[70]

Gramsci once again highlighted Germany's strategic position when, despite lacking sufficient information, he analysed the 'March Action' unleashed by the KPD. He said that 'the movement had its origins in conditions that, at the present moment, are typical of almost every country in which the class struggle has reached its peak of harshness and exasperation'.[71] He then drew a passionate and also striking analogy between the Spartakist rising of January 1919 and the agitation by that part of the German proletariat which identified with the communists, thus suggesting once again Gramsci's theoretico-practical link with Spartakism, especially with Rosa Luxemburg.

What eluded Gramsci was not only the tactical error of these two confrontations, which both ended in serious defeat, but also the fact that conditions had been profoundly altered by the offensive of capital. It is possible to observe, here, that Gramsci followed the 'leftist' political orientation that prevailed not only in the Communist Party of Italy, but also in almost the whole of the West, feeding the hopes that the revolutionary movement would soon return. At the same time, however, Gramsci indicated the novelty of fascism as a reactionary mass movement and the tragic aspect of the proletarian movement's defeat.

In the estimation of the PCd'I – which was largely Gramsci's appraisal too – by analogy with what was going on in Germany, the political process was headed for a coalition between socialists and liberal democrats, and not to any lasting kind of dictatorship, because fascism would be abandoned by the bourgeoisie as soon as it had fulfilled its repressive role. Especially for that reason, the communists were more concerned with consolidating the *scission*, seen as a necessary preparatory moment for resuming the proletarian revolution, and targeting the PSI, than with understanding what made the fascist phenomenon so particular. Since they did not recognise that the proletarian class had entered a process of strategic defeat by the offensive of capital, the communists were unable to contribute to the reversal of the process of fascism and its reorganisation of the power bloc. This mistake and the insufficient understanding of that movement led to an irreversible defeat.

---

70   Gramsci 1974, p. 101.

71   Gramsci 1974, p. 120.

A symptom had appeared in the parliamentary elections of 15 May 1921, when the communists, owing to their 'putting the Socialists on trial' and the 'abstentionist' path followed by a large part of their militants, had far fewer votes than could have been expected by comparison to the results of the Socialist Congress at Livorno. The PSI's good result, as compared to the communists' relative failure, offered a new argument for Serrati to insist that the scission and the Comintern's position was a mistake. Gramsci, a candidate in Turin, was not among the fifteen communists who were elected. The fascists, as part of the National Bloc coalition which brought together liberal and conservative groups, elected thirty-five deputies, including Mussolini, who had the highest number of votes in Milan.

Gramsci, at odds with the prevailing view in the PCd'I and contemplating other possibilities, considered with anguish the possibility of fascism's rise to power, this being the goal of any political movement. The risk of a successful fascist *coup d'état* was real 'because only an insurrection of the broad masses can break a reactionary coup de force', even though there was no preparation for this action, as the socialists did not conceive it possible. Though Gramsci does not say it clearly, neither did the PCd'I take such a possibility seriously. Its slogan for armed insurrection was directed at an immediate seizure of power and the overthrow of the bourgeoisie, and not conceived as a mass action capable of inverting the advance of fascism. Gramsci was anyhow correct in saying that 'a *coup d'état* by the fascists, by the general staff, the landowners and the bankers, is the threat which has hung over this legislature from the start'.[72]

An agreement between the socialists and fascists for ending violence in public spaces and bringing the fascists into the parliamentary game was being considered as early as June, and thus there was the possibility of some socialist participation in the government. At first Gramsci considered natural an agreement between socialists and fascists, because 'both no longer have a function to fulfil in the country: they have therefore rightly become government parties, "practical" parties'.[73]

A few days later he returned to this view, saying that 'the same process will take place in Italy as has taken place in the other capitalist countries. The advance of the working class will be met by a coalition of all reactionary elements, from the fascists to the *popolari* and socialists'.[74]

---

72   Gramsci 1999b, pp. 88–9.

73   Gramsci 1999b, p. 101.

74   Gramsci 1999b, pp. 102–3.

Later, Gramsci saw things very differently, believing that 'the very probability of socialist collaboration with the government increases the danger of a fascist *coup de main* ... And it is also certain that fascism will not want to lose the position of predominance which it occupies in so many regions today'.[75] Continuing in that direction, he soon after said that 'there are now in Italy two repressive and punitive apparatuses: fascism and the bourgeois State. A simple calculation of utility suggests that the ruling class at some point will wish to amalgamate these two apparatuses, and destroy any resistance from the tradition of civil servants with a *coup de force* aimed at the central organs of government'.[76]

It is, therefore, clear that Gramsci just like the rest of the communist movement was unable to establish the precise connection that existed between fascism and the petit-bourgeois masses, on the one hand, and big capital and state institutions, on the other. This was mainly because fascism was considered exclusively in its repressive and violent aspect, and its reach as a movement capable of making possible a reorganisation of the power bloc and the establishment of a mass-based régime was not understood. Without this realisation, the need for the working class to carry out a strategic retreat could not be acknowledged.

Gramsci was making these reflections while the Third Congress of the Comintern was taking place in Moscow, during which the Italian delegation aligned itself with the trends of the communist left and opposed the attempt of the Comintern once again to approach the PSI, and the PSI's delegates returned to Italy convinced that they should increase their own number of members to counter the losses made to the PCd'I at Livorno. The PCd'I was criticised for concentrating its activity on consolidating the scission and making permanent attacks on 'centrism'. The understanding that the PCd'I should become the organised revolutionary vanguard of the working class, though not necessarily the majority of this class, ensured that the Italian delegation had great reservations about the Congress's final report, which called on the communist parties to go 'to the masses'.

The decision by the Comintern's Executive Commission to send observers to the Eighteenth Congress of the PSI, which took place in October 1921, particularly displeased the communist leadership, who disagreed with the political tactics approved at the Second Congress, sensing veiled criticism of the decision taken in Livorno to found the new party. Even though the 'third inter-

75   Gramsci 1999b, p. 109.
76   Gramsci 1974, pp. 257–60.

nationalist' socialist fraction founded by Lazzari had limited weight, Serrati's maximalist majority judged the bourgeois state to be on the path to disintegration and thought that the PSI and the working class should preserve themselves for the right moment. In practice, this position was not very different from the PCd'I's, but it made impracticable the reformists' steps towards an agreement with the liberals for ruling the country, and with the fascists (who had become a political party a few weeks before) for ending the violence, including the dismantling of the 'Arditi del Popolo', organisations of armed resistance to fascism which had 'spontaneously' arisen in the previous months.

The political conditions for a unitary action of the proletarian movement against fascism would have been present, were it not for the fact that both the PCd'I and PSI believed that the proletarian revolution was going to come soon – not realising that the advance of fascism and the offensive of capital were gaining momentum. Instead, the PCd'I would confront the Comintern exactly on the issue of the united front, and the PSI would not be able to withstand its dynamics of fragmentation.

4   The Origins of the United Front Policy in the Communist International

After the assassination of Rosa Luxemburg and Karl Liebknecht in January 1919 by the republican social-democratic government, Paul Levi became the leader of the KPD, a party of the German working class with great ideological mobility. Faithful to the conceptions of Rosa Luxemburg, he attempted to isolate the 'anarcho-syndicalist' and 'leftist' trend of the party, marginalised at the Heidelberg Congress which took place in October 1919 and saw virtually half the members leave the party.[77]

Meanwhile, the KPD sought a rapprochement with the vast proletarian base of the USPD, which was leaning towards the left and solidarity with Soviet Russia, a tendency made clear by the strengthening, at its December 1919 Leipzig Congress, of those who showed themselves favourable to leaving the Second International. In October of the following year, the new majority favourable to

---

77   The KAPD – Communist Workers' Party of Germany – was founded in 1920 and accepted as a sympathiser of the Comintern, but was unable to consolidate itself. It was soon weakened by the return of many of its members to the KPD, which for a while bore the name of VKPD, after having admitted the left of the USPD.

the Comintern was consolidated, as a preparation for the congress of communist unification in December 1920.[78]

Now the KPD would be able to count on a significant proletarian and popular base, which would once again allow it to raise the flag of proletarian unity and for the communists once again to fight for the leadership of the movement as a whole. However, there was still a strong trend within the party defending the so-called 'theory of the offensive', which insisted that, as long as the revolutionary situation existed, offensive tactics should be adopted, whether or not there was support from the majority of the working class.[79]

On 7 January 1921, the KPD sent an open letter, written by Paul Levi and Karl Radek, to all the trade union organisations and workers' parties of Germany, namely the KAPD, the USPD and the SPD, proposing a common action in defence of working-class living standards, and demanding the dismantling of paramilitary organisations, the liberation of political prisoners and the reestablishment of diplomatic relations with Soviet Russia. This outline of a united front policy proposed by the KPD was refused by most of the organisations who received the proposal, and it also received strong criticism from those within the party who stuck by the 'theory of the offensive'.

Faithful to the goal of proletarian unity, when Paul Levi represented the KPD at the Livorno Congress of the PSI, which sealed the Italian communists' scission, he was opposed to this latter on the grounds that it failed to include the maximalist majority of the workers' movement. In contrast with what had happened in the months after the Comintern Second Congress, when the tactics of a forced scission with the reformists had yielded good results in Germany, France, Czechoslovakia and Sweden, in Italy the scission left the communists isolated as the maximalists chose to unite with the reformists.

Even though he had obtained support from the central executive leadership of the party, Paul Levi was in the minority in the plenary meeting of the Central Committee, and for that reason resigned the leadership, soon being followed by others who supported the policy suggested in the 'Open Letter'. Levi was replaced by Heinrich Brandler, and the others who resigned were replaced by opponents of this tactic. The proponents of the 'theory of the offensive' gained strength not only in the KPD but also in the Comintern as a whole. In Germany

---

78   In 1922 the defeated minority of the USPD went back to the comfort of its traditional home in the SPD.

79   A similar process involved the SFIO in February 1920, when a significant 'centrist' fraction chose to join the Comintern, aligning itself with extremist and revolutionary syndicalist tendencies, creating a hybrid Communist Party of France.

there was an effort by the KPD and the KAPD to draw closer, even considering a merger between these organisations.

Without a clear political line and suffering from pressures derived from a dispute within the ECCI, the KPD was unable to give direction to the proletarian agitation of the second half of March. Divided between two opposed political orientations, and possibly incited by members of the ECCI (especially Bela Kun), the communists launched a strike and attempted insurrection as a response to the armed intervention in Saxony under the orders of the social-democratic government. Armed conflicts ended with the defeat of the attempted revolution and a massive loss of supporters, thus providing the opportunity for Paul Levi to make harsh criticisms of the divisions within the KPD leadership, even though the 'March Action' had been saluted by the ECCI as a sign of support for the Party leadership.

In a letter to Paul Levi and Clara Zetkin, Lenin said that he agreed with the new tactic outlined in the 'Open Letter', but that he disagreed with their resignation from the party leadership and doubted that interference by Bela Kun had precipitated the 'March Action', the tactics deployed being too ultra-left. The fact that Paul Levi had brought forth his disagreements through channels other than the party's own led to his suspension and later to his departure from the communist movement.[80]

Certainly, the recently founded PCd'I was happy to see the rise of the German communist fraction, hoping not only to find an immediate justification for the Livorno scission, but also a stimulus for the revolutionary movement to resume in Italy soon. Gramsci, in agreement with the 'theory of the offensive', wrote at the time that 'the communists deny that the present time can be considered "reactionary"; indeed, they affirm that the complex of present events is the most evident and abundant proof of the final decomposition of the bourgeois régime'.[81]

Just when the KPD was publishing the 'Open Letter', which was a sign of the growing disagreements among the communist parties in the West, in Russia Bukharin argued for the 'theory of the offensive', going against Lenin's orientation. In reality, two different strategies for dealing with the reflux of the international socialist revolution were taking form. Leftist communism understood that the international socialist revolution was being forced into a minor retreat – its success being inevitable – and so the working-class offensive should continue, taking advantage of the recent incorporation of mass support for the communist movement in the West.

---

80   Agosti 1976, vol. 2, pp. 344–5.

81   Gramsci 1974, p. 145.

Lenin, on the other hand, observed that the revolutionary impetus was becoming exhausted after the defeats of the Italian workers' movement and the failure of the Red Army in Poland. Of utmost importance, then, was to consolidate the communist parties by enlisting new members and using the contradictions between the imperialist countries to the advantage of the defence and survival of Soviet Russia. Thus any untimely action that could lead to the isolation of communists within the workers' movement or to the isolation of Russia in the international arena should be avoided. Paul Levi's defeat gave new strength to leftist communism within the Comintern and brought added complications to the decisions that had to be taken in Russia, at the moment when civil war and imperialist intervention were coming to an end.

At the beginning of 1921, there were great signs of discontent in Russia among those who had brought the revolution to victory. The peasant revolt in the Tambov region, the strike and protest by the workers of Petrograd (stemming from the reduction in food rations) and finally the Kronstadt uprising made the Bolsheviks see that the revolution urgently needed a change in course. The Tenth Congress of the RKP(B), which took place in March 1921, marked the turning point, aiming at a reconstruction of the worker-peasant alliance and at the same time at establishing a diplomatic policy that would take advantage of the contradictions between the imperialist powers, just as the offensive of capital against the world of labour was beginning.

Measures such as the establishment of a tax *in natura* instead of the forced requisition of the harvest, the reestablishment of monetary and market relations, and the slowing down of nationalisations represented the first steps of the future NEP – New Economic Policy. These measures, together with the trade treaty with Germany signed in the same month, as well as the treaties of friendship signed with Persia, Afghanistan and Turkey, implied a tacit recognition of the failure of the international communist revolution, in the East as well as the West, even if a new revolutionary offensive was believed to be coming soon.

While the socialist revolution did not resume, concessions to the Russian peasants and the use of diplomacy's weapons were inevitable. The meaning of this political turn was far more profound and lasting than it would seem at the time, as it actually started a second phase in the development of the communist refoundation, which faced insurmountable difficulties and whose most noteworthy element was the political formula of the united front.

From the very beginning, there was open or covert resistance from leftist communism, fearing a weakening in Russia's anti-imperialist stance and the possible restoration of capitalism implied in the concessions to the peasants. They insisted on the idea that a revolution in the West should take place at any cost, and communists should always be on the offensive, in the vanguard, possibly entering the fight even before the working class, so as to break its passivity. This perspective prevailed among Russian leftist communists and the leadership of the Comintern under Zinoviev.

The tortuous and oscillating trajectory of the workers' movement and particularly German communism, as well as the strength of leftist communism within the West as a whole, made it extremely difficult for the communist refoundation to reach a new stage of development arising from the defeat of the international socialist revolution. The new political orientation approved at the Tenth Congress of the RKP(B) owed more to the emergency situation in the country than to any conviction of the need for profound strategic change. For many Bolsheviks in tune with leftist communism, these were only temporary concessions to the peasants, which would end as soon as a revolution broke out in the West.

Only from a historical point of view can we see that the defeat of the international socialist revolution and the offensive of capital had unsuspected depths; that Russia, the East, would once again become a peculiarity; and that the focal issue would once again become the strengthening of the worker-peasant alliance. In backward countries such as Russia, the socialist revolution could only be victorious with the help of the industrial and agricultural proletariat of the imperialist countries. Otherwise, a strategic alliance between proletarian power and the far larger peasant mass, to which many concessions had to be made, would be necessary. In the West, though, the heart of the matter was the need to find new forms of proletarian unity against the offensive of capital.

While the socialist revolution did not get its momentum back, in Russia there was only space for the first steps of socialist transition, in the form of state monopoly capitalism aimed at the building of large industries, increasing labour productivity (which included the use of Taylor's method of 'scientific labour organisation') and making a slow passage from small-scale agricultural family production to large-scale production. The essential measures for starting this process would be the reestablishment of mercantile relations in agriculture and the system of concessions in industry, creating relations with the world market.

These measures would be necessary to secure the united front (even though the term 'united front' was not yet in use) of workers and peasants in the first stage of the transition, which would have in the Worker and Peasant Inspection Commission its institutional form of control over the party and the proletarian state. Thus the first steps of the socialist transition in Russia would necessarily be taken through state monopoly capitalism, something more backward than what the imperialist countries had, but under a political authority that defended the interests of the working class against the bourgeoisie.

In some of his final writings Lenin sought a greater understanding of the notion of state capitalism as the first stage of the transition in a backward country, highlighting how important it was for peasants to organise themselves in cooperatives, which should exist alongside private enterprise and public socialist companies. Since the working class had already taken state power, 'now the emphasis is changing and shifting to peaceful, organisational, "cultural" work'. This cultural work must be aimed at recreating public administration as inherited from Tsarist times and organising the peasants in cooperatives, because 'the system of civilised cooperators is the system of socialism'.

Lenin realised that the reconstruction of public administration and the preservation of the worker-peasant alliance were necessary elements of the whole transitional period. The control of a new bureaucracy by a collectively organised worker-peasant alliance at a high cultural level would allow for the advance of socialism in Russia, though its rhythm would ultimately be conditioned both by the RKP(B)'s ability to prevent the scission of the united front of the two classes, and the pace of the world revolution.

In the West and in the countries located in the periphery of imperialism, the counterpart to this orientation was meant to be the united front policy. However, insurmountable difficulties prevented its concrete realisation and theoretical development, anticipating the enormous limitations faced by the second phase of communist refoundation, those which brought about its historical defeat. There was an indication of the complexity of the situation in the dispute over the KPD's 'Open Letter' and the subsequent expulsion of Paul Levi, whom the Comintern's Executive Commission accused of trying to create a sort of right wing of the International, among other things, and in the different understandings of what the NEP meant, a situation that would exist as long as the NEP itself existed.

The communist refoundation and the political formula of the united front had to overcome the challenge of establishing themselves between leftist communism (extremism) as displayed in the 'March Action' and 'theory of the offensive', and the social-democratic left that gravitated around the so-called 'Austro-Marxists', pejoratively referred to as the Two-and-a-Half International, which Paul Levi joined. Therefore, we can see that the foundation of the PCd'I happened at a time of strategic redefinition after the defeat of the international socialist revolution and the beginning of the offensive of capital, while the PSI took a step back from its allegiance to the Comintern and returned to its policy of 'class collaboration'.[82]

---

82   A year after the Paul Levi case and the foundation of the PCd'I, Lenin admitted that he was wrong regarding Levi and Serrati, and started to treat them 'as contemporary models of the extreme left of petty-bourgeois democracy'.

The Third Congress of the Comintern, which took place between 22 June and 12 July 1921, witnessed a lively debate between the communist left, which upheld 'the theory of the offensive', and those who believed that a new tactics should be proposed in order to face the offensive of capital, which was thought to be only a temporary weakening of the revolutionary process. The communist left had great representation in the West: in France, Austria, Hungary, the Netherlands, Czechoslovakia, Italy, and of course Germany. In Germany and Czechoslovakia, a deep opposition to leftist communism arose, arguing that any revolutionary initiative could provoke a reaction that would be a disaster for the working class, considering that communists were in the minority.

Leftist tendencies were also represented among the Russian party, by important figures such as Zinoviev and Bukharin – Lenin convinced them, however, that it was important for the Russian delegation to appear united, because of the need to explain the implications of the New Economic Policy, which was just then being put into practice. This was one of the elements that settled the dispute against the substantial leftist delegation present at the congress. While Lenin explained the meaning of NEP within the context of the reflux of the socialist revolution, Karl Radek outlined the new tactics aimed at defending the immediate interests of the working class and at conquering the masses, which had to be educated for the conquest of power.[83]

The Third Congress of the Comintern necessarily ended in compromise, but it was acknowledged that the revolutionary process had to go for a longer stretch, during which the communists had to attract a majority of the working class through the struggle for partial demands, to be fought for in an organised manner including all exploited strata of workers in both town and country. The themes related to these new tactics were debated not in relation to a greater and necessary theoretical advance that would highlight the nodes of the new political formula for facing off the capitalist offensive, but rather in relation to the national situations of Czechoslovakia, Germany and Italy.

The final report of the Third Congress of the Comintern brought the understanding that communism had become a movement capable of 'threatening capital', but that the power of capital could only be broken 'when the communist idea took shape with unrestrained impetus in the vast majority of the proletariat guided by the communist masses'. For the moment, the bourgeoisie was capable not only of restraining any insurrection by force, but also 'capable, should it be necessary, of provoking premature insurrections of the proletariat

---

83   Still, the similarities with certain formulations by Rosa Luxemburg are quite remarkable!

preparing for struggle and defeating the proletariat before it had the opportunity to create an invincible common front'.[84]

In order to create the united front of the proletariat, it would be necessary to draw 'the vast masses of workers away from the influence of social-democratic parties and the treacherous union bureaucracy'; and this could only be done in the everyday struggle for better working and living conditions. The trade union movement was seen as a decisive terrain for this effort, considering that this would be 'the fight for enemy positions in our own territory; such is the problem of creating a front before which capital is forced to give in'. The political formula of the united front appears clearly as a way of addressing this problem and 'the danger lying in the perfected strategy of the ruling and owning classes and in the strategy – still in its first stage of development – of the working classes struggling for power'.[85]

The united front of the proletariat is thus seen as a means to counter the offensive of capital and prepare a new revolutionary strategy. It did not indicate, however, that the revolutionary phase had ended, nor that this strategy had to be developed in theory and in practice to the extent that the difficult tasks proposed were met, among these tasks the fight for the political and cultural leadership of the workers' movement. So, this important international event, which established the political formula of the united front as a distinctive point of the second phase of communist refoundation, put an end to the moment of the *scission*, enshrined 'to the masses' as a slogan and called for the formation of a 'united front of the proletariat'. However, it also expressed with absolute clarity that this formula was born under the sign of feebleness and indefiniteness.

---

84   Agosti 1975, vol. 2, pp. 471–8.

85   Ibid.

CHAPTER 2

The Paradox between Communist Scission and United Front

1 **How the Communist Scission in Italy Consolidated Itself over the Dispute within the Communist International and the Fascist Offensive**

Even after the Comintern's Third Congress, Gramsci continued to believe that the situation favoured the international socialist revolution. He had hopes that the deep social crisis in Poland would lead to the collapse of the ruling anti-Soviet régime and create good opportunities, because 'in the countries with a more objectively revolutionary situation, such as Germany, Czechoslovakia and Italy, the international environment will be more favourable to the proletariat in reorganising itself and victoriously organising the system of soviets atop the ruins of imperialism ...'[1]

As for Italian politics, Gramsci dedicated great attention to the polemic against the PSI and its leader Serrati, in which he also indicated that the new policy established at the Third Congress, with its implicit perception that a new phase in the struggle of the working class had begun and thus a new policy was needed, had not yet been well understood. Gramsci and especially the leadership of the PCd'I held the theoretical view that the moment of the *scission* and the revolutionary offensive was still current.

The policy of a united front with the socialists could not be put into action, because Gramsci believed that 'the Socialist Party is a counterrevolutionary party',[2] and understood that 'a united front means only one thing: the regrouping of the great proletarian masses around a concrete programme for immediate action in the realm of trade unions'. This would be justified by the fact that Italian trade unions appeared less as organs for the defence of corporate interests and more 'as organisations established by the sympathisers of certain political persuasions'.[3]

---

1 Gramsci 1974, pp. 334–6.
2 Gramsci 1974, p. 433.
3 Gramsci 1974, p. 439.

This political orientation was based in a plausible understanding of the final orientation of the Third Congress and on a certain interpretation of the process of class struggle in Italy, which 'would be an enigma if one neglected to take as the central focus of one's historical vision the ceaseless endeavours of certain governmental strata to incorporate into the ruling class the most eminent personalities from the working-class organisations'.[4] In this methodological suggestion, we can find the seeds not only of the notion of transformism but also of hegemony, which would be important threads in Gramsci's mature reflections.

For Gramsci, the state and the political régime in Italy were established as the northern capitalists bureaucratically superimposed themselves over the central and Southern agricultural classes. The development of industrial and financial capital in the North encouraged a rearrangement of alliances, and so the alliance of the propertied classes from north and south was cast aside in favour of an alliance with the urban proletariat, as a foundation for a parliamentary democracy which enabled the strengthening of trade unions and cooperatives.

However, 'the system of cooperatives and all the other organisations of resistance, insurance and production of the Italian working class were not born out of some original and revolutionary creative impulse, but depended on a whole series of compromises in which the strength of the government represented the dominant element'.[5]

It was by precisely these means that the bourgeoisie shaped a system of alliances which forged a petit-bourgeois stratum within the working class, with vested interests in the established order. But that which the bourgeoisie always allowed to grow under its control became a challenge after 1919, when the Socialist Party began to question its rule, such that 'fascism became the instrument for blackmailing the Socialist Party; for producing a scission between the petty-bourgeois elements, encrusted like barnacles upon the established interests of the working class, and the rest of the Socialist Party – which limited itself to feeding on ideological formulae'.[6]

So, on the one hand using fascist violence without directly involving the institutions of the state, and on the other 'intensifying to the point of absurdity the policy of compromise which is traditional for the Italian ruling classes, the bourgeoisie has succeeded in obtaining what it had patiently been preparing

---

4   Gramsci 1999b, p. 133.
5   Gramsci 1999b, p. 135.
6   Gramsci 1999b, p. 136.

for twenty years' – that is, the gradual assimilation of the reformist proletariat by the bourgeoisie. There could be no stronger reason to proceed to the scission actually implemented in Livorno, because, 'for the proletariat to become an independent class, it was necessary for the edifice of false economic might that had been built up in twenty years of compromise to disintegrate'.[7]

The challenge was to find out how the political process was creating 'a series of substantial transformations', the basis of which could be found 'in the attempt to bring to the Italian state the deep strata of the working masses from the cities and the countryside and thus deliver the state from its crisis; the instruments in this action are the two typical "social-democratic" parties: the Popular Party and the Socialist Party'.[8]

In Gramsci's opinion, besides, these parties were 'fulfilling a common task: that of laying the foundations for the future social-democratic Italian state'. Even fascist violence itself was seen as a means to reach this goal, it being recalled that 'nowadays, even in the fascist party, there are clear symptoms of social-democratic rottenness'. The recurring crises in parliament as well as fascist violence were 'elements of a phase of accommodation' during which 'all in all, the socialists are not asking for anything other than to make their own contribution to the common task of rebuilding and strengthening the state'.[9]

Gramsci's thoughts on the consequences of the defeat of the autonomous labour movement were correct to the extent that he realised that the offensive of capital and the crisis of the liberal state could only be solved through the emergence of a new mass political régime countering the socialist revolution. The mass basis of the new régime would be provided by the small bourgeoisie embedded in the PSI and the peasantry represented by the Popular Party, an alliance that could also involve the fascists, which by that time were redefining their identity, and thus bring a solution to the crisis.

Even if it is true that an intricate and rapid political process aggravated the crisis within the PSI and weakened the Popular Party, while fascism extended its influence over the petit-bourgeoisie and drew strength from its ever-closer alliance with big capital, it does not follow that there was any underestimation of this new political force and its possibilities. The essential point was that a capitalist state with a reactionary regime based on petit-bourgeois masses, directly opposed to working-class autonomy and the socialist revolution, was

---

7   Gramsci 1999b, pp. 136–7.
8   Gramsci 1974, pp. 453–5.
9   Ibid.

the only solution to the crisis within the framework of bourgeois domination – and Gramsci and the PCd'I had understood this.[10]

After the report on the activity of the leadership was presented at a plenary meeting in December 1921, the congress theses could be disseminated for debate within the party. The local assemblies in preparation for the PCd'I Second Congress met in February 1922. After Gramsci's opening speech, the Turin section unanimously approved the general political orientation proposed by the party leadership. The assembly was cautious about the tactic of the united front, an orientation which came from the Comintern and the German experience, stating that 'there are conditions of time and place in which the Communist Party can and should compromise with other parties which enjoy the trust of the more backward strata of the working and peasant classes, and also must insist on calling on these parties to break every relationship with the bourgeoisie in order to create a political coalition within the exclusive terrain of the working classes'.[11]

These conditions would appear only when the institutions of the coming proletarian power were established and the masses were turning to the left. However, since 'in the countries of central and western Europe this historic process has just entered its initial phase' and the proletariat had suffered a defeat in Italy, 'the only tactic possible at this moment is the united front of trade unions'.[12]

---

10   The greater part of the literature on the history of Italian communism and Gramsci's intellectual history tends to stress the fatal mistake of underestimating fascism, as if it were possible, in the heat of the moment, to foresee the concrete form the fascist régime would consolidate a few years later, as well as its specific way of organising the state and the masses. It does not seem right to say that the PCd'I believed that there was some intimate relationship between fascism and democracy, a common idea in certain sectors of the international communist left. Ever since Trotsky's analyses of fascism at the beginning of the 1930s, this presumed underestimation tended to be mistakenly repeated in studies dedicated to the relationship between the PCd'I and fascism. Actually, the point on which the Italian communists insisted at that moment, and Croce too, in his own way, was that there was an intimate relationship between fascism and liberalism, not fascism and democracy. More generally speaking, we can say that a united anti-fascist front was sought in a moment when the working class was defeated and divided, and the process of fascistisation was being driven forward by the offensive of capital. The risk in these interpretations is that they can be confused with a certain strategy used by the PCd'I in the 1960s and 1970s, and with the notion that democracy means liberal democracy. For Gramsci, in particular, when there is not mere silence there is indulgence for his having had some intuitions about the nature of fascism.

11   Gramsci 1974, pp. 497–8.

12   Ibid.

Almost at the same time, during the First Plenary Meeting of the ECCI in February 1922, once again the PCd'I held to its opposition to the united front policy, which was finding more and more support within the Comintern. Its allies were the Spanish and the French, who refused to make contacts with socialist leaders. At the same time, the PCd'I was preparing its Second National Congress, to be held in Rome on 20 March. Trotsky and Radek, soon after the ECCI Plenary, had the opportunity to examine the congress theses of the PCd'I and initially proposed they should be rejected, because their political orientation ran counter to the decisions of the Comintern Third Congress and to the political line there determined, which entrusted the communists with the task of becoming the majority of the proletariat through the united front tactic. Ultimately, it was agreed that the theses would be discussed as a contribution to the Comintern's Fourth Congress, to be held in November of that year, thus postponing the predictable dispute.

The fact remains that the leadership that arose from the November 1920 meeting of the communist fraction, which had sealed an accord among the leftist communism of Amadeo Bordiga, the *L'Ordine Nuovo* group and smaller currents, remained firmly attached to the political line established at that time and simply further explicated its conceptions. These conceptions converged with leftist communism, which carried weight in many parties. Basically, the PCd'I did not grasp the changed period that had been developing since March 1921, on which the Third Congress of the International had begun to draw possible conclusions, albeit still without the necessary depth. But maybe it would be best to observe that, given the understanding of capitalist crises and conception of the socialist revolution which served as their guides, the Italian communists did not consider this change to be the heart of the matter, but rather the organisation of the antagonistic subjectivity within the revolutionary party, which would be crucial for taking power.

In their analysis of the Italian situation, the socialist revolution still had a long path ahead of it, with the retreat of the working class, as in Germany, allowing for the emergence of a peculiar 'social-democratic' solution to the crisis of the liberal-bourgeois state, based on a coalition between Catholics and socialists. As Gramsci had insisted, however, a reactionary *coup de force*, such as the 1920 Kapp Putsch, also in Germany, could not be ruled out. In this context, fascism was seen as a constitutive element of the offensive of capital, aimed at breaking the autonomy of the working class and at its subordination to state institutions. Once the workers' resistance had been broken, these institutions could assimilate fascism within the framework of the 'social-democratic' solution itself. So, there was no fundamental opposition between the possibilities which the bourgeoisie had before it. It was always a matter of placing the labour movement within the parameters of the bourgeois state. This analysis was apparently corroborated by the transformation of fascism into a party and by its intention to contest parliamentary elections.

Between a 'social-democratic' solution or a reactionary coup which could eventually put fascism in power, the communists believed that capital would choose the former path. Thus they only accepted the perspective of a united workers' front in workplaces and trade unions, within the terms of the tactics already indicated by the Comintern, since this fit with the leftist communist view then prevalent in the PCd'I and its understanding of the socio-political process. The struggle against the PSI became a struggle against the instrument which capital was using to achieve its goal at that moment, as well as an unyielding defence of the political autonomy of the workers. In this way, no one realised that the worsening of the crisis of the PSI and the Popular Party created the possibility for fascism to establish itself as a mass reactionary régime, absorbing the social bases of those political groups.

The communists sought to base their particular united front policy in the trade unions, acting in all organisms dedicated to the defence of the working class against fascism and the capitalist offensive, and advocating that the trade unions unite around the CGL and join the Red Trade Union International. The congress theses on this topic, written by Gramsci and Tasca, note the importance of transcending the union as a form of workers' organisation, pointing to the need for factory councils and control over production.

A relatively small and heterogeneous opposition began to take shape within the PCd'I after the Comintern's Third Congress. Angelo Tasca was part of it. He had already entered into a serious polemic with Gramsci during the period of the factory councils. Antonio Graziadei was also part of it. Graziadei had proposed himself as the man who could preserve the unity of those who had supported the Third International in the socialist congress that decided the scission. Both defended, albeit with caution, the political orientation of the Comintern and the tactic of the united front also on the political terrain. So, too, did other militants, who may have been more emphatic, but did not have such a great capacity for expressing their ideas. Even though it enjoyed the encouragement and the sympathy of the Comintern's delegates Humbert-Droz and Kolarov, this view did not become more widespread.

Gramsci's intervention in the congress debate over the issue of the united front confirmed his convergence with the theses proposed by Bordiga and Ter-racini. He believed the tactical orientation of the party should not include any 'generic formula' that pointed towards admitting the possibility of a 'political united front'. As Gramsci said at that time, 'I am convinced that not just the Popular Party, but also a certain part of the Socialist Party must be excluded from the proletarian united front, in accordance with the conception of the theses approved by the Enlarged Executive Committee [of the PCd'I] because to make an agreement with them would mean making an agreement with the bourgeoisie'.[13]

For Gramsci, then, an alliance with the Popular Party was not possible because its base consisted mostly of the peasantry. Neither was an alliance with the Socialist Party possible, given the ambiguous nature of this party, which tried to represent both workers and peasants. Since an alliance with the peasantry could only be possible if they confronted the state, and not when 'the struggle they wage is inspired by motives which belong to the sphere of the bourgeois civil code',[14] with the defence of private property, he understood such alliances as unacceptable compromises, especially considering the bourgeoisie's effort to enlarge its social base in order to solve its social crisis.

It can be seen that the only conception of a united front acceptable to Gramsci would involve the industrial and agricultural proletariat allying with a view to the programme of the socialist revolution. So the goal set could not be anything other than attracting the working-class base of the PSI into joint action, because the PCd'I was essentially a workers' party. The influence of Bordiga at this point elided analytical mediations, and almost ruled out the perspective of a worker-peasant alliance.[15]

Gramsci had a different estimation of the situation in Germany, a country which had three worker-based parties at this time, since 'the tactic of the united front has no value except for industrial countries, where the backward workers can hope to be able to carry on a defensive activity by conquering a parliamentary majority', a tactic unfeasible in Italy considering the greater number of agricultural workers. Thus, 'the trade-union united front, by contrast, has an aim which is of primary importance for the political struggle in Italy', as this would be the only proper locus for creating the united workers' front without falling into 'trade-unionist' mistakes.[16]

Amadeo Bordiga had the opportunity to present these conclusions from the Second Congress of the PCd'I when he participated in the meeting of the three international organisations of the proletarian movement, which took place in April. Besides his opposition to the concessions made by the Comintern, the disagreements with the ECCI clearly came to light during a discussion of

---

13   Gramsci 1999b, p. 185.

14   Ibid.

15   An influence which, as we have already seen, was not extraneous to Gramsci's understanding of Italian reality. See note 85.

16   Gramsci 1999b, pp. 185–6.

the Italian situation. This meeting anticipated the political confrontation that would unfold during the Second Enlarged Plenary Meeting of the ECCI, set for June 1922 in Moscow.

Together with Graziadei and Gramsci, who had been nominated by the congress to represent the party before the International, Bordiga joined the Italian delegation to Moscow, as well as Ersilio Ambrogi, who waited for them in the Russian capital. Among the activities of the Second Plenary was the evaluation of the 'Italian question', a task for which a specific commission was designated. It was coordinated by Zinoviev, head of the Comintern at the time, and he also met with the PCd'I delegates. The ECCI, as expected, considered the theses of the PCd'I mistaken and to be at odds with the decisions taken by the Comintern since its Third World Congress.

Zinoviev authored a confidential decision, far harsher than the one made public, and sent it to the Italian communists. This document demanded that 'the PCd'I immediately and absolutely stop hesitating about the tactic of the united front', adding that 'it is impossible to admit in any case a distinction of principle between the united front in the realm of economic struggle and the united front in the realm of political struggle'.[17]

It is clear, beyond any other consideration, that the Comintern did not duly consider Gramsci's arguments on the specificity of the Italian situation, stating that the only possible political way to create a united front in Italy would be a trade-union united front, given the character and non-economistic tradition of the Italian trade unions. Gramsci thus insisted on the view that proletarian unity should be forged in the factory and in the organisations for the defence of the workers' immediate interests. The fact that the PSI had become a constitutive element of the bourgeois state prevented the realisation of such a political alliance.

There was also the demand that the PCd'I take up the slogan of the 'workers' government', though the Italians believed that this would only be possible when the actual seizure of power by the proletariat was near. It must be noted, however, that the meaning of this demand, as presented by Zinoviev, was far from expressing a consensus within the Comintern itself. In fact, at that moment, for Zinoviev, 'it is understood that this idea of a workers' government must not be seen as a parliamentary combination, but rather as the revolutionary mobilisation of all workers for bringing down bourgeois rule'.[18]

---

17   PCd'I 1976, pp. 114–15.

18   Relazione del partito comunista d'Italia al IV congresso dell'Internazionale Comunista 1976, pp. 114–15.

One last demand indicated that 'the PCd'I should take the initiative of the proletarian united front against fascism,'[19] a question over which there was disagreement both in form and contents, since the PCd'I believed that the united front should exist as a united front of the industrial and agricultural proletariat, bringing the communists and Maffi's socialist left closer together in the trade unions. It should not come about, as the Comintern thought, by means of a rapprochement with the PSI as a whole, especially not with Serrati, nor with the Popular Party. The unmediated radicalism of the PCd'I's politics gave priority to the direct struggle against capital and against the political power of the bourgeoisie, as condensed in the state.

Even though they were sure that accepting the Comintern's decisions would sow great confusion among militants, not doing so could lead to the Comintern turning against the party leadership. Thus a decision was made to insist on the attitude adopted until then – to adopt only formally the political line defined by the Comintern, adapting it to the understanding of Italian reality that came through the lenses of their particular 'leftist communism'. The importance of sticking by the discipline of the International became greater with the fact that a new scission was taking shape within the PSI, and the Comintern anticipated a merger of this split fraction with the PCd'I, just as had happened in Germany between the USPD majority and the KPD. The resistance of the PCd'I and Gramsci, who remained in Moscow, though obstinate, did not prevent the Comintern from openly supporting the fraction of Maffi, Lazzari and Riboldi at the coming congress of the PSI.

From July onward, the PCd'I began to spread the slogan of the 'proletarian government', fascism strengthened its offensive and the workers' resistance placed its final energies in regional general strikes throughout Piedmont and Lombardy. The failure of the attempts to create a coalition government joining liberals, Catholics and socialists together for the defence of legality and checking political violence – a coalition that could have included even the fascists – led the reformist wing of the PSI to call for a general strike in the name of legality, through the Alleanza del Lavoro. Having opposed every prior call by the communists when the resistance had displayed greater vitality, the reformists now called and ended the strike at a moment when the defence lines of the working class had already been broken, and so all they did was to open the gate for fascism's decisive attack, which took the form of street fights lasting several days.

---

19   Ibid.

As the final defeat of the proletarian movement neared in early October, the Nineteenth Congress of the PSI assembled with the sole purpose of confirming its scission, which was now a certainty. The possible merger of the maximalist wing of the PSI with the PCd'I was seen as an important victory for the International's united front tactic. With this goal in its sights, the ECCI sent a letter appealing to the socialist congress, directed at the maximalists, observing that 'the most elementary and most urgent task for Italy lies in this: in gathering as soon as possible all the revolutionary forces, and with them opposing the proletarian bloc to the bloc of reformist, fascist and imperialist forces'.[20]

Since the reformists were slightly in the minority, they left and founded the Unitarian Socialist Party, while the rapprochement of Serrati's maximalists and Maffi's 'third internationalists' assured the survival of the PSI, which would immediately have to face the issue of merging with the PCd'I, as presaged by the Comintern. Renewing its decision to join the Comintern, the PSI soon sent a delegation to the Fourth World Congress, hoping to present itself as the most faithful follower of the political line of the united front. The PCd'I, on the other hand, believed that the pressure for the merger which the Comintern had exerted challenged its own leadership's legitimacy in the context of the International.

The visit of a Comintern delegation led by Rakosi, a Hungarian whose mission was to prepare the merger between the two parties, anticipated the conflicts the PCd'I delegation would have to face in Moscow, though there was resistance to the merger also within the PSI. The PCd'I faced a dilemma between the force of discipline and the cohesion of its leadership; the PSI's dilemma was whether or not to sacrifice its historical identity.

A few weeks later, fascism finally rose to power with the mission of solving all the contradictions within the ruling power bloc and guarding the way for financial capital's rise to preponderance, all with the support of a régime based on the petit-bourgeois masses. In Moscow, Gramsci wrote an article showing that the origins of fascism and Mussolini's government were in the offensive of capital begun in 1920 with the creation of the National Confederation of Industry [CNI, the Confederazione Nazionale dell'Industria]. Giolitti returned to a government that had Bolini as its Minister of War, carrying out a plan to enlist sixty thousand demobilised officers – whose remuneration was guaranteed for four more years – in the 'fasci di combattimento' [the 'combatants' leagues'], which 'had previously remained merely a small organisation of socialist, anarchist,

---

20   Agosti 1974, pp. 589–91.

syndicalist and republican elements who had been favourable to Italian participation in the War on the Entente side'.[21]

There began the rapprochement of the big landowners with the captains of
industry, as well as the activities of fascist 'squadrismo'. Unfortunately, Gramsci's analysis of this phenomenon could not continue because he had health
problems at precisely that moment when he would have addressed the process
of fascistisation.

2   The United Front Policy in the Communist International and in the
        USSR: Theoretical Weakness and Political Defeat

Germany's socio-political process, where the offensive of capital was apparent in the decline in workers' purchasing power and an attack against liberal-
democratic institutions, gave impulse to the communists' united front tactic.
They were willing to give outside support to a coalition government formed by
the SPD and the USPD in the region of Thuringia, and made several appeals for
joint protests and for international solidarity. The new orientation was implemented by leaders who had previously opposed it, but even so a new left wing
in the KPD remained opposed to the united-front tactic because it meant an
alliance with social democracy. Putting the new tactic into practice was a task
permeated with great difficulties in almost every European country, with the
communist parties resisting it in various degrees.

The main problem that presented itself to the communists at this moment
lay in interpreting the content and meaning of the political formula of the
united front (the counterpart of which lay in the issue of the NEP). In a position
that made concessions to left communism, which insistently rejected the new
political line, Zinoviev maintained that the international socialist revolution
would soon resume, and thus the united front policy would have the effect of
proving to the masses the hesitancy of the social-democratic leaders.

People like Radek (and quite probably Lenin, too), who understood that
what was at stake was a deeper and longer reflux of the proletarian movement
as a whole, were able to come closer to seeing a new strategy for the socialist
struggle in the political formula of the united front. Naturally, in each reading
the political relationship with reformism implied a different, almost opposed
content. This implicit ambiguity in the political orientation of the Communist International fed the social democrats' mistrust towards the possibility of

---

21   Gramsci 1999b, p. 195.

joint work with the communists, thus limiting the concrete reach of a certain variant of this formula – that which most stressed the conditions of bourgeois democracy.

Not only was the new policy ambiguous in its theoretical and practical formulation, it also faced strong opposition from the very first moment. In Russia, there was no open, vehement opposition to the NEP, partly on account of a decision by the Tenth Congress of the RKP(B) prohibiting the formation of fractions. It is also well-known that a large part of the party leadership saw the NEP only as a temporary retreat and not as a strategy for socialist transition. Rather, it was thought that this latter should be developed and articulated with the strategy for the international socialist revolution, summed up in the political formula of the united front, as proven by the consequences of the political-ideological dispute in the USSR that began shortly before Lenin's death.

Open or discrete opposition to the new tactic was more or less visibly present in all communist parties in the countries most important to the Comintern. In Germany, Czechoslovakia, France and Italy, the united front policy was either viewed with mistrust or mutilated in its application. The communist parties resisted passing from the moment of the scission to the policy of a united front with reformism. The main reason for this was a fear of sacrificing their newly acquired identity, but there was also a certain inability to develop this identity in confrontation with other cultural and political trends of the working-class and socialist movement. However, this resistance to the new political line also entailed some awareness of the specificities of the West as compared to Russia. There was a fear that the Comintern would collapse if it acknowledged that the Austro-Marxists' analyses of capitalism's tendencies to reorganise itself in the political offensive of the bourgeoisie were partially correct, and the mainly catastrophist tendencies in the Comintern's own analyses mistaken.

Ambiguity and the difficulty in clearly defining the strategic content of the political formula of the united front soon appeared in the debates of the KPD. After the Comintern's Third Congress, Karl Radek, who represented the ECCI in the KPD at that time, defended the use of parliamentary-democratic means in order to arrive at a 'workers' government'. Should they affect the interests of capital, the measures taken by such a government could provoke a reaction from the bourgeoisie, and this reaction would work as a catalyst for factory councils and the struggle for proletarian dictatorship. The communists should participate in any such government every time there was a real intent to fight against capital.

This view of the united front and the workers' government as a parliamentary coalition was rejected by August Thalheimer and Clara Zetkin on behalf of the KPD majority, which stated that communist participation in a government based on a parliamentary majority was inconceivable, even if it was formed by reformist parties with a working-class base, because this government would be the last defence of capitalist order and the last stage of bourgeois democracy. The communists could naturally support a social-reformist government from the outside whenever it introduced measures that favoured the workers or any time it was threatened by political forces that were clearly bourgeois or reactionary. For the greater part of the leadership of the KPD, therefore, governmental participation could only take place upon reaching the threshold of rupture with bourgeois institutions and when the dictatorship of the workers' councils was about to be established, when the majority of the working class was willing to break with the dominion of capital. A trend even further to the left thought any accommodation with social democracy to be undesirable, believing it to have completely passed to the political camp of the bourgeoisie, and thus arguing that the struggle for proletarian unity could only take place in the realm of production and the fight for workers' power.

In December 1921, an ECCI meeting decided that the united front tactic was the key for the communists to conquer the masses, but the restrictions on the leaders of the social-democratic parties remained significant indeed. In an attempt to get around the resistance towards the new policy, the document produced in this meeting stated that the working masses were 'beginning to shift to the left', though, 'on the other hand, under the influence of ever stronger attacks from capital, among the workers there is now a spontaneous tendency to unity, which is literally impossible to contain'.[22]

The workers' united front could include agreements with the social-democratic parties as long as they did not affect the communists' autonomy and right to criticism, and it should be applied in accordance with the realities of each country. The year 1922 began with an appeal from the ECCI together with the Red Trade Union International for the formation of a proletarian united front. The explanation of the need for a united front presented as an important novelty the implicit suggestion that such a policy could define a whole phase, of greater or lesser length, in the struggle for the conquest of the majority of the working class for the socialist revolution. The document acknowledged that 'the chains of the past, the influence exerted by the capitalist school, the press and the Church are still strong', and that the working class was still far from revolution. However, even though the workers still did

---

22   Agosti 1976, vol. 2, pp. 521–31.

not dare to undertake the struggle for power, they should unite 'at least in the name of life pure and simple, in the struggle for a piece of bread, in the struggle for peace'.[23]

Finally, this document acknowledged the need for an everyday socio-cultural struggle so that the communists could attain the capacity for leadership within the mass movement as a whole. Beginning with obstructing the offensive of capital and the fight for everyday demands, the united front policy could rapidly become an offensive strategy, though this suggestion was far away from sinking roots in the Comintern.

Soon after, from 21 February to 4 March 1922, there was a plenary meeting of the ECCI (the first in a series) for the purpose of clarifying the tactic and winning over the recalcitrant. The united front tactic and the conclusions of the Comintern's Third Congress were reaffirmed, but there was no theoretical improvement in the understanding of the new policy, not only because there was still strong resistance, but also because the reading of the historical moment was replete with serious mistakes. The political formula of the united front, in all its reach, could only become a new revolutionary praxis and a new subjectivity if it were associated with a proper reading of the social conflict. During this meeting, PCd'I delegate Umberto Terracini once again spoke on behalf of a current contrary to the united front tactic, also comprising the French and Spanish communists. However, ultimately, even if not out of conviction, everyone formally agreed to follow the political line reaffirmed at the congress.

The united front policy met with resistance from all sides, from the left wing of the communist parties as well as the social democrats. This restricted its implementation and its reach, even if certain localised and isolated successes were achieved. The Berlin conference with the three international political organisations of the working class showed the difficulties as well as the possibilities of this orientation. Even if the result of the meeting was not very auspicious, in a certain sense it strengthened the tendency within the communist parties favourable to the united front, especially in Germany, Czechoslovakia and Poland. But there was still great resistance coming from France and Italy, for different reasons and in various ways. While the PCF saw the crystallisation of internal conflicting trends, the PCd'I reacted almost en bloc against the International's attempts to impose the political line established at the Third Congress.

---

23   Agosti 1976, vol. 2, pp. 532–8.

The Second Plenary Meeting of the ECCI, which took place in June, opted for a wait-and-see attitude towards the PCF [French Communist Party] congress, to be held that October. But the PCd'I had already concluded its own congress, establishing a policy very different from the one proposed by the leaders of the International, which was wagered on the PSI suffering a new scission even before the Comintern's Fourth Congress due to be held in November. There was a further progression of the collision course between the Comintern and the PCd'I in a confidential document written at this meeting, demanding the organisation of the united front.

As the date of the Comintern's Fourth Congress approached, the debate as to the possibility of a 'workers' government' arose as a deepening and a consequence of the political formula of the united front. This issue had presented itself time and again in Germany ever since the struggle against the 1920 Kapp Putsch, when it was first raised by the unions.[24] The external support provided by the KPD to the regional governments led by the SPD and the USPD ensured that actual communist participation was discussed, as well as the possibility of a workers' government nationally. By the end of 1921, after the KPD received the ECCI's approval for the conception of the united front and the 'workers' government' as understood by Radek, the Czechoslovak communists also addressed this question, approving the slogan of the 'workers' government' in September 1922, though not disregarding the specificities of their own country.

As leftist communism lost ground and the resistance to the tactic of the united front largely became restricted to the PCd'I, referring only to the practical implementation of this political formula, it was possible for the question of the 'workers' government' to become the main focus of the Comintern's Fourth Congress. However, just as the left tended to interpret the policy of the united front as a new way of fighting the reformist leaders, establishing alliances only 'from below' instead of understanding it as a policy aimed at uniting the political forces of the working class, the same happened in the case of the 'workers' government'. With the communists looking to establish a mass line that could stop and reverse the offensive of capital, as well as create the conditions that could elevate the member parties of the Comintern to the leadership of the movement, there emerged two different views of the political formula of the united front and the 'workers' government' idea that appeared as its consequence.

---

24   In March 1920, a philo-monarchist coup was prevented by the immediate action of the working class, especially the German trade unions.

To the left of the Communist movement, 'workers' government' could only mean the implementation of the 'dictatorship of the proletariat' – even if this part of the left was not homogeneous. There were those who accepted alliances and occasional agreements with social democracy and also those who insisted on separation from this latter. Zinoviev's more nuanced formulation, which aimed at a balance between the different views, was also defeated, and it was Radek's conception that prevailed, one that indicated a possible connection among the united front, different forms of workers' government, and the beginning of the socialist transition. The workers' government, the goal established for the united front, would not only be one way among others of containing the offensive of capital, but also a possible way to start a strategic counter-attack. To that extent, the possibility that the socialist revolution would begin with the election of a workers' government formed by a coalition of the socialist forces bolstered by a broad mass movement was now under discussion. There was a clear attempt to seek an alternative strategy for the socialist revolution in the West, even though, once again, the risk of converging with the formulations present in Austro-Marxism did not go unnoticed.[25]

Given the impact of fascism's rise to power in Italy, the Fourth Congress attempted an initial approach toward the problem by characterising the new régime as a product of 'agrarian reaction', a formulation which was qualified somewhat in the debate between those who, like Bordiga, saw in fascism a form of capitalist reaction following a revolutionary crisis, and those who, like Radek, saw new elements in a political movement of the petit bourgeoisie. Their difficulty in identifying the specific nature of the fascist dictatorship was always associated with the more general question of not realising that the workers' movement was carrying out a strategic retreat before the offensive of capital, which had in fascism its expression and result.

The failure to identify the correlation of forces prevented an orderly retreat as well as the due preparation of the counter-offensive, a movement which the political formula of the united front really would have made possible. The theoretical and cultural limits which prevented the development of this formula, as well as its disfiguring by those who resisted it, only aggravated the process of the defeat of the revolutionary movement from late 1920 onward.

---

25   This strategy became stronger and established itself in the communist movement with the new conditions brought by the defeat of Nazi-fascism after the Second World War. Its highlights were the 'Italian road to socialism', which was Togliatti's initiative, and Berlinguer's Eurocommunism.

Just as the chances of the international socialist revolution succeeding after 1917 depended largely on the working class of Germany and Russia rising to power within a relatively short time-span, so, too, was the success of the political formula of the united front conditioned by the results of the NEP and by the situation in Germany. However, the KPD congress which took place at the end of January 1923, soon after the occupation of the Ruhr by French and Belgian troops, set the stage for a fierce debate on the themes of the united front and the workers' government.

The majority of the central leadership, which included Brandler, Thalheimer, Clara Zetkin and other followers of the Spartakist tradition, acquiesced without conviction to Karl Radek and the ECCI's notion that the united front should include the whole of the SPD (even though its left was to be the main ally), and that the communists should take part in the regional coalition governments in Thuringia and Saxony, following working-class policies within bourgeois democracy and using the instruments of bourgeois democracy in order to participate in government with the help of the mass movement. The leftist opposition, which had strong support in some of the most industrialised areas of the country, defended, through Thälmann, Maslow and Ruth Fischer, a united front only 'from below' and understood 'workers' government' as a synonym for 'dictatorship of the proletariat', emerging from an insurrectionary process.

An escalation in the offensive of capital worsened the situation of the working class, particularly in Germany, and also brought about a new effort to isolate the USSR. The nationalist and fascist tendencies in Germany were gaining strength and a coup in Bulgaria deposed the Peasants' Union government. The Third Plenary Meeting of the ECCI, in June 1923, discussed the situation while echoing the ongoing debate in the USSR on the difficulties and perspectives of the NEP. The 'worker-peasant government' slogan was approved, expressing a concern for widened social alliances as well as including the most backward countries of the imperialist order. At the same time, the difficulties in converging with social democracy were felt, as the incorporation of the Vienna International by the Amsterdam Socialist International weakened the position of the left wing of social democracy, which had been bridging the gap between the extremes of the workers' movement.

Foreign occupation, the failure of Hitler's Munich Putsch and the deterioration of the social-economic situation created very positive conditions for the development of the united front policy in Germany. Even though Radek's proposal that the communists' alliance policy be enlarged so as to reach the social bases of nationalism and fascism – namely, the petit bourgeoisie – had increased the party's size and lessened its isolation, this policy was unable to guarantee working-class unity, and still less prepare an insurrectionary movement with a real chance of victory. The lack of a clear and decisive mass political orientation effectively promoting Communist hegemony, giving priority to establishing a dialogue with social democracy of specific intent and acting in every sphere of socio-cultural and state life, enabled nothing but a merely politicist and superficial practice of the united front.

The anti-fascist day of protest on 29 July, which had to take place indoors because of a government prohibition, seemed to calibrate the axis of the united front policy. The 9 and 10 August strikes against precarious living standards, called by the communists without social-democratic support, led the government to resign. The safest indication that the united front policy was unable to impose itself as a strategic alternative was the fact that the ECCI, which had until then attempted to restrain the left of the KPD, now began to consider the situation as prone to socialist revolution, at the same time as the SPD was negotiating its entrance into the government coalition. In spite of the resistance presented by the left wing of the social democrats, a republican government came to power with a broad coalition, including the SPD, in an attempt to overcome the financial crisis and renegotiate Germany's war reparations to France. The consequence of these developments was a reflux of the mass movement.

In these circumstances, the continuity of the united front policy as defined by Radek and the Fourth Congress could have been the formation and the strengthening of regional workers' governments and common work with the social democrats, demanding that promised fiscal penalties on big companies be fulfilled, as well as the dismantling of paramilitary fascist and monarchist organisations. Another option would be to fight for the strengthening of the workers' organisation within the factories, with a view to increasing the pressure on the governments in which the social democrats participated, and making concrete government action a condition for offering them external support, as was proposed in Brandler and Thalheimer's view.

The crisis worsened, and once-promising elements of the political formula of the united front were left aside: both Radek's variant, which was wagered on the virtues of bourgeois democracy, and Brandler and Thalheimer's, which placed its energies in the self-organisation of the masses and in a revival of the councils. The result of an action whose putschist character was clear – on account of an unresolved strategic attitude toward bourgeois democracy – could not have been anything but failure.

In September, as the Comintern and the KPD confidently prepared the insurrection in Germany, in Spain and Bulgaria reactionary coups deeply affected the already shaken communist organisations. In October, the communists joined the regional governments of Saxony and Thuringia, but the central government and the army (with the assent of the social democrats) demanded the dissolution of the 'proletarian centuries', a force then recently created to help the insurrection.

On 21 October, during the meeting of the factory councils, the KPD proposed an insurrectionary general strike. The social democrats remained static, forcing the communists to retreat. Even so there was an attempt at insurrection in Hamburg, without any success, and on 29 October the army occupied the main cities in Saxony. They deposed the workers' government, which was replaced by a social-democratic government aligned with the central government.

This fresh defeat for communist insurgency had lasting and irreversible effects on the communist movement. Germany was of pivotal importance for revolutionary strategy at the time, and the first crisis of the NEP was emerging in the USSR. Initially, the grave social situation, and then the NEP's relative success, as well as Lenin's authority, had secured the unity of the RKP(B) and the application of the united front policy within the context of the conditions and needs of the Russian revolutionary East. Trotsky, betraying his shallow conception of the NEP and the united front policy, already at the Twelfth Congress of the RKP(B) in April 1923 presented his disagreement with the bias he observed toward agrarian production and the peasantry as against the need for industrialisation and broader plans to go beyond the NEP.

Even though his remarks met with little attention, Trotsky insisted on his opinions, adding criticism to the bureaucratisation of the party and the state as well as concerns with 'workers' democracy'. Trotsky began his fight soon after the failure of the German workers' insurrection in October with a document signed by forty-six important militants, a document he used to seek a greater hearing for his ideas. Trotsky's disagreement with the majority, which defended the continuity of the policy already in force, was motivated by demands for faster industrial development and by greater democracy within the party, so as to allow for the return of factions.

Trotsky was defeated at the Thirteenth Congress of the RKP(B), which took place a few days before Lenin's death, in the beginning of 1924, and which reaffirmed the importance of the worker-peasant alliance. Then Trotsky became more and more inclined towards splitting with the group of leaders who had made the revolution in 1917, and towards allying himself with those who had been part of leftist communism and its variations. The difficulties of the NEP, the fact that different sectors of the Bolshevik Party contested it either quietly or openly, the defeat of the insurrections attempted in Germany and other countries, as well as Lenin's death, were elements which contributed greatly to undermining the policy of the united front.

3   Gramsci in Moscow and the Solution to the Dispute between the
       PCd'I and the Communist International

Right at the beginning of the Fourth Congress of the Comintern, which opened
on 5 November 1922, only one week after fascism came to power in Italy,
there was a clumsy and gravely mistaken attempt to interpret the fascist phenomenon. The analysis of the Italian communists, especially Gramsci, was
comparatively much closer to grasping the essence of this new socio-political
movement than was the Comintern.

   In a letter appealing to the workers and peasants of Italy, the Comintern
stated that 'Fascists are above all a weapon in the hands of the landowners.
The industrial and commercial bourgeoisie anxiously follows the experience
of unrestrained reaction, seeing it as a kind of black Bolshevism'.[26]

   The report from the PCd'I presented to the Congress, in its turn, updated
the theses from the Second Party Congress until a few weeks before fascism's
rise to power. Written by Bordiga, the document affirmed that there was no
chance that the liberal state would be restored, emphasising that 'the situation
can yield two very different outcomes: either the proletariat and the unions
will dwindle and fall under a régime of slavery, or there will be a revolutionary
response from the masses, who in this case will have to face the coalition of
fascism, the state and all forces which uphold the democratic foundations of
the present institutions'.[27]

   The programme of action expounded by the PCd'I during the Fourth Congress of the Comintern established three fundamental targets to be destroyed
so as to extinguish the state power of the bourgeoisie: 'the state apparatus,
with all its resources of political and military strength; fascism, with its potent
counterrevolutionary organisation; and social democracy, which deprives the
revolutionary struggle of a large portion of the proletariat thanks to its pacifist
preaching'.[28]

   It was considered indispensable for the development of the PCd'I that members of other worker-based parties gradually came over to its own ranks, and
thus any project of merging with the PSI should be rejected. For now, only
the individual entry of socialists belonging to the 'third internationalist' fraction would be acceptable. There was also a negative answer to the question
of whether 'among the demands of the PCd'I it would be possible to include

---

26   Agosti 1976, vol. 2, pp. 615–17.
27   Agosti 1976, vol. 2., p. 30.
28   Agosti 1976, vol. 2, p. 41.

a solution to the question of the governmental régime that is not that of the proletarian dictatorship'. For the PCd'I, 'there are no other forces inclined to direct anti-fascist struggle besides those willing to fight a revolutionary struggle against the state: communists and libertarians'.[29]

Thus their goal could be nothing less than 'a government by workers and peasants, a phrase which means the same as proletarian dictatorship'.[30] Their influence and insertion among the masses would be obtained to the detriment of socialists, populars and republicans, in the fight against fascist reaction and for the revolutionary unity of the trade unions, noting that 'the united pro-letarian front for demands opposing the bosses' offensive is the fundamental platform of the present activity of the Communist Party of Italy and the way for it to achieve the foremost position in the leadership of the Italian prolet-ariat'.[31]

The key to the political line of the PCd'I lay in the understanding that the crisis of capitalism and the Italian state had no solution within the existing parameters, and that the bourgeoisie would only be able to recompose its power with unstable forms, either by means of a liberal-Catholic-reformist party coalition or open fascist dictatorship. From this came the notion that the united front should aim, without mediations, directly at revolution and proletarian dictatorship.

Even though Zinoviev had distanced himself from this conception during the Fourth Congress of the Comintern, the fact remains that on various occa-sions both before and after that Congress he stated that he believed the workers' government and the dictatorship of the proletariat to be synonymous, because he still believed that the revolutionary movement would soon resume. The political formula of the united front was a tactical expedient of only limited duration, this being at least partially aimed at exposing the social-democratic leaders. This observation contributes to understanding how political positions later came to distinguish themselves from each other within the leadership of the RKP(B).

Therefore, there are points of contact between Zinoviev and the PCd'I which have not been explored because the Bolshevik leader was concerned with maintaining a certain balance within the Comintern and, at that moment, there was a strong tendency towards isolating the communist left. The con-tempt with which Zinoviev regarded the possibility of fascism betrayed his

---

29   Agosti 1976, vol. 2, p. 54.

30   Agosti 1976, vol. 2, p. 51.

31   Agosti 1976, vol. 2, p. 54.

view of the crisis and the capitalist offensive. Radek, on the other hand, warranted that the defeat of the international socialist revolution was of deeper significance, and would last far longer, and so held that a lasting and systematic investment in the united front policy was necessary. Hence his more nuanced perception of fascism as the product of an alliance between big capital and the reactionary mass movement of the petit bourgeoisie.[32]

In any event, the positions of the majority of the PCd'I, represented by Amadeo Bordiga, were sharply criticised at the congress in the speeches of Zinoviev, Trotsky, Bukharin, and Zetkin, as well as others, such as Tasca and Graziadei, who were part of the Italian delegation's minority. Not surprisingly, the main point of disagreement was the issue of the merger with the PSI, around which hung different views of the united front and the role of social-democracy at that historical moment. The congress commission had approved the immediate merger of the PCd'I and PSI, such that the majority aligned with Bordiga was placed before a *fait accompli* further reinforced by a letter signed by the leaders of the Russian party, the implications of which were not hard to discern: a new majority was to be formed through the convergence of the Communist minority and the maximalists, thus aligning the PCd'I with the trends more toward the right within the International and creating an internal instability that would render the party incapable of resisting fascism.

Faced with this risk, Gramsci, with greater resolution than Bordiga, decided to mount a resistance according to Scoccimarro's proposal, displacing the issue onto the conditions and manner of the merger. The terms presented by the PCd'I were so restrictive that in practice they meant a return to the conditions set out in the PCd'I's report to the Fourth Congress, which only accepted the individual adhesion of members of the 'third internationalist' trend of the PSI. Eventually a compromise was reached, but the socialist delegation also presented conditions and justified the need for the national PSI leadership's agreement. The resistance presented by both sides plus a new wave of fascist repression rendered the merger impossible and aggravated the internal situation both in the PCd'I and the PSI. The Comintern's manoeuvres to encourage the merger, in the hope that a stronger party would emerge to implement the united front policy, actually made the workers' resistance to fascism far weaker.

Fascist violence became institutionalised with the new régime, and started to coordinate its actions with the repressive forces of the state. Now both had the same command. While the intensity of fascist squadrism had not decreased, at the beginning of 1923 an offensive by the recently installed régime

---

32   Spriano 1967, p. 240.

against the institutions of the workers' movement, which was still resisting, was put into practice. A wave of attacks against newspapers, party and trade union headquarters, including beatings and murders, made victims of anarchists, communists and socialists. The PCd'I was strongly hit, and the greater part of the central leadership was arrested, including Amadeo Bordiga, most regional leaders, and about five thousand militants, which amounted to a quarter of the party.

Faced with Comintern pressure to complete the merger with the PSI and carry out the political line approved at the Fourth Congress, and still having to face the fascist attacks, the original leading group of the PCd'I gave in. A division in the Italian delegation, briefly apparent in Moscow, now came to the surface. The majority was divided between those who, like Bordiga, refused any interference from the Comintern and preferred to be in the opposition in the international arena, attempting to unite the left communists, and those who understood that an accord with the Comintern was essential, in spite of all the disagreements, for facing fascism. This was Gramsci's position. In March, Ruggiero Grieco wrote a collective resignation on behalf of the leadership and sent it to the ECCI. It argued that it was impossible to act in such circumstances without a clear tactic. As the leadership of the PCd'I did not agree with the Comintern's line, they stepped out of the way so as to facilitate the merger with the PSI and the implementation of the new policy.[33]

Gramsci was preparing to return to Italy together with the commission for the merger between the communists and socialists, when he learned that the fascist régime had issued a warrant for various leaders of the PCd'I, including himself. Thus Gramsci remained in Moscow until a new decision regarding himself and his new responsibilities could be taken. Even though Gramsci was committed to the merger, because he understood it to be inevitable and believed that it would open a new phase in the life of the party – which now had to face fascism, the new occupant of the bourgeois state – he thought that the struggle was above all a battle for control over the merger process so as to avoid the PCd'I being aligned with the more rightist sectors of the International, which would likely be the case if the initiative were left to Tasca and the maximalists.

In a letter sent from Moscow in March, Gramsci drew attention to the risk that, considering the PCd'I's resistance against the merger and especially the weaknesses displayed before the wave of repression unleashed by fascism, 'the left of the Socialist Party might be too highly esteemed and the Comintern

---

33   Spriano 1967, pp. 257–8.

might direct its greatest hopes toward it'. Besides, 'it would be a disaster to give an air of failure to something that was decided in a World Congress [of the Communist International] and so what matters is that we continue working on the merger', even if on an extended deadline.[34] Gramsci also conveyed the news that the Comintern had decided to create a secretariat devoted to the struggle against fascism, with offices in Berlin and Vienna, the latter specifically aimed at coordinating the work of the PCd'I, to which 'comrade Gennari should be appointed'.[35]

As the fascist onslaught tore the party to pieces, Gramsci started to realise the limits of the political strategy which had brought the party into existence and led it to this point. He understood the point of view of the Comintern and admitted that, considering the difficulties of the situation, 'the only possible tactic would be the International's'. The pressure coming from both the Comintern and the realities of fascism led Gramsci to agree to the merger between the PCd'I and the PSI, though under very specific terms, and, as a consequence, he adopted the united front policy which was being developed and clarified by communists in various countries. In order to put into practice these ideas, which were still not too solid, Gramsci proposed the creation of a fortnightly newspaper which could be named *Common Sense*, after an English publication. Such a suggestion brings to mind the name of Tom Paine (a likely inspiration for the English editors) but also that of Georges Sorel. This is probably why Gramsci suggested that such a name would be able to express 'an agenda', the agenda which the Comintern intended to spread among the masses.[36]

Gramsci realised ever more clearly that the link with the Comintern and the application of the decisions of the Fourth Congress was indispensable to the survival of the party and to making sure that the *scission* consummated in Livorno did not remain a matter of 'doctrine' but rather assumed the characteristics of a new *tradition* with the ability of taking the proletariat to power. Meanwhile, Bordiga chose publicly to denounce the Comintern's interference and to refuse the merger with the PSI, seeing this as a better way to defend the original leadership. Seeking to counteract the imminent breakup of the PCd'I leadership, Gramsci decided that it was time to regroup the comrades from the old *L'Ordine Nuovo*, which would also serve the purpose of preventing that tradition from being exploited by Tasca's right wing, as well as to ward them and the maximalists, who were about to join the party, off the leadership. In

---

34   Gramsci 1992, p. 503.
35   Gramsci 1992, p. 509.
36   Gramsci 1992, p. 114.

this case, there would be a reversion of the *L'Ordine Nuovo* group to the period before the merger, when it remained organically connected with maximalism.

Gramsci then felt that there was a need to 'create a nucleus within the party, one that is not a fraction, of comrades who possess a maximum of ideological homogeneity, and for that reason are able to give practical action a maximum of directive consistency'. The mistake of avoiding 'taking theoretical and practical disagreements to their full conclusions', which had been the practice of the *L'Ordine Nuovo* group, would have to be overcome so that the theoretical and practical differences with Bordiga's trend could be clarified. As for the problem of the PSI, Gramsci acknowledged the deep roots of the social-democratic tradition and argued that with the united front 'a vast and careful political action is required, breaking up this tradition day by day, breaking up the organ that embodies it. The tactic of the International fits that purpose'.[37]

Gramsci was now aware that it was of the utmost importance to create a new leadership anchored in the tradition of *L'Ordine Nuovo*, so as to win over the masses that followed the PSI and thus dismantle that organisation. At this point, the essential thing was to prevent the PCd'I from falling into the historical bed of social democracy, a risk that was present in Angelo Tasca's 'rightist faction'. Keeping good relations with the Comintern and having a fair understanding of its policy were essential elements of this strategy, because, as Gramsci noted, 'we are in a questionable position, in view of the international situation. The tactic of the united front, laid down with considerable precision by the Russian comrades, both technically and in the general approach to its practical application, has in no country found the party nor the men capable of concretising it'.[38]

Gramsci apparently began to understand the meaning of the political formula of the united front, and more: the Sardinian revolutionary began to realise how the experience of *L'Ordine Nuovo* and the factory councils was a small affluent of a large political and cultural river that had the historic meaning of a true *communist refoundation*. His observations about organisational issues, the need for ideological divergences to be clarified, as well as this initial understanding of the meaning of the political formula of the united front brought Gramsci very close to Lenin.

Fascist repression, the resignation of the PCd'I's leadership and the victory of the opponents of the merger at the Twentieth Congress of the PSI, which took place in the middle of April 1923, were factors decisively contributing to

---

37   Gramsci 1992, pp. 118–23.
38   Gramsci 1999b, p. 227.

the failure of the agreement sealed in Moscow between the two parties putting both within the scope of the Comintern. In June, during the Third Enlarged Plenary of the ECCI, Angelo Tasca presented the majority trend of the PCd'I as responsible for the failure of the merger and the policy proposed by the Comintern, having received the approval of the socialist fraction favourable to the merger. Faced with this, all majority leaders united, Gramsci included, in defence of the party.

It was most important at that moment to oppose Tasca, as the leadership's resignation would probably be accepted, and the space for a new group would be cleared. The majority position still held that there were irremediable contradictions in the fascist government and its bases, and these would provide the revolutionary movement with new possibilities. Gramsci, who had been accused by Zinoviev of having a dubious nature, stated at this meeting, not without a certain caution, that 'after the time of the Fascist government the time of the decisive struggle of the proletariat for conquering power will begin. This time is somewhat distant'.[39]

The report from the executive commission of the PCd'I presented at the Third Enlarged Plenary of the ECCI, which was to a great extent written and organised by Gramsci, analysed the difficulties fascism faced in its intention of uniting Italy's ruling classes and preserving the petit bourgeoisie as its support base, and also pointed to problems in fascism's conquest of the state. However, the greatest difficulty lay precisely in bringing to certain sectors of middle capital the same alliance made with financial capital. Hence why 'the opposition to Fascism presented by the largest papers of the bourgeoisie is an expression and a reflex of a process which has yet only begun, but which, in the future, will unfold as a gradual reduction of the social basis of Fascism'.[40]

The National Fascist Party was identified as a mass party of the petit bourgeoisie, which, as it took power, would try to establish the political unity of the ruling elite, leading to tensions and complaints among the petit bourgeoisie and its own mass membership, thus allowing for a shift towards liberalism, but also for a differentiation within fascism itself. The document analysed the contradictions of fascism and was animated by the hope that it would not be able to consolidate itself. Towards the end, it indicated that the PCd'I should 'act on the general political arena to raise against fascism every social force that can be used to that purpose ... to instigate a tight revolutionary unity of workers and peasants ...'[41]

---

39   Spriano 1967, p. 279.
40   Somai 1989, p. 819.
41   Somai 1989, p. 817.

That document expressed a moment of transition in the political direction of the PCd'I, even if the unitary determination of the leadership still prevailed. One could see that the document's understanding of fascism was quite complex, as it tried to identify the social basis of the régime, the interests to which it remained connected, and its goals and contradictions. It is possible to observe a certain continuity in the elaboration of the analysis of the political process and the question of fascism. The document did not give up on the idea that the crisis of capital could end either in fascist dictatorship or in a liberal reformist régime, in which fascism could perhaps also take part, depending on its internal contradictions and the contradictions of the ruling classes. In this sense, an opportunity for the rise of the workers' movement could always be considered possible.

Even though there is no explicit reference to the united front policy, it is indicated and specified for the concrete situation, in the tasks of the party. Thus, contrary to a certain 'common sense' that suggests a diluted version of fascism as a form of reactionary violence manipulated by the big owners of land and industry, the communists attempted to understand the phenomenon and its contradictions and specificities; in this, it certainly went far beyond the documents issued by the Comintern.

During the final resolutions of the Third Plenary, the ECCI demanded the actual application of its decisions, especially the application of the united front tactic, according to Italian conditions. The nomination of a new executive commission for the PCd'I was also decided. It was to be composed of three members from the majority and two from the minority. Doubtless, the rightist fraction won ground, here, especially if we consider that some in the majority insisted on refusing this solution, following the line of Bordiga (who was still in prison). To Bordiga, going over to the opposition was the best way to resist the right wing and the maximalists as well as the Comintern's interference; hence the need to organise a fraction. Bordiga was consistent and understood that the leadership should go over to the right wing and that he should resign from the CC. He did so in August and was followed by Grieco and Fortichiari.

Gramsci's persuasion led Togliatti, Scoccimarro and Gennari (substituting for Fortichiari) to accept the job, as his strategy for the internal struggle demanded that the greatest number of positions was occupied so as to prevent the advance of Tasca's and Graziadei's right wing, as well as the PSI's 'fusionists', who, in the face of fascism's victory and taking advantage of the Comintern's decisions, contested the very legitimacy of the 1921 scission. However, the fact remained that the disintegration of the mass workers' movement in the socialist tradition was still continuing, just as the original leadership of the PCd'I was at risk of disintegrating, rendering fascism's victory absolute.

Gramsci insisted on showing that the heart of the matter was not the merger with the PSI, but 'whether the PCd'I has understood the overall Italian situation, and whether it is capable of giving a lead to the proletariat ... whether the leading group of the PCd'I has assimilated the political doctrine of the Communist International ...' The point was to attract elements from the PSI and help them overcome the crisis for the good of the working class, considering that:

> The Italian socialist movement of the last thirty years has been an apparatus for selecting new leading elements for the bourgeois state. The same goes for the *popolari*. Fascism is the last and most decisive of these movements, which seeks to absorb the whole new social stratum that has been formed, by dissolving the bonds between leaders and masses.[42]

Therefore, the fulcrum of the problem did not have to do with legalistic questions regarding the organisational merger, but with effective action for the autonomous unification of the proletariat, which should transcend the tradition of Italian socialism, redeeming the 'spirit of separation' and creating a new morality and a new culture based on labour. Such a goal could not be dissociated from the formation of a leading group connected with the Comintern and the theoretical conception it upheld, even if remaining aware of its national autonomy.

The Comintern also put pressure on the PSI, which saw another important moment in its crisis during August and September with the expulsion of its 'third internationalist' wing. Soon after, in a fresh wave of repression, the new executive commission of the PCd'I was arrested, aggravating the crisis in the original leadership group. Meanwhile, in Moscow, Gramsci announced the Comintern leadership's decision to create in Italy a new paper aimed at the workers' movement, one in which there was to be space for every trend that remained on the terrain of class struggle, from anarchists to republicans and trade unionists. The editorship, however, was to be shared between communists and 'third internationalists', always taking care that the latter did not make the publication a mere tool in their own private fight with the leadership of the PSI.

The new daily should thus be an organ of the united front policy, hence the suggestion of naming it *L'Unità* (a name which also recalled the periodical once edited by Salvemini). Besides the search for proletarian unity on the terrain of

---

42   Gramsci 1999b, pp. 231–2.

the class struggle, the name was also justified as a reference to national unity, because, as Gramsci added, 'since the decision of the Enlarged Executive on the workers' and peasants' government, I think we must pay special attention to the Southern question – in which the problem of relations between workers and peasants is posed not simply as a problem of class relations, but also and especially as a territorial problem, as one of the aspects of the national question'.[43]

Thus Gramsci returned, thanks to a new directive from the Comintern, to the thinking presented on the eve of the Livorno Congress, now indicating that a debate on the Southern question in the pages of the paper – suggesting the 'Federal Republic of Workers and Peasants' as a slogan – could have an effect 'especially among the left layers of the *popolari* and bourgeois democrats, who represent the real tendencies of the peasant class and have always had in their programmes the slogan of local autonomy and decentralisation'.[44]

The political formula of the united front began to materialise in the context of the Italian social formation. The idea that in Italy such a policy could only find concrete expression in the trade unions had been left behind. Now was the time to search in the concreteness of the Italian social formation for the elements that could constitute the united front, such that an understanding of the country's reality, its social struggles and its regional specificities became indispensable for the fight against fascism and the construction of a new state.

The united front policy should thus bear a strongly national mark, which would demand a deep knowledge of the socio-historical reality of the country. Gramsci, however, observed that all this was still to be done. Referring to the communists, he admitted:

> We do not know Italy. Worse still: we lack the proper instruments for knowing Italy as it really is. It is therefore almost impossible for us to make predictions, to orient ourselves, to establish lines of action which have some likelihood of being accurate. There exists no history of the Italian working class. There exists no history of the peasant class.[45]

The political defeats of the Comintern – especially in Germany – the beginning of the struggle for power in the USSR, and Bordiga's acquittal in the lawsuit that had kept him in prison since February, created a new political situation. If, on

---

43   Gramsci 1999b, p. 235.

44   Gramsci 1999b, pp. 235–6.

45   Gramsci 1999b, p. 245.

the one hand, it took its toll on the possibilities of practical and theoretical progress in the formula of the united front, on the other it saw this strategic orientation take root in the PCd'I. It was precisely in the context of the practical difficulties presented by the consolidation of the mass base of fascism and by the disputes within the Bolshevik leadership that Gramsci was able to bring the political formula of the united front above the level of a mere tactic, bringing forth the complex articulation between resistance to fascism and socialist transition.

4 Gramsci between the Communist Refoundation and the Theoretical Regression of Bolshevism

In Moscow, Gramsci acquired an international point of view, from which he could look with new and penetrating eyes not only at the revolutionary experience of Russia, but also the whole trajectory of the Italian workers' and socialist movement and its possibilities. It was during this time that he was able to realise that the universal character present within Bolshevism lay precisely in its ability to comprehend the particular: that the international socialist revolution depended on the most correct and profound analysis of particular national and popular situations. The most evident theoretical-political implication of this – an implication Gramsci had already foreseen – was that the specificity of the PCd'I could only become explicit within the context of the Comintern, and not outside of or opposed to it. Similarly, the Italian social form could only be effectively understood within the context of Europe and the world. Thus, it was only after his stay in Russia, and after the definitive defeat of the German revolution, that Gramsci walked the path of communist refoundation, the dimensions of which would be set by resistance to fascism and the political formula of the united front.[46]

Gramsci then joined the trend of communist refoundation which, at that moment, was emerging within the nucleus responsible for formulating the Comintern's policy: Lenin in particular, but also Trotsky, Radek, Bukharin, Zinoviev and others. However, Gramsci assimilated not so much the Lenin of the theory of democratic revolution, nor the Lenin of the *scission* (a point at which he had arrived through different paths), but rather the Lenin who began a new phase in the communist refoundation, who took on the theoretical-practical problems of the transition and the new forms of workers' anti-

---

46   For further considerations on this topic, it is particularly worth reading Paggi 1984.

capitalist struggle which would be necessary after the first wave of socialist revolution emanating from Russia was defeated. This, Gramsci's Lenin, is the Lenin of the political formula of the united front, not only as a tactical defensive movement, but as a strategy for rising to power and keeping it, aiming at socialist transition.

However, the communist movement as a whole was entering a phase of theoretical regression, owing mainly to Lenin's infirmity and death, the beginning of the process of the scission within the leading Bolshevik group, and the intrinsic limits of a socialist transition standing isolated as a landmark in conditions of extreme material backwardness. Gramsci's thinking started from a broad spectrum of theoretical influences – Machiavelli and Vico apparently the most important among them – which he blended together in order to define the nexuses of a communist refoundation anchored in Marx and Lenin.

The concrete problem – let it be stressed once again – was that of defining a line of resistance to fascism that also prepared the working class for resuming the revolutionary offensive. At first sight, the political formula of the united front involved a series of fragmented or dissimilar questions: how to preserve the centrality of the factory and the social relations of production as the basis of political action, whilst also demonstrating the need to come out of the factory and conquer social allies among other strata of workers, especially in the countryside, as well as reaching out to spheres of subjectivity and material representation such as trade union and cultural institutions.

The perspective of totality would be given by the revolutionary political party of the proletariat. Or else it would come through the establishment of the workers' party, with a capacity for uniting the class and creating a spectrum of alliances. This would coincide with the perspective of totality, which, in its turn, only fully takes shape amidst the socialist transition. The political formula of the united front defines the strategy to be followed in order to achieve this long-term historical goal.

Endowed with new theoretical and political tools, Gramsci began to criticise the varieties of leftist communism present in Italy. These had appeared in the *L'Ordine Nuovo* experience, but mainly in the trend led by Bordiga. Gramsci found in the considerable presence of leftist communism in Germany and Italy all the weaknesses and difficulties of the united front policy in those countries and, more generally, the West.

Naturally, left-wing communism was able to realise that the West's specificities demanded a political strategy different from the one used in Russia. The problem actually lay in the particularisation of the socio-historical conditions of the West, with the loss of the universal aspects of the proletarian and socialist revolution: in this aspect, it coincided with the interpretation given by the social democrats. The 'maturity' of capitalism seemingly pointed toward a certain working-class exclusivism in the revolutionary process, and thus the form and the pace of the revolution would be different, since the revolutionary class would take some time to identify itself with its vanguard party.

The complexity and the slower pace of the revolutionary process in the West, dictated by the presence of solid institutions of the working class which acted within the current order, was not the essential point of disagreement between leftist communism and the communist refoundation. The main issue, which distinguished the theoretical trend of the refoundation as a whole, beginning with some of Lenin's youthful writings, was the hegemony of the proletariat in the revolutionary process.[47]

To speak of hegemony implies defining a line of political action that concerns the social formation as a whole and projects the pure contradiction between labour and capital in its abstract form. It means to redefine the relationship between economics and politics, investigating the forms of subjectivity which preserve the power of capital in production whilst also observing the materiality of the superstructure. It means to pay attention to the role that culture and intellectuals play in preserving order. Hegemony is exerted over allies, hence the need to define lasting social alliances, and in the cases of Russia and Italy these could not but be with the rural proletariat and the poor peasantry.

The struggle for the hegemony of the proletariat thus demanded a form of revolutionary party different from that taken as a vanguard by left-wing communism. What was required was a party that was part of the class and not its abstraction, a party that acted in every social and political determination in radical opposition to the apparatus of the bourgeois state, not confining itself to the dimension of factory work alone. From a theoretical and practical point of view, the political formula of the united front then presented itself to Gramsci as that most adequate for taking and preserving power, as well as the formula that clarified the nexus between the universal and the particular in the socialist revolution, both in Russia and the West. It was impossible, here, not to hear the loud echoes of the problems of political science as presented by Machiavelli!

In Italy, the political formula of the united front would be part of a strategy to confront both liberalism and fascism – a clear symbiotic relationship being seen between these forms of bourgeois power – and also to build the hegemony of the proletariat. When Gramsci realised the connection between the theme of hegemony and the revolutionary party of the working class, he distanced

---

47   For the origins of the concept of hegemony in the Marxist tradition, see Anderson 1976, pp. 16–18.

himself from Sorel and came closer to Lenin, overcoming the intermediary stage of the alliance with Bordiga. There was a redefinition of the very notions of the scission and politics. While maintaining the 'spirit of separation' with regard to the order of capital, typical of Sorel, now it was necessary to recognise, as Lenin did, the need for a new policy, a revolutionary policy, endowed with a strategy aimed at destroying the capitalist order and its system of power.

It is of the utmost importance to understand that Gramsci was walking both the path of the communist refoundation and that of the theoretical development of the political formula of the united front as he assimilated the decisions from the Third and Fourth Congresses of the Comintern and the first three Plenary Meetings of the ECCI, as well as the political literature produced by the three main Bolshevik leaders during this period – the peak of the elaboration produced by the International, just before the beginning of a significant regression. This latter was a theoretical regression which reintroduced certain economistic and voluntarist elements[48] present in the social-democratic tradition and in left communism, and which affected the same principal actors who had developed the previous formulation with Lenin.

Initiated in the milestone year of October 1923, this theoretical regression, as previously indicated, stemmed from the defeat of the international socialist revolution, from the isolation of Russia and the extreme backwardness of its productive forces, and from the struggle between capital and labour losing centre stage to national peasant movements. Its essence lay in an objectivist view of the economy, which, in the face of the backwardness of the productive forces and the impossibility of associated (truly socialist) labour actually arising as the guiding thread of the revolutionary process and the transition, brought forth the perspective in which the dimension of subjectivity, proper to the sphere of politics, was elevated to a position of centrality, leading to the belief that reality should conform to socialist intentions.[49]

---

48 A new eruption of thought forms mixing up the subjectivity and objectivity of social being brought about a regression of dialectics and praxis as fundamental elements of Marxist communism and Leninist refoundation. As the final milestones of a time of great theoretical flourishing, two works may be mentioned, both published in Russia in 1924: Evgeni Pachukanis's *Marxism and the General Theory of Law* and Isaak Illich Rubin's *The Marxist Theory of Value*.

49 Actually there are different degrees of revolutionary radicalism which mutually reinforce each other: the preponderance of the nucleus of the West in the contradiction between capital and labour theoretically makes possible the revolution of associated labour and triggers a more advanced socialist transition, whereas the peasant-based, anti-imperialist revolutions of a national-democratic-bourgeois nature at best allow for state monopolist

This difficult objective situation can explain why the second phase of the theoretical refoundation of communism occupied itself so much – especially in Gramsci and Lukács – with the materiality of the subjective dimension. The variation appeared in the forms in which this process could be manifested. Thus, while Gramsci saw in the political formula of the united front a universal dimension and a path to be trodden and broadened – in order not only to assure Soviet power, but also to understand and defeat fascism and build proletarian hegemony in Italy and the West – in Russia the Comintern walked the path that would lead to the emptying-out of its potential, thus creating a paradox and a theoretical fracture in Marxist culture between East and West. Gramsci's arrest and the fascist victory, on the one hand, and the objective conditions that led the USSR to state socialism, on the other, led the communist refoundation to exhaust itself in the countries where the bourgeois revolution was 'passive' or had failed.[50]

From a concrete historical standpoint, the theoretical regression started with the intertwining of the consequences of the first crisis of the NEP and the conclusion of the scission of the Bolshevik leadership group, along with the repercussions of the German October defeat within the Comintern (aggravated by the defeats in Poland and Bulgaria). Then a broad redefinition of alliances and political positions began, both in the USSR and the Comintern and many of its sections, with the predominance of a marked dislocation and retreat in the theoretical formulation and in the political practice of the united front – these latter being caused by their analyses of the capitalist crisis and, within this context, of the role of fascism and social democracy.

In the USSR, the problems posed by the crisis of the NEP stimulated the debate on questions related to the socialist transition, such as the development of the productive forces, the worker-peasant alliance, the bureaucracy and

---

capitalism as an embryonic stage of the revolution. The defeat of the international socialist revolution in 1921 changed the concrete situation in revolutionary Russia, leaving it isolated from that second point of view.

50   Naturally there is no place in this reading for posing Gramsci as an exponent of so-called 'Western Marxism'. This phrase comprises the theoretical production of intellectuals who were not involved with the revolutionary praxis of the workers' movement, such as the most famous names of the 'Frankfurt School' or in certain cases those who were connected to workers' parties in Western Europe at the time when the 'Cold War' made this region peculiar. By way of antonomasia, 'Eastern Marxism' could be understood as the state ideology which arose in the USSR and spread to other countries and as the communist movement. The innovative elaborations produced during the Chinese Revolution, for instance, cannot be understood as such.

workers' democracy. However, this debate took place within the context of the defeat of the international socialist revolution and of the great backwardness of the productive forces. These elements provided leverage to the regrouping of capitalist and pre-capitalist socio-cultural and economic forms, which undermined the material basis of the communist refoundation, immersed as this was in the revolutionary process, leading to a theoretical and cultural regression, manifested as subjectivism. Thus the scission of the Bolshevik leadership group, which brought about a permanent redefinition of tactical alliances and a situation in which each leader tried to take possession of one aspect of Lenin's thought in their quest for power, not only manifested this regression but also prevented the emergence of a new theoretical synthesis.

The initial problem was, however, to bring the economy back to its pre-war levels, which was generally achieved only in 1927. Soon the need for industrial planning was acknowledged, and for this reason a specific state agency was created not only to ensure continued growth, but also to preserve a certain harmony between the different areas of production. The need for planning and 'the scientific organisation of labour' reinforced the position of the technical managers who came from the old régime, as well as the management of productive units by a single person, to the detriment of self-management and the soviets.

As the war ended and the NEP began, there was a remarkable flourishing of the traditional rural commune across the vast agrarian sector, organised around family production and aimed at subsistence. The surplus could go to the market, and this established a link, even a weak one, with the cities. The sharing out of the land, typical of the commune tradition, would be carried out every nine years, according to the established legislation, so as to minimise the tendencies to capitalist accumulation. In Central Asia rural social relations had preserved characteristics pertaining to Oriental-Turkish social forms. The inability of industrial production to provide for the needs of the countryside gave strength and visibility to the rising merchant petit bourgeois (the so-called 'nepmen'), whom left communists identified as evidence of the strengthening of capitalist tendencies in the USSR.

With a view to maintaining its role as the leading organ of social life and conductor of the socialist transition, the RKP(B) understood that it should marshal that portion of the working class which was slowly being reconstituted, and use it to extend the materiality of the state, with a growing number of administrative and repressive organs. The limitations of the socio-historical foundations of the socialist transition in the USSR are to be found in its material backwardness, together with the prevalence of the subjective sphere and the strengthening of the state and the party. Administration prevailed to the detriment of an unsustainable self-management, just as the political state prevailed to the detriment of civil society. It was the only way to keep the production process going. The penetration into the new state of technical-managerial officials trained under the old régime, as well as the clear theoretical and cultural deficiencies of the masses who joined the party, were elements which contributed not only to proving the historical limitations of the communist refoundation, but also to legitimising its theoretical regression in the USSR and the Comintern.[51]

Defeated in 1923 during the Thirteenth Congress of the RKP(B), Trotsky's opposition, which revolved around the demand for greater control over the bureaucracy and a broader 'workers' democracy', held back for a little while, perhaps because Trotsky felt partially answered by the decision to increase significantly the working-class base of the party, or perhaps because he was waiting for the situation in the Comintern to become clearer after the 'German October'. Trotsky's remarks on the problems of the development of the transition had apparently been absorbed and neutralised, but in fact the first episode of the scission was only just beginning. Avoiding open conflict during the Thirteenth Congress of the RKP(B), which took place in May 1924, and also during the Fifth World Congress of the Comintern (June and July 1924), Trotsky returned to the debate in October, publishing a collection of essays named *The Lessons of October*.[52]

Trotsky recovered and developed certain aspects of his pre-Bolshevik theoretical formulations, especially the idea of 'permanent revolution', which emphasised the unmediated development of the revolutionary process. Then Trotsky made a clear effort at theoretical differentiation and particularisation, recovering the theory of permanent revolution, originally formulated in 1905, at the same time as he attempted to preserve his connection with Lenin's elaborations. He saw that the offensive of capital, as well as the reorganisation of production at which it aimed, would increase the developmental disparity of the productive forces of the USSR and the USA, as the USA rose as the great capitalist power. On the other hand, as he noted, there was no possibility whatsoever of advancing the transition without creating a large working class and strong industry.

---

51   The bibliography on the USSR is very large, but some works of reference deserve highlighting: Bettelheim 1979–83; the work of E.H. Carr; Boffa 1976; Ellenstein 1976; and many others. A very useful theoretical discussion on the issue of the socialist transition can be found in Martorano 2002. As examples of the various current historiographical tendencies on the USSR and the Comintern, see Furet 1995; Dreyfus et al. 2001; Agosti 1999; Losurdo and Giacomini (eds.) 1999.

52   Trotsky 1937.

Given these observations, as well as his conviction that the international socialist revolution would catch its breath in a short while, Trotsky concluded that there should take place in the USSR a process of industrialisation and accelerated recomposition of the working class, so as to create the material bases for the transition and perhaps enable the possible establishment of a 'workers' democracy', even if at the expense of the peasantry and the alliance promoted by the 1917 Revolution. The main allies in the socialist transition of the USSR would be the working classes of Germany and especially China, indelibly articulated with the international socialist revolution. Provided with this theoretical reevaluation, Trotsky tended to stray from the course of communist refoundation, with which he was falsely identified for a certain time, toward leftist communism, even though he also returned to the similarities his political thought had with the Mensheviks, among these a difficulty in acknowledging national specificities.[53]

It can be said that Trotsky realised the enormity of the historical limitations of the socialist transition in the USSR, which lay both in the backwardness of the productive forces and especially in the proneness to capitalist accumulation which was present within small-scale rural commodity production. Trotsky detected the energy with which capital was developing the USA, and so he believed it was inevitable, in the interests of the socialist transition, to clash with the Russian peasantry in order to advance the urgent need to develop the productive forces – without which there would be no strong industrial proletariat, nor a workers' state. He also believed the link with the world working class to be indispensable, and thus identified the fulcrum of the problem in the reactivation of the international socialist revolution. Moving from a fair assessment of the concrete historical limitations of the Russian East, Trotsky leapt into subjectivism when he estimated the correlation of forces, especially in the international arena, thus remaining attached to the essential need to develop the productive forces.

Trotsky understood that the political formula of the united front was adequate for a period of retreat for the workers' movement, but the occupation of the Ruhr in Germany, as a 'brief revival of the imperialist war', led him to remark that 'in 1923, the situation in Germany actually developed, suddenly and radically, towards revolution', such that this policy no longer made sense. The German revolution had thus apparently begun a new period, its main characteristic being that 'democratic-pacifist elements from bourgeois society would

---

53   See Hobsbawm 1980, pp. 116–30 and 131–65.

rise to power', because 'fascism cannot last long; it cannot be the normal state of a bourgeois society'.[54]

The reformist period into which Europe was entering after the supposedly temporary defeat of the German revolution was, in Trotsky's view, warranted by 'the main factor in the contemporary history of mankind: the United States'.[55] This country, which had been consolidating its power since 1898, had a considerable reputation as a 'pacifist', which enabled it to meddle in European affairs and advance its project of establishing supremacy over the whole planet. Even if, for Trotsky (and the Comintern as a whole), the main imperialist contradiction was the opposition between the United States and Britain, for him it was crucially significant that the social-democratic parties of Europe had 'educated and made an effort to educate the working masses in the religion of Americanism; in other words, they create a new political religion out of Americanism, which is the role of American capital in Europe'.[56]

Thus, in Trotsky's reading, it was clear that America 'came to Europe to bring order, not to accumulate ruins', and thus a lasting nexus between Americanism and social-democratic reformism was emerging. A new phase of wars was beginning, though, and it would strengthen the workers' resistance, which would be able to overcome 'the gospel of Americanism' in Europe as well as China. Depending on how Britain resolved the conflicts of interest that opposed it to the United States, especially in Latin America, it would be the very first country to face the dilemma of either going to war or aligning itself with the American empire.[57]

The same dilemma would present itself to Europe as a whole: if European capital decided to confront America, it would go to war; if it capitulated immediately, it would have to face revolution. However, the element that would actually be decisive for the world revolution lay within the very fortress of Americanism. It was reformism in its most perfected form. Trotsky called attention to new forms of corporatism rising in the USA as means of organisation of the 'labour aristocracy', which led to 'a sort of social opportunism, amidst which the servitude of the working class is automatically reinforced'.[58]

Such reformism ensured domestic support for American imperialism, and it could only be enabled by the immense power of capital. It did not go unnoticed by Trotsky (and others before him) that the nature of the American social form

54   Trotsky 1971, pp. 13–15.
55   Trotsky 1971, p. 19.
56   Trotsky 1971, p. 28.
57   Trotsky 1971, p. 30.
58   Trotsky 1971, p. 54.

favoured experimentation and innovation, as well as a tendency to mechanise work and to substitute machines for men. Trotsky remarks that, owing to the Fordist organisation of labour,

> America no longer knows apprenticeship: it no longer spends its time in learning, because labour is expensive; learning is replaced by a division of labour in minimal parts that demand little or no apprenticeship. And who unites all the parts in the labour process? It is the endless chain, the transporter. This is the real teacher. In a very short time, a young peasant from southern Europe, from the Balkans or the Ukraine is transformed into an industrial worker.[59]

This is the explanation for America's superiority, and 'this is why European socialism will learn the technique of the American school',[60] which also benefited from a rational relationship between production and population. In Trotsky's view, though, the world revolution would only hit America in a second wave, forced in part by a revolutionary victory in Europe and Asia, even if these latter were more backward in terms of their productive forces. As we know, a large part of Trotsky's predictions did not come true – but what really matters is his clear perception of the expansive tendency of Americanism and Fordism as supports to the most powerful reformism and imperialism of the twentieth century.

Gramsci had great intellectual respect for Trotsky during the time he spent in Moscow and Vienna, until the moment when the issues of the united front formula, the worker-peasant alliance and the conception of the party set them apart. Gramsci's analyses of the Italian situation converged with Trotsky's for a while, especially concerning the persistence of a revolutionary phase and the bourgeoisie's possibility of taking a democratic-pacifist course. Gramsci also shared with Trotsky the view that social democracy would be a better tool for the Americanisation of Europe than fascism. It is still imperative to note how the formulation of the themes of Americanism and Fordism, relatively marginal in the Comintern, was approached by Trotsky and resumed by Gramsci in his prison years. Gramsci preserved many points in common with Trotsky.

It also must be noted that the view of social democracy as a possible tool for Americanism was also espoused by Lukács some time later, in 1928, when he wrote the theses of the Second Congress of the KMU, to be held the following

---

59   Trotsky 1971, p. 56.
60   Trotsky 1971, p. 57.

year. Lukács notes that in the USA 'the bourgeoisie was able to create forms of democracy in which every possibility is given to free development, to the accumulation and the extension of capital, and in which the outer forms of democracy are warranted, even though the working masses cannot have any sort of influence over the political direction, strictly speaking. America is not only economically but also politically an ideal of the current ruling bourgeoisie'.[61]

Similarly, 'social democracy ... tends to stimulate the creation of an American-style democracy in every European State'.[62] Lukács also saw a general tendency towards the fascistisation of the trade unions during the epoch of imperialism. By this he understood, in very general terms, the subordination of the trade unions to the capitalist state. However, the solution given by Italian fascism clashed with the interests of certain sectors of the trade union bureaucracy. It was not the most adequate answer to the intentions of the European bourgeoisies and the trade union bureaucracies connected with social democracy. The most desirable option would be the mediation of conflicts through state interference, with the preservation of political democracy.

Even though both the European bourgeoisie and the trade union bureaucracy wished to come closer to the American ideal, the tradition of working-class struggle as well as European imperialism's lesser expansionist capacity made it difficult for this intention to be realised. Even if marginally, it is possible to see that the reflection on the importance of Americanism had an impact on communist culture, and that the interest Gramsci shows for it in his prison writings are an important part of a broader concern, though a largely insufficient one. It was not something absolutely new.

Meanwhile, the polemic on the foundations of the NEP, the worker-peasant alliance and the socialist transition continued to go on in the USSR, particularly opposing Preobrazhensky, an exponent of the left communists – who had converged with Trotsky – and Bukharin, who had the support of most of the party leadership, but who had also come from the leftist trend of Bolshevism.[63]

To Preobrazhensky, since Russia was a country that began its transition process from a point of significant backwardness, there would be a need for primary socialist accumulation, which would feed the state-run urban industrial economy, the true foundation of the socialist transition. The source of such

---

61   Lukács 1928.

62   Ibid.

63   Until 1921, Bukharin and Preobazhensky had also been close collaborators. Bukharin's change of perspective happened while Lenin was sick, a time during which the two revolutionaries spent time together and in which their mutual affection became stronger.

primary accumulation could only be the production surplus of the mercantile peasant economy and the small mercantile bourgeoisie, hence the need for an unequal relation between the two economic sectors of this immense country. Besides, it was also necessary to prevent the strengthening of the mercantile economy from giving impulse to the formation of an agrarian bourgeoisie that could claim state power in a possible alliance with imperialist capital.

Thus the specificity of the transition in the USSR would be marked by the contradiction between two social forms, which would develop until their clash was inevitable. As such, socialism's victory would entail industrialisation and production planning to the detriment of the agrarian bourgeoisie (the *kulaks*) and its potential allies in the country and the cities, who benefited from the existence of market relations and aimed directly at a social fracture within the cooperatives. In this formulation of the socialist transition, the NEP and the worker-peasant alliance carry out a very limited role, as primacy is given to the unity of the agrarian and urban proletariat.

Karl Radek was one of the most original, determined and productive champions of the political formula of the united front in the Comintern between 1921 and 1923. Coming from the Spartakist group, he established an alliance with Trotsky in defence of 'the workers' democracy' after the defeat of the 'German October' and his return to the USSR, and also approached the left communists. Amidst this political oscillation, his opportunity to become the theoretician of the political strategy of the united front was greatly reduced, and maybe even lost, exactly as had happened with Trotsky.

Zinoviev tended – and this was typical of him – to seek a balance between the trends in the debate. He criticised Trotsky's theory of permanent revolution and its implications for the role of the peasantry in the revolution and the transition. He warned Bukharin about the possible stimulus to the richer peasants to the detriment of those poorest, and also understood the NEP as a tactical retreat until the world revolution was reactivated, which he expected to take place shortly. Speaking against Stalin, he argued for the importance of world revolution to the transition, opposing this to the idea of 'socialism in only one country'.

Exactly like Stalin had done before when he lectured at the Moscow Academy of Teachers, Zinoviev eventually wrote a book, *Leninism*, in which he attempted to give a systematic overview of Lenin's ideas and tried to justify his political and theoretical positions in the discussions that preceded the Fourteenth Congress of the RKP(B). Thus Zinoviev made a significant contribution to the theoretical regression of Bolshevism, as he believed in 'works that systematically espoused the essence of Leninism to be indispensable, books which make an effort to define Lenin's real ideas on burning questions. The future of the international workers' movement largely depends on their solution'.[64]

Bukharin, who had been very close to Lenin in his final days, believed that the worker-peasant alliance should be considered essential both to achieving power and to keeping it during the process of the socialist transition, as it would provide a broad consensus. Expressing the indelible need for the workers' hegemony, Bukharin believed that he was speaking generally when he said that 'the fatal hour for the state of capital and the landowners will arrive only when the working class is completely removed from the influence of the bourgeoisie, snatching from it large strata of the peasant masses, helping them to tread a new and autonomous path'.[65]

In the specific case of the USSR, given the situation of incredible backwardness in the development of the productive forces, it would only be possible to emerge from this very slowly, by means of a state policy that encouraged industrialisation in harmony with urban and agrarian demands. Since rural production for the market had an inclination toward the overt accumulation of capital, the state and the party should work so that the rural communes, which were now being revived, could turn into cooperatives and mechanised collective farms, instead of private capitalist property.

However, on the other hand, only capitalist economic rationality would be able to stimulate the accumulation of wealth, and so the agrarian bourgeoisie would have a very important role, even if under heavy taxation. The goal would be to ensure the transference of resources to the poor peasantry. The growth of the agrarian bourgeoisie would be limited by the expansion of state capitalism and by the strengthening of cooperativism. As time went on, and without the need for the class struggle to become more intense or for a new revolution, the economic and cultural standards in the countryside would increase, so that the transitional state would be based exclusively on the working class of both town and country.[66]

State monopoly capitalism, supported by the worker-peasant alliance, would gradually create the material and cultural conditions for the socialist transition in the USSR. However, just as the world socialist revolution had taken a blow, it also would proceed more slowly. The view was that 'capitalist stabil-

---

64   Zinoviev 1926, p. 7.
65   Bukharin 1980, p. 60.
66   The formulation of the agrarian policy presented by Bukharin was accused of harking back to Stolypin's policy from Tsarist times, as it strengthened the agrarian bourgeoisie, and was then called neo-Narodnik for placing its hopes in the cooperatives typical of the old rural commune.

isation' could take a long time and that the heart of the contradiction had been displaced to the periphery of imperialism, to the colonised peoples' struggle for emancipation and to the peasantry. Bukharin, therefore, tried to develop a strategic view of the NEP and the worker-peasant alliance as an anchor for the transition.[67]

Bukharin emphasised that Soviet power had inherited the feudal features of Russian capitalism, manifested in the presence of the enormous peasant mass. However, in spite of the backwardness, the path of the socialist transition could be tread, even if it was known that 'the ultimate guarantee against the return of the old régime, supported by foreign armies, is nothing but the international revolution, which our Party must favour, participate in, and bring about'.[68]

Even if restricted to these brief observations, it is possible to see that only Bukharin had a strategic view of the worker-peasant alliance and the political formula of the united front during the transition period, even though he was also immersed in the prevalent theoretical regression – engulfed as it was by the original historical limitations of this attempt to make the socialist transition. The theoretical rapprochement of Gramsci and Bukharin took place precisely and exclusively in terms of their strategic view of the political formula of the united front and the worker-peasant alliance. Only during his prison years did Gramsci's analysis disagree with Bukharin's on the lasting results of the capitalist offensive. All the other more prominent leaders of the socialist revolution in Russia saw in the political formula of the united front only a defensive tactical move, to be overcome as soon as a new revolutionary outbreak allowed.[69]

Even though Bukharin can be seen as an obstinate follower of the political indications of the late Lenin, especially on issues regarding the united front, the worker-peasant alliance and the NEP, he cannot be seen as part of the communist refoundation. Not only were there difficulties in his use of the dialectic, between objectivity and subjectivity and the philosophy of praxis, but he also had to face the concrete historical limitations which led to a lack of theoretical and strategic autonomy, a subaltern alliance and eventually political defeat.[70]

---

67   When we speak here of state monopoly capitalism, we mean a system in which the workers' state owns the monopoly of major industry, the banking system and foreign trade. We do not intend any connection with the 1970s theoretical debate, which took place mainly in France, regarding the nature of the capitalist state at that historical moment.

68   Bukharin 1980, p. 92.

69   Hobsbawm 1980, vol. 1, pp. 657–95.

70   Lenin himself had foreseen Bukharin's theoretical limits in his relation with Marx's philosophy, an opinion supported in 1925 by Lukács. So, even before Stalin and Zinoviev,

For a little while, Bukharin's alliance with Stalin brought a preponderance of the orientation that highlighted in the worker-peasant united front the core of the socialist transition in the USSR, under the conditions of the 'capitalist stabilisation'. This political orientation reached its height after the Fourteenth Conference of the RKP(B) in April 1925, and so it remained until 1927, when it began to face various insurmountable difficulties. The influence of Bukharin in the Comintern was also significant and, without a doubt, so too was Gramsci's reflection on the political formula of the united front and on the worker-peasant alliance as the basis for the revolutionary process in Italy.

However, it was Stalin who conceived the affirmative resolution of the concrete historical limits of the socialist transition in the USSR, as well as the theoretical regression that compromised the praxis of the communist refoundation, even though this was obviously not his conscious intention. Parallel to the Thirteenth Congress of the RKP(B), in May 1924, Stalin gave a series of lectures, soon to be published under the title *On the Foundations of Leninism*. This attempt at the systematisation of Lenin's thought on the one hand drew the dialectical power out of the theoretical-practical work of the recently deceased revolutionary, but on the other it served as an example, soon to be followed by Zinoviev, of how 'Leninism' could become a new and powerful 'common sense' among the leaders of the new state.

Beginning with the polemic with Trotsky, the idea of 'socialism in only one country' was conceived, supposedly as a distinctive aspect of 'Leninism'. Based on the interpretation of Lenin's writings, first Stalin opposed himself to the formula of the 'permanent revolution' advanced by Trotsky, emphasising the relative lack of weight given to the peasantry as well as the difficulties Russia had to face in overcoming its backwardness and actually placing itself on the course of socialist transition, without the progress of the world revolution. Then he developed the notion that the socialist transition could come very close to its realisation or tipping point within the limits of only one country, should it possess the USSR's potential in terms of its geographic expanse, natural resources and workforce.

The first part of his assertion could make reference to Lenin's notion that the first steps of the transition could be taken in only one country in the form of state monopoly capitalism, even if the country in question had a backward capitalism. This kept Stalin and Bukharin as allies, but the practical consequences

Bukharin had already worked towards 'systematising' communist theory, beginning with *The ABC of Communism* (1920), soon followed by *Historical Materialism* (1921). The latter volume was targeted by Gramsci's criticism in his *Prison Notebooks*.

of the second part of Stalin's assertions brought about the rupture between them. Stalin put forth a view of the socialist transition which represented a theoretical regression to the sphere of subjectivity, emphasising the role of the state, which ultimately would become stronger in the transition process – and not weaker, as Marx and Lenin had intended. As a consequence of Stalin's theoretical formulation, the transition would culminate in the crystallisation of a national state socialism. The political formula of the united front and the international socialist revolution itself would remain attached to the corporate interests of the Soviet state.

The scenario was extremely limited. The socialist transition was still in its very first steps and associated with a theoretical regression in which everyone spoke on behalf of Lenin without achieving any theoretical-practical synthesis. Stalin's formulation emerged as that most adequate to garnering the support of the mass of the party and the state bureaucracy, partially inherited from the old Tsarist régime. However, the fully matured version of Stalin's conception only appeared when state socialism became a concrete reality in the late 1920s, as the NEP was overcome and the socialist transition was frozen.[71]

Trotsky, again in the minority and isolated, was taken out of the army command already in the beginning of 1925. Now Zinoviev and Kamenev opposed themselves strongly to the deepening of the NEP, insisting that the united front formula was only a tactical manoeuvre and pointing to the theoretical error of the idea of 'socialism in one country'. At the same time, there was a hard-fought struggle for control of the institutions of both party and state, which culminated, in the December 1925 Fourteenth Congress of the RKP(B), in the complete defeat of the opposition led by Zinoviev and Kamenev. The obstinate struggle for the unity of the leading group, which went back at least to the Tenth Party Congress (1921), ran parallel to the process of the scission and the-

---

71   Stalin's socialist intentions are undeniable, even though the real process led to a peculiar form of state socialism. The notion of state socialism has been present in the history of the workers' and socialist movement since so-called 'utopian socialism', with Lassalle also being one of its proponents. Marx fought against both. It returned to the debate of the Socialist International. In the case of the post-1929 USSR, the phrase 'state socialism' refers to a form of appropriation of the labour process which generates capital both in parcellised work and in common work as organised by the state, which concentrates property and is responsible for the unequal distribution of the surplus, in the absence of common work by voluntary association. State socialism as such appears as a form of 'passive revolution' that restores the feudal-absolutist state. See Del Roio 1998, Chapter Five.

oretical regression. The result was the growing preponderance of the sphere of subjectivity and the gradual elimination of political debate and exchange of ideas.

From then on, there was a tendency toward the rapprochement of all the oppositions that had arisen since 1921. This united opposition, which came together in 1926, could once again count on the outstanding figure of Trotsky, along with Zinoviev and Kamenev. The elements that knit together their weak unity were their critiques of the Stalinist formula of 'socialism in one country' (not even Bukharin fully agreed with it) and of the management of economic policy, which, as they observed, benefited a new agrarian and mercantile bourgeoisie. The alliance of these new social forces and the state and party bureaucracy combined to block the socialist transition, under the banner of 'socialism in one country'. In order to try and reverse this situation, the 'united opposition' demanded better conditions for the working class, a more accelerated pace of industrialisation and the implementation of a five-year plan.

Even though they represented half of the leadership group that had made the revolution, the united opposition only achieved weak repercussions in the new mass party the RKP(B) had now become. The effort to advance the opposition platform inside the party was truncated, but a few points were filtered out and promoted during the following years, such as the need for fast industrialisation and the implementation of a global development plan, which would have as an indirect result the strengthening of the state bureaucracy.

Through these methods, which tended considerably to lessen the degree of debating ideas and the democratic process within the party, the opposition coalition was broken in October. Its main leaders capitulated, and even though they claimed to maintain their opinions they admitted that they had undertaken political activities typical of factionalism, something prohibited by party regulations. Nevertheless, Trotsky and Kamenev lost their places in the Political Commission of the Party and Zinoviev ceased to be president of the Comintern. Unlike the others, who capitulated, Trotsky insisted on his struggle against the 'majority' of the RKP(B) during the whole of the next year, until he was expelled from the party.

CHAPTER 3

The Communist Refoundation and the United Front in Gramsci

1 The Influence of the Theoretical Regression on the Political Actions of the Communist International

The process of the political scission and the theoretical regression had a great impact on the evolution of Comintern policy. Its effects were amplified by the defeat of the revolutionary initiatives in Europe and always led to a form of organisation that was more centralised. On the other hand, the repercussions of the defeats at the end of 1923, especially in Germany, were felt by the RKP(b), the Comintern and various other communist parties.

Radek's return to the USSR in December of that year, along with his support to demands made by Trotsky and others for a broader 'workers' democracy' – as opposed to the growing bureaucracy – aggravated Zinoviev's and the ECCI's initial criticism of the responsibilities of the KPD leadership group regarding the failure of the October insurrection. Since Radek was formally associated with the Brandler-Thalheimer leadership, his support for Trotsky penalised those German militants who were identified as the 'right wing' of the Comintern and who had been conducting the application of the united front policy even though they had basic disagreements with the ECCI's representative regarding the theoretical-practical status of the united front policy.[1]

Then there was an unusual rapprochement between the trends more to the right of the Comintern, those that had more deeply identified with the united front policy – leaders from the KPD, the KPP (Poland's Communist Party) and the KSC (Czechoslovakia's Communist Party) – with some of Trotsky's political demands in the USSR. Even though Brandler and Thalheimer, whose position was already delicate, tried to dodge any such involvement, it is undeniable that they were the principal knock-on victims of the Comintern's turn to the left, which entailed a new interpretation of the united front policy.

---

1 There is a large bibliography, for the most part strongly ideological, on the history of the Communist International. Given the spirit of the present book, a couple of titles deserve mention, as they partially provided its basis: Hajek 1975 and Agosti 1974–9.

As president of the Comintern and one of the most important leaders of the USSR, Zinoviev attempted to find a balancing-act position in the ongoing debate. As he realised that the left of the KPD, which opposed the united front policy proposed by the Comintern, was becoming stronger in the wake of the October defeat, and that the right could associate itself with Trotsky, Zinoviev tried to find support in the old majority, now gathering around Hermann Remmele.

The faltering progress of the political formula of the united front was deeply shaken by the meeting of the ECCI Presidium which took place in December and January, with the purpose of discussing the question of Germany. Karl Radek (with Trotsky's and Piatakov's support) defended the continuity of the policy of a united front with social democracy. The left opposed the united front policy as a whole, believing that it had caused the defeat. With Zinoviev's support, the position that came to prevail understood that the united front should only come 'from below', namely with the purpose of attracting and exposing the social-democratic leaders, who were now increasingly presented as a 'wing' of fascism. Thus the slogan of the 'workers' government' or of a 'worker-peasant government' would be nothing other than an agitational slogan aiming at the establishment of the dictatorship of the proletariat.[2]

The process by which the leadership of the KPD distanced itself from the leadership of the Comintern, which was deeply affected by the rise of a new opposition within the RKP(b), led to the substitution of Brandler and Thalheimer, and to the smoothing of the way for the victory of the left at the April 1924 KPD congress. Thus arose the concrete possibility of an international articulation of leftist communism with the purpose of emptying out the united front policy which had been developing since the Comintern's Third Congress. But even though such an articulation did not establish itself, the pressure of the left was enough to disfigure the foundations of the original formulation. The intermediate formula of a united front 'from below', the content of which was uncertain, also won a consensus in the PCF and KPP, and had obvious connections with the internal dispute of the RKP(b), which opposed most of the leadership to Trotsky and his allies.

---

2 It must be noted that the March 1921 and the October 1923 defeats had opposite meanings: the first strengthened the united front policy, while the latter weakened it. It is also possible to see that Trotsky's support to Radek over the German question came as reciprocation for Radek's support on the Russian question, as months later (as seen above) Trotsky would cite the military occupation of the Ruhr as marking the end of the validity of maintaining a united front with social democracy.

When the Comintern's Fifth World Congress began on 17 June 1924, the lefts were strong and on the offensive politically. In order to contain this impulse and preserve the work developed by the leadership since the previous congress of the International, Zinoviev attempted to tone down some of the positions which had been upheld in the preceding months. As to the political formula of the united front, it should come 'from below', but in certain cases and circumstances it also could come 'from above'. The 'worker-peasant government' should be understood as a synonym for the dictatorship of the proletariat, but, in certain places, such as Italy, the fascist dictatorship could be replaced by an intermediate formula, designated as 'new democracy'.

The Fifth Congress gave little importance to the problem and merely concluded, in two paragraphs, that 'fascism is one of the classical forms of counter-revolution in a time of decline for the capitalist social order, a time of proletarian revolution', and also that 'fascism is an instrument in the struggle of the haute bourgeoisie against the proletariat', even though it acknowledged that 'considering its social structure, fascism is a petit-bourgeois movement'. From such a simplification, it went on to the mistake of judging that 'given the gradual dismantling of bourgeois society, every bourgeois party, especially social democracy, takes on a more or less fascist nature' and, besides, that 'fascism and social democracy are two aspects of the same instrument of the dictatorship of big capital'.[3] It was a significant regression as compared to the views expressed by Zetkin, and especially by Gramsci on behalf of the Italian delegation at the Third Plenary of the ECCI on June 1923, and it created many difficulties for seeing the united front tactic as a long-term formulation.[4]

Instead of a synthesis that defined revolutionary praxis, it was ambivalence and the permanent search for a balance between fragmentary opinions that resulted from the actualisation of theoretical regression, which essentially manifested itself in an inability to clarify the nature of the capitalist offensive. The 'pacifist-democratic' phase heralded for the main imperialist countries was understood either as an expression of the weakness of bourgeois power (Zinoviev) or else as a demonstration of the strength and confidence of the bourgeoisie, which could even put fascism to one side in favour of the state adopting reformist policy forms (Trotsky).

The political defeats of the workers' movement by the end of 1923, as well as the financial and economic stabilisation owed to new techniques developed

---

3   Agosti 1974–9, Vol. 1, pp. 163–4.
4   Here we find a formidable echo of Bordiga's line of reasoning, in spite of all the confrontations he had with the general political orientation of the Comintern.

during the war, only reaffirmed the vigour of the capitalist offensive. Reality indicated that the paths opened by the Third World Congress should be deepened and better explored, preventing the analytical subjectivism from an expected new revolutionary wave from obscuring the formulation of the necessary political programme. Only Karl Radek and Clara Zetkin (the remnants of the Spartakist leadership group) strongly defended the political orientation resulting from the previous congresses and the centrality of the political formula of the united front, exposing the fallacy of counterposing 'from below' to 'from above' in the application of this tactic.

The beginning of the theoretical regression gave new life to left-wing communism and allowed for the emptying out of the political formula of the united front, which never went beyond an embryonic stage. Its most obvious limitation, and also the cause of its failure, was the persistent expectation that the united front policy offered short-term results, that the crisis of capital and the new revolutionary wave would lead the proletariat to an armed insurrection dragging social democracy or at least part of it along in its wake. Considering the limitations imposed by concrete conditions and circumstances, it was not possible to develop theoretically the political formula of the united front and of the worker-peasant government, and, specifically in the heart of the West, the issues of taking power and the socialist transition.

The offensive of capital had brought a phase of economic and institutional stabilisation that led the communists to become isolated and their influence to be diminished. The view that social democracy was the left wing of fascism, besides being a grave analytical error, made the political formula of the united front impotent and pushed the communist parties away from the masses and the skilled working class, then emerging from the use of technical innovations which had arisen in the recent war and were now being used by large industry. Various kinds of difficulties arose in the communist parties of France, Germany, Poland and Czechoslovakia. Italy once again seemed a special case, only now in the opposite sense: it was the country where the united front policy bore some fruit in spite of the turbulent situation.

From the organisational point of view, in an effort to combat so many theoretical and analytical disagreements, it was decided that a Comintern Programme (which would only be ready at its Sixth Congress, in 1928) and centralisation, now called 'Bolshevisation', should be emphasised. This would imply a stronger presence of the leading bodies of the International in the life of the national sections, stronger ideological definition, and obligatory party reorganisation, starting with organs concerned with industrial matters. The result was that the scission in the leadership of the RKP(b) spread to all the International, and so too did the corresponding theoretical regression.

The expectation that the crisis of capital would worsen and the workers would again take the initiative, which had justified the Comintern's turn to the left, was not fulfilled. The Fifth Enlarged Plenary of the ECCI, in March 1925, acknowledged the mistakes in this forecast and began to pay attention to the East. Bukharin's speech on the importance of the peasantry in the world revolution reflected the temporary success of the political formula of the worker-peasant alliance inside the USSR, with the development of the NEP and the emphasis given to the relative economic success of the workers' state as opposed to the failures in the West, and also the possibilities for revolutionary developments in China.

Rosa Luxemburg's theory on the extended accumulation of capital, which had already been repudiated at the Fifth Congress, was complemented by criticism aimed at 'Luxemburgism' in party organisation, counterposed to 'Bolshevisation'. The KPD lefts led the campaign against 'Luxemburgism' after the defeat of October 1923, and their critical views prevailed over the theories of Rosa Luxemburg in their fight against the Spartakist current, the greatest proponent of the united front policy.

Clearly, the context was the resistance existing in the West (Germany, Poland and Czechoslovakia) as well as the ECCI's decision in favour of 'Bolshevisation', which could perfectly suit the theoretical conception of the party Gramsci had been developing in Italy. The Spartakist trend would only have any influence on the KPD again during the brief period in which Bukharin was in the leadership of the International, between Zinoviev's fall and the Sixth World Congress, when this group were known as 'the conciliators'.

The Spartakists' fear was that Bolshevisation would imply the analytical dissolution of the historical specificity of Germany and Central-Eastern Europe, which would be the certain consequence of the imposition of a particular understanding of the united front formula (reawakening certain fears expressed by Rosa Luxemburg shortly before her death). Left-wing communism, which by then had established itself in the KPD leadership with a political conception entirely opposed to the united front policy, laid even greater stress on the specificity of the West. This had the potential to open the way for a challenge to the Soviet preponderance implied in the 'Bolshevisation' formula, involving fractions from various sections such as the Poles and Bordiga in Italy.

Divisions among the ultra-left group allowed Thälmann to take over the KPD leadership in 1925 – albeit not without great struggle – and this only strengthened its already established alliance with Stalin. On the other hand, the conditions arose for the stabilisation of a leading group in the KPD and for a broader conception of the united front policy in the Comintern, more in agreement with the USSR's political conditions. The condensation of a new leading group, simultaneously favourable to 'Bolshevisation' and the united front policy, had Gramsci's open sympathy.

The Sixth Enlarged Plenary of the ECCI met in February 1926, as Zinoviev's leadership of the RKP(b) and the Comintern entered a slump.[5] New players entered the scene as a result of the latest changes in leadership in certain important Western parties, and they expected new and fierce clashes. Even so, as Zinoviev outlined a new correlation of forces in his speech, he once again mentioned the united front as a long-term political tactic, and thus he was elected president of the ECCI for one more term. From the organisational point of view, the demand that party structures be based on factory cells was softened, taking into consideration not only the potential of territorial organisation, but also acknowledging that the previous decision had led many communist parties to lose cadre.

Soon after the meeting had been concluded, the conflict within the USSR Party and state leadership was rekindled as the so-called 'united opposition' arose. At the same time, it was possible to see a conservative tendency in Europe and in international politics, opening up the prospect of renewed conflict, and possibly a war targeted against the USSR. As for the Comintern, the defeats of the workers' movement in Great Britain and Poland instigated fresh disagreements, which reached their highest point in the RKP(b) between July and October 1926.

The utter defeat of the 'united opposition' in the RKP(b) took by surprise the whole sector of leftist communism that still maintained its principled opposition to the united front policy, and also excluded or forced into submission those who had reservations over this policy and the NEP as its necessary and symmetric counterpart. At the same time, however, this movement demanded a fresh correction in Bukharin's view of the NEP, and he accepted some of the criticism from the opposition, which accused him of benefiting the 'middle' peasantry to the detriment of the semi-proletarian peasantry, creating an imbalance that would contribute to the strengthening of Stalin's theoretical and political positions.[6]

During the Seventh Enlarged Plenary Meeting of the ECCI (in November 1926), the opening remarks were given by Bukharin, who would for some time

---

5   After its Fourteenth Congress, which took place in December 1925, the RKP(b) began to call itself the Communist Party of the Soviet Union (Bolshevik), even though the famous acronym CPSU only entered regular usage in the 1950s. In this book, we chose to use the denomination RKP(b).

6   Agosti 1974–9, vol. 1, pp. 389–432.

remain the most important representative of the Comintern. He discussed the current historical phase as a renewal of capital, with implications for the technical basis of the accumulation process itself, such that a deep crisis providing an opportunity for the proletariat was improbable. Therefore, the goal should be the strengthening of the communist parties and the development of the political formula of the united front. This united front was to be extended also 'from above', while the USSR would continue with the NEP. The perspective of a revolution in the West seemed to have been postponed indefinitely. Bukharin drew particular attention to the revolutionary process in China, which, though it was bourgeois-democratic in nature, allowed for a worker-peasant alliance which could tread a 'non-capitalist path' and become a strong component of the world revolution.

Stalin opened the discussion on the Russian question, defending the possibility of socialist transition in Russia without help from the Western proletariat, believing the endogenous development of the productive forces to be feasible. This implied that Soviet power should be able to beat the 'Soviet bourgeoisie' with its own strength and that the contradictions between the imperialist countries and the forces of the national anti-imperialist movements, especially in China, would provide the USSR with the necessary resources. Within this framework, the Soviet state would play a decisive propulsive role in the world revolutionary process.

The differences between Bukharin and Stalin began to surface in a very nuanced manner, but they would mark the beginning of a new phase in the internal conflict of the Bolshevik leadership, leading to the failure of any attempt to develop the NEP as a path to socialist transition in the USSR. While Bukharin understood that the Soviet agrarian bourgeoisie could be assimilated during the transition process, Stalin believed the use of state force would eventually be inevitable.

The Seventh Plenary of the ECCI was the last great dispute into which the oppositions entered, both in the RKP(b) and the Comintern. 'Left-wing communism', which still resisted in Germany, stuck by the position that the USSR was on a fast track to capitalist restoration, by means of an alliance between the state bureaucracy and the rich peasantry. The possibility of an alliance between this small and heterogeneous tendency with the Russian 'united opposition' brought the 'majority' together in a solid front that smoothed over its differences.

The 'united opposition' stressed the risk of the revolution being 'debased' by bureaucratisation and the excessive economic role played by the peasantry, which could have serious implications leading to a retardation in industrialisation and to the USSR continuing to depend on the world market. The theoretical regression that had affected the Comintern was apparent, in this debate, through the countless canonical citations from Marx, Engels and Lenin, used by each side to back up their positions. By the end of the meeting, the 'united opposition' was identified as a bearer of 'social-democratic' errors.[7]

Bukharin's period of greatest theoretical and political influence coincided with the NEP's high point in the USSR and the revolutionary ferment in China, which brought to the centre of the discussion the problem of the role of the peasantry in the revolutionary process and the socialist transition itself. The ECCI only spoke specifically about China in March 1926, during the Sixth Enlarged Plenary – almost a whole year after the revolutionary process had begun – drawing attention to the fact that China was a markedly agrarian country.

The very advance of the Chinese revolution and the appearance of the peasantry on the stage brought a realignment of forces and with it a reflection on the united front policy that had been executed until that moment, national-democratic and anti-imperialist in nature. As the process developed, with the formation of a political alliance of the bourgeoisie with the so-called 'warlords' for the sake of national reunification, the peasantry organised itself and promoted changes in social relations in rural areas.

The Chinese question became a matter of political dispute within the RKP(b) and the Comintern. Trotsky and Zinoviev proposed that the Chinese CP should make a definitive break with the Guomindang, in defence of the idea of the 'hegemony of the proletariat'. Bukharin and Stalin, on the other hand, believed that the united front policy should remain centred on anti-imperialism. The difference between them was that while Stalin thought that the basis for revolutionary victory was in the urban industrial centres, even for want of any peasant revolt, Bukharin believed that the advance of the revolutionary peasantry could alter the correlation of forces within the anti-imperialist united front.[8]

These events helped to push Gramsci away from Trotsky, with whom he had identified at least until the end of 1924. Trotsky's political and theoretical position in the splitting of the Bolshevik leadership contributed to this. On the other hand, Bukharin's formulations and especially the need to think through the specificity of the Italian social form led Gramsci to go deeper in his reflections on the peasant question.

---

7 Spriano 1969, pp. 72–87.
8 It has been observed that, at the same time, in China, Mao Zedong was reaching conclusions similar to Bukharin's on the fundamental role to be played by the peasantry in the Chinese revolution and the socialist transition. See Sader 1982, pp. 37–57.

2   Gramsci in Vienna and His Confluence with the Communist Refoundation

Gramsci's trip had been delayed for many months. Finally, by the end of November, he left Moscow and went to Vienna, where he arrived on 3 December 1923. In his first weeks there, Gramsci tried to clarify what his political responsibilities would be and which resources he could use in his activities. Living modestly in the periphery of Vienna, Gramsci very soon applied himself to bringing *L'Ordine Nuovo* back to life. His purpose was to create a periodical that touched upon the matters most pressing to the working class, without slipping into mere reporting or compiling of the news, and one that presented itself as an organ aimed at the united front. That is to say, he wanted an organ which did not depend directly on the party, presenting itself as a 'review of working-class politics and culture', so that it could also circulate in intellectual milieux.[9]

Gramsci was, above all, concerned with contributing to the education and the intellectual progress of the working-class vanguard. Apparently, this was Gramsci's reaction every time that he realised he was politically isolated. At that moment, he was also considering organising a yearbook of the working class, which would have about seven hundred pages. Enthusiastic about beginning the third phase of *L'Ordine Nuovo*, Gramsci believed that 'such a publication would not be without impact on the education of our more qualified and responsible comrades, and could also garner sympathy for our party in certain intellectual milieux'.[10]

At the beginning of 1924, in a letter to Ruggero Grieco, Gramsci suggested that in the presentation of *L'Ordine Nuovo*, third series, it should be said that '*L'Ordine Nuovo* aims at creating in the masses of workers and peasants a revolutionary vanguard capable of establishing the State of Workers' and Peasants' Councils and preparing the terrain for the advent and establishment of communist society'.[11]

In his effort to educate the vanguard, Gramsci also proposed a new publication, more strictly intellectual in nature, to be called *Proletarian Critique*. All these educational and cultural activities would be part of a broad effort of preparation of the 'future cadre of the mass party', which also included the creation of party schools, especially abroad, a correspondence course and the publication of a series of basic works.[12]

---

9   Gramsci 1992, pp. 132–5.
10   Gramsci 1992, pp. 146–50.
11   Gramsci 1992, p. 169.
12   Gramsci 1992, pp. 184–91.

As for the internal situation of the party, Gramsci remained convinced that Angelo Tasca's minority still acted with the purpose of 'always being able to show that the opinion of the majority [of the party leadership] continues and continued to create difficulties for the political work of the Comintern in Italy'.[13] On the other hand, Amadeo Bordiga insisted that most of the leadership collectively sign a document defending the political orientation of the Second PCd'I Congress, which led Gramsci to believe that his isolation was inevitable and would last for some time. Already at the beginning of 1924, Gramsci reaffirmed his refusal to sign the manifesto proposed by Bordiga, even at the risk of weakening and dividing the majority before the internal opposition.[14]

Gramsci seemed already convinced of the need to stay away from Bordiga, all the better to fight the 'rightist' trend forming around Tasca, even though he believed himself alone in this conviction. The basic disagreement between Bordiga and Gramsci had to do with the conception of the revolutionary party and the policy proposed by the Fourth Congress of the Comintern and the Third Enlarged Plenary of the ECCI, with which Gramsci claimed to fundamentally agree. Unlike Togliatti, he believed there was an immediate need to begin the formation of a new leading group, one that could occupy the 'centre' of the party's political spectrum, as this would be the only possible way to reestablish a relationship of collaboration and trust with the Comintern without converging with the path followed until then by Tasca and the minority group to the right of the party.

'I do not know yet exactly what to do. It is not the first time that I have found myself in this situation ...', Gramsci wrote, acknowledging his position of virtual isolation and remembering the harsh disputes which had affected the *L'Ordine Nuovo* group in 1920, during the process of the *communist scission*. As Gramsci recalled, 'and just as then within the Socialist Party it was necessary to depend on the abstentionists if one wished to create the basic nucleus of the future

---

13   Gramsci 1923, p. 156.

14   Even though Amadeo Bordiga was in prison during the whole preparation of the Third Enlarged Plenary of the ECCI, he wrote the project for a manifesto to be sent by the PCd'I leadership, defending the decisions of its Second Congress and attacking the decisions at the Comintern's Fourth Congress, including the united front policy and the projected merger with the PSI. It was decided that any decision on this matter would be delayed, considering the delicate circumstances faced by the Italians at that moment, not only in terms of the International but also the fascist repression. However, when Bordiga left prison at the end of October, he once again insisted on the document, even though he made some compromises, softening his criticism of the maximalists and refusing nomination for the PCd'I executive committee.

party, so today it is necessary to struggle against the extremists if one wishes the party to develop and stop being nothing more than an external faction of the Socialist Party'.[15]

Thus Gramsci began a second phase in the movement of the *scission*, which would take him definitely to converge with the *communist refoundation* begun by Lenin, according to which education had a decisive role in the formation of a properly oriented leadership. Even though Gramsci believed that he would remain alone, he was determined to fight on two fronts within the PCd'I, both against Tasca's 'right' and Bordiga's 'extremism', in order to 'take the doctrine and tactics of the Comintern as the basis for an action programme for our activity'.[16]

After receiving a letter from Alfonso Leonetti, an old comrade from the Turin struggles, Gramsci suddenly changed his tone, replying: 'Your letter pleased me very much, because it showed that I am not alone in having certain anxieties and in considering certain solutions to our problems necessary'.[17] However, Gramsci said he was against pure and simply recreating the *L'Ordine Nuovo* group, and even challenged the continued existence of such a group as he pondered their past and present disagreements, as well as the political mistakes committed during the process of the *scission*, among them the fact that the group was confined to the Piedmont region.

Upon the suggestion of Umberto Terracini, Gramsci wrote a long letter explaining the broad lines of political orientation that he would like to see prevail in the PCd'I as the result of a new correlation of forces and trends, an orientation more fitting to the international situation of which Italy was part. Therefore, it was of the utmost importance to clarify the political positions that existed among the communists of Russia and Germany, these countries being decisive in setting the pace of the world revolution.

Gramsci takes for granted that, in the case of Russia, Lenin played the role of a mediator between a more leftist trend formed by Trotsky, Radek and Bukharin, and a more rightist trend formed by Zinoviev, Kamanev and Stalin, and he also synthesised them. Regarding Trotsky, Gramsci noted that

> throughout the history of the Russian revolutionary movement Trotsky was politically to the left of the Bolsheviks, while on organisational questions he often made a bloc with or actually could not be distinguished

---

15   Gramsci 1999b, p. 251.
16   Gramsci 1999b, p. 251.
17   Gramsci 1999b, p. 268.

from the Mensheviks. It is well known that in 1905, Trotsky already thought that a socialist and working-class revolution could take place in Russia, while the Bolsheviks only aimed to establish a political dictatorship of the proletariat allied to the peasantry that would serve as a framework for the development of capitalism, which was not to be touched in its economic structure. It is well known that in November 1917, while Lenin and the majority of the party had gone over to Trotsky's view and intended to take over not merely political power but also economic power, Zinoviev and Kamenev remained in the traditional party view.[18]

Gramsci thus interpreted the events of 1917 as Lenin coming closer to Trotsky's positions to the detriment of the Bolshevik right, which continued to defend the political orientation traditionally espoused by the party. The centrality of the factory as the nodal point of Gramsci's political theory, as well as Trotsky's belief that the revolution should intervene in industrial management from its very beginning, present a clear point of rapprochement between the pair. Reading historical events in such a manner, Gramsci justifies his obvious sympathy towards the left and Trotsky's positions in the debate that took place by the end of 1923.

> In the recent polemic which has broken out in Russia, it is clear that Trotsky and the opposition in general, in view of the prolonged absence of Lenin from the leadership of the party, have been greatly preoccupied about the danger of a return to the old mentality, which would be damaging to the revolution. Demanding a greater intervention of proletarian elements in the life of the party and a diminution of the powers of the bureaucracy, they want basically to ensure the socialist and proletarian character of the revolution, and to prevent a gradual transition to that democratic dictatorship – carapace for a developing capitalism – which was still the programme of Zinoviev and Co. in November 1917.[19]

Thus Trotsky's and the opposition's stance were apt to the extent that they attempted to prevent the renewed prevalence of the old Bolshevik thesis that a democratic dictatorship should direct capitalist development. According to Gramsci, the only really important novelty within the Bolshevik leadership was Bukharin's shift to the positions defended by the right, which at the time

---

18   Gramsci 1999b, p. 272.
19   Gramsci 1999b, pp. 272–3.

comprised the majority of the party. Apparently, he did not discern Lenin's own shift to more rightist positions, and made no effort to hide his sympathy for Trotsky as well as a certain revulsion toward Zinoviev and Stalin, thus placing himself more to the left within the Comintern political spectrum.

The greatest evidence for this lies in Gramsci's view that a revolutionary situation still lingered both in Germany and Italy, making the weakness of the existing leaderships an even more serious problem to be addressed. He saw the leftist and the rightist trends in each leadership as incompetent.

In the case of Germany, Gramsci believed that the KPD leadership should be replaced. Brandler and Thalheimer should yield their places to Fischer and Marlow, as they represented 'the majority of the revolutionary proletariat', even though they presented serious objections to the united front tactic. Later, when this leftist group differentiated itself as Thälmann arose as a leader sticking to leftist positions while turning toward the united front tactic, Gramsci looked on the process with great sympathy.

However, it is more important to take note of Gramsci's criticism of the application and the conception of the political formula of the united front as elaborated in Germany by Levi and Radek, and to which Brandler and Thalheimer felt forced to accede, not without resistance.

> Wanting at all costs to find allies for the working class, they have ended up by forgetting the function of the working class itself. Wanting to win the labour aristocracy controlled by the social-democrats, they have thought they could do so not by developing a programme of an industrial nature, based on the Factory Councils and on workers' control, but by seeking to compete with the social-democrats on the terrain of democracy and thus leading the slogan of a workers' and peasants' government to degeneration.[20]

Gramsci's criticism ultimately stressed the 'spirit of separation' present in the cultural tradition of the German workers' movement, its great independence from bourgeois state institutions and its capacity for self-organisation and centralisation. The only possible conception of a united front, within such a perspective, was the united front that assimilated new popular and working-class layers to the 'spirit of separation' in order to confront capital within the production process itself. The terrain of democracy, on the other hand, would be more favourable to the class enemy.

---

20   Gramsci 1999b, pp. 273–4.

Even though from a strategic point of view the defeated group in the KPD stood further to the right, the fact remains that the political mistake of October 1923 was 'putschism'. As Brandler and Thalheimer felt they were losing the majority of the party, they soon shifted to the left. However, the united front policy did not allow for such sudden movements, even though it did enable a momentary convergence of Trotsky's and Radek's positions and those of the KPD leadership. The defeat of the German October, therefore, had a direct impact on the unfolding of the political struggle in the USSR.

From Gramsci's analysis it can be seen that even though he was situated on the left wing of the Comintern, he opposed the left's 'extremism' and, more importantly, he outlined the political formula of the united front as a strategy that should start from the centrality of workers and their management of production. Gramsci denied that the Comintern was turning to the left, because he himself had adopted that position – thus he did not realise that Germany's and Italy's supposed revolutionary situations were not real, and that the offensive of capital was already bearing fruit.

As Gramsci discussed the problems of the Italian situation, his disagreements with Bordiga became more and more explicit, and centred on the relationship between the PCd'I and the Comintern. This implied a discussion of the whole question of the international dimension of the communist movement and its universal nature. Bordiga believed that the specificity of the Russian East, which had allowed the victory of the revolution, had nothing to do with the more advanced West. Given a developed capitalism with a large working class, what was at issue was to organise a vanguard party able to draw this working class away from the influence of reformism and confront the capitalist state.

In advanced capitalism there would be no need for social and political alliances that were not part of the logic of the conflict between capital and labour, and it followed that the political formula of the united front was a serious theoretical and practical mistake. Thus Bordiga followed, in his extremist attitude, the same determinist logic of social democracy, which believed the difference between West and East to be insurmountable.

At the same time as Gramsci seemed to echo various formulations from Luxemburg and Lenin, he also advanced the original formulation which he would later develop in the *Prison Notebooks*, in a passage explaining why Bordiga's formulations were mistaken:

> Firstly, because the political conception of the Russian communists was formed on an international and not on a national terrain. Secondly, because in central and western Europe the development of capitalism has not only determined the formation of the broad proletarian strata, but

also – and as a consequence – has created the higher stratum, the labour aristocracy, with its appendages in the trade-union bureaucracy and the social-democratic groups. The determination, which in Russia was direct and drove the masses onto the streets for a revolutionary uprising, in central and western Europe is complicated by all these political superstructures, created by the greater development of capitalism. This makes the action of the masses slower and more prudent, and therefore requires of the revolutionary party a strategy and tactics altogether more complex and long-term than those which were necessary for the Bolsheviks in the period between March and November 1917.[21]

The fundamental disagreement, therefore, did not concern the specificity of the Russian East as compared to the West. Both Bordiga and Gramsci saw that the revolution in the West would be more complex because capitalism was more developed and reformism had a stronger presence. What separated the one from the other was the question of the universality of the Russian Revolution and the communist movement, and the revolutionary strategy to be employed.

Now, the political formula of the united front takes the notion of hegemony as a given. So it was the theme of the hegemony of the working class – and, therefore, the theme of alliances and political mediations – that separated the two revolutionaries, and this had direct implications for the way the party and its activity would be conceived and organised. For Gramsci, the united front in Italy should aim at concretising the slogan of the 'worker-peasant government': starting from the real situation in the country, confronting the labour aristocracy and reformism, and 'seeking the alliance between the poorest strata of the Northern working class and the peasant masses of the Mezzogiorno and the islands'.[22]

Gramsci's ongoing correspondence with some of his comrades from the old *L'Ordine Nuovo* group persuaded him of the concrete opportunity to organise a current situated between the extreme left and the right of the party, opening up the possibility for a new majority and a new leadership. An important step would be to organise this tendency with a view to the party conference due to be held in Como the following May, and to the presentation of a conference document. In Gramsci's evaluation, the fact that the bourgeoisie was regaining control over the productive forces and that social-democracy was shifting to

21   Gramsci 1999b, pp. 282–3.

22   Gramsci 1992, p. 259.

the right enabled a recovery of liberalism across the whole of the West. Thus the overcoming of fascism could take place through a liberal-bourgeois path with a preponderance of reformism within the workers' movement.[23]

Gramsci realised the fundamental importance of dialogue with the anti-fascist intellectuals, and also saw how they were soaked in pessimism and a lack of clear horizons. The explanation for this situation lay in the lack of a concrete pragmatic perspective that effectively gave meaning to the 'worker-peasant government' slogan. Given that 'the broad masses, which the intellectuals automatically claim to represent, have no precise direction, and do not know how it will be possible to get out of the present tumult', there was a need for a precise analysis of the Italian situation, addressing every possibility: 'is it possible for the slogan of a Constituent Assembly to become relevant once again? ... Is it possible that we will go from fascism to the dictatorship of the proletariat? What would be the possible and likely intermediate stages?'[24]

The need to go through intermediate stages seemed more likely as the city of Milan, which had the largest industrial proletariat in Italy, came under reformist hegemony. Gramsci then realised this was 'the greatest difficulty of the Italian revolution', because 'the greatest vital centres of Italian capitalism are located in Milan; Italian capitalism can only be decapitated in Milan', and thus this would be 'a national and, in some ways, also an international problem'.[25]

Gramsci realised that, as a key, the united front should join together the most advanced social sector – which meant the Milanese working class, even though it was under reformist hegemony – and the most backward sector – the Southern peasantry, for whom 'class problems also tend to be "territorial" ones, since capitalism appears as an outsider to the region, and so does the government that takes care of capitalism's interests'. The opposition to fascism and also to the liberal-reformist path – two variants of bourgeois class power – would leave open to the peasants the possibility of either following the Southern democratic petit bourgeoisie, at the risk of breaking the state apart, or else sealing the worker-peasant alliance. Gramsci was aware that 'in the present situation, as the existing proletarian forces decline, the Southern peasant masses become ever more important in the revolutionary arena'.[26]

Answering a letter from Piero Sraffa, an old *L'Ordine Nuovo* collaborator, Gramsci wrote an article explaining why he had outlined the united front policy

---

23   Gramsci 1992, pp. 260–1.
24   Gramsci 1992, p. 283.
25   Gramsci 1978, p. 8.
26   Gramsci 1978, pp. 171–5.

in the way that he did. In order to counter the opinion of his old friend, now a professor of economics in Cagliari, who had been led by the weakness of the working class to see no solution other than supporting the liberal-democratic opposition so as to complete the bourgeois revolution, Gramsci argued that

> Our party is an organised fraction of the proletariat and of the peasant masses, i.e. of the classes which are today oppressed and crushed by fascism. If our party did not find for today independent solutions of its own to the overall, Italian problems, the classes which are its natural base would turn en masse towards those political currents which give some solution to these problems that is not the fascist one.
>
> If that occurred, the fact would have an immense historical significance. It would mean that the present is not a revolutionary socialist period, but we are still living in an epoch of bourgeois capitalist development. It would mean that not only the subjective conditions of organisation and political preparation are lacking, but also the objective material conditions for the proletariat to attain power.[27]

Thus we see that, for Gramsci, the historical period of the international socialist revolution begun in 1917 was still ongoing, and importantly so in Italy. In order to defeat fascism as well as any other form of preserving the power of capital, it was necessary immediately to ensure the organisational, political and cultural autonomy of the working class. However, since this class was a minority within the country as a whole, a minority concentrated in the north-western region amidst a situation of defeat and isolation, the creation of a united front with other proletarian strata and the Southern peasantry was indispensable for the goal of making a 'worker-peasant government'-possible.

While Gramsci was in Vienna, in January 1924, the CC of the PCd'I presented a document suggesting the political orientation of the periodical *L'Unità*, which campaigned for the Proletarian Unity coalition, advocating the unity of revolutionary forces and the goal of the 'worker-peasant government'. This document stated that: 'The CC considers the electoral struggle as a moment in the Party's activity aiming at the formation of a united front in defence of the economic and political interests of the working class, all denied by Fascism ... [It] believes that every electoral agreement must have a programmatic nature that can serve as the basis for a permanent united front of action'.[28]

---

27   Gramsci 1999b, p. 323.
28   Communist Party Archives, 1924. 229/29. Fondazione Istituto Gramsci, Rome.

The situation was not too hopeful when it was considered that the régime approved electoral laws that would largely benefit its own list of candidates and that the PSI and PSU would form their own coalition, in conditions better than those of the communists. Just to make things worse, Amadeo Bordiga, the most prestigious communist leader, refused nomination to lead the coalition. Even so, the PCd'I, which hoped to obtain eight to twelve seats in parliament, had a result far better than expected, electing nineteen deputies (six from the socialist third-internationalist fraction – *terzini* – which would enter the PCd'I in August). Gramsci was elected in the Veneto region.

In mid-April the PCd'I discussed its electoral results and the political perspectives of the united front tactic. Togliatti opened the debate noting that the PSU, the party that received the largest amount of votes among any of the fragments of the old PSI, was 'a reserve force of the bourgeoisie, a wing of fascism', such that 'the united front tactic can only be applied to them from below, in order to put the masses against the leaders who betray them'.[29] He proposed a merger with the *terzini* and the creation of a united front with the PSI, but without nurturing any illusions and remaining wary of the risk of spreading 'liquidationism' among the masses. The goal of this united front tactic should be extracting from the PSI whatever remained of its left wing and thus 'favouring its elimination from the arena of proletarian competition'.[30] Even though Togliatti believed any alliance with the Popular Party to be impossible, he insisted on the centrality of the question of the worker-peasant alliance.

3   Gramsci in Rome: The United Front Policy and Anti-Fascism

Gramsci went back to Italy in order to take part in the Como Conference, which took place in the middle of May 1924. Three trends with clearly defined positions emerged at this meeting, though ultimately there was a conspicuous distortion in the balance of forces: the so-called 'centre' trend, largely inspired by Gramsci, had the majority of the CC, but only came in third place in terms of the number of delegates present, representing the intermediate levels of the party.

The 'leftist' trend thus ratified the line approved in the Rome Congress (March 1922), opposing the united front policy and the decisions of the Fourth World Congress, while also drawing attention to the probable mistake of having established a relationship with the PSI for the purposes of a merger. The 'right'

---

29   *Rivista Storica del Socialismo*, 1964, p. 532.
30   Ibid.

confirmed its view that a mistake had been made in the very origins of the PCd'I, which went back to the Livorno Congress itself, and that the leadership really was responsible for the defeat of the Italian proletariat, owing to their resistance to taking on board the united front policy and merging with the PSI.

The 'centre' also chose the 'right' as its main adversary, not only because of the risks it foresaw in that line for the survival and the autonomy of the party, but mainly because the Comintern had been turning to the left since the beginning of the year. It believed that the foundation of the PCd'I had been a necessary action, but since the Fourth Congress it had pointed to the probable error of opposing the Comintern, and proposed corrections to the united front policy. As for immediate merger with the *terzini*, the 'centre' and the 'right' were in agreement, whereas the 'left' continued to oppose it.[31]

The need to conform to the situation of the Comintern and to try to broaden the consensus at the top of the party forced many compromises on the trend led by Gramsci, a trend that was already maturing theoretically within the communist refoundation but also had to cope with the regression in the international communist movement as a whole. Even so, Gramsci tried to focus on the positive aspects of the meeting, insisting, however, on the revision of the Theses of Rome and the construction of a new platform. He then said that at that meeting 'our Party for the first time confronted the question of how to become the party of the broadest Italian masses, and become the party that realises the hegemony of the proletariat within the framework of the alliance between the working class and the peasant mass'.[32]

As a large Italian delegation began to head for Moscow in order to take part in the Fifth Congress of the Comintern, a political crisis suddenly exploded, making the fascist régime tremble. With the apparent goals of restraining the CGL union leaders' thirst for establishing forms of collaboration with the fascist régime, as well as assembling the democratic opposition, Giacomo Matteotti directed harsh criticism at the régime from his parliamentary tribune. The result was his kidnapping and murder on 11 June, which two days later led the opposition to withdraw from parliament until the case was resolved. This was the so-called Aventine Secession.[33]

Antonio Gramsci, also meant to be on his way to Moscow, together with Mauro Scoccimarro began effectively to lead the party, thus testing the antagonistic united front policy. At first there was an attempt to involve the whole

---

31   Spriano 1967, pp. 355–7.

32   Gramsci 1978, p. 182.

33   A reference to the retreat of the people of ancient Rome, who demanded citizenship rights, to the Aventine mount in 494 B.C.

opposition in a rapid action that took advantage of the political crisis, which Gramsci fundamentally saw as a crisis of the petit bourgeoisie. However, the efforts of the constitutional democratic opposition, joined by the two socialist parties, were directed at providing an institutional way out of the régime's crisis, such that popular discontent would be channelled into the creation of a new democratic and parliamentary régime. The PCd'I's break with the Aventine opposition, caused by the latter's hesitation and refusal to mobilise the masses, apparently left the communists in a position of isolation. The fact, however, was that the party managed to garner strength and sympathy, even in spite of the failure of the general strike called for 17 June.

Similarly, the political orientation of the CC broadened its internal support against the 'left' trend, which insisted on more decisive political action, and the 'right', which defended the unity of the anti-fascist opposition as a whole. Gramsci argued against this view in a meeting of the CC by the middle of July: 'The first task of the proletariat, even in a situation like this, is to assume an autonomous stance', and 'certain speeches betray the thought that we live in a colonial country, where the proletarian revolution is not possible if the "oppositions" will not first conclude their national revolution'.[34]

However, Gramsci was never satisfied with the simplistic notion, so common among various sectors of the International, of a united front 'from below', aiming only at the goal of proletarian dictatorship. On the contrary, he favoured broader social alliances including sectors of the small bourgeoisie, particularly the intellectuals that expressed it, aiming at intermediate goals. Thus Gramsci criticised the republican and socialist leaders, because 'they did not want to sanction in the centre the alliance made in the periphery between the proletarian and petit-bourgeois revolutionary forces'.[35] He was referring to the radically anti-fascist position taken by the young intellectuals gathered around the magazine *Rivoluzione Liberale* [Liberal Revolution] from Turin, edited by Piero Gobetti, and the magazine *Il Caffè*, from Milan, edited by Riccardo Bauer. Gramsci concluded: 'we Communists demanded of the oppositions nothing different from what these liberal groups reproached them for not doing. Even when we demanded action that would force the fascist government to quit, we had no intention of imposing goals of our own'.[36]

In August, in accordance with the decisions at the Fifth Congress of the Comintern, the *terzini* were accepted into the PCd'I and a new leadership

---

34   Gramsci 1978, p. 462.
35   Gramsci 1978, p. 192.
36   Caprioglio 1997, p. 266.

was established. It was formed by the 'centre', the 'right' and the *'terzini'*, with Gramsci nominated general secretary, while Bordiga's 'left' decided to stay out. In the discussion on the Italian crisis, Gramsci believed fascism to be fatally wounded. The régime's birth and death were associated with the crisis of the middle classes, the only truly national social stratum. Fascism may not have been able to resist the crisis, but its collapse should be followed by intermediate phases and goals, during which the proletariat and the communists should preserve their autonomy.

The alliance with the democratic constitutional opposition would compromise the move to more advanced stages in the struggle, because 'the broad working masses are disorganised, dispersed and fragmented among the undifferentiated population'. The current phase was 'rather a preparatory phase, of transition to the struggle for power: in short, a phase of agitation, propaganda and organisation', aiming 'to create a broad factory movement that can develop until it gives birth to an organisation of city-wide proletarian committees, elected directly by the masses. These committees, in the social crisis that is looming, can become the strongholds of the general interests of the entire working people'.[37]

We see how Gramsci's strategy was anchored in the need for autonomous and antagonistic working-class organisation on the basis of the production process itself, and that this should be the distinctive characteristic of the configuration of a united front based on factory councils and workers' and peasants' councils. The mistake in this analysis stemmed from his interpretation of a general crisis of capitalism and the immediacy of the socialist revolution, even though Gramsci did have a clear view of the need for connected intermediate phases. Gramsci had not yet realised that the crisis did not have to do merely with the petit bourgeoisie, which was preparing to seal a lasting alliance with monopoly capital, but also with the skilled industrial working class that had been lost between reformism and factory self-management, and was strongly repressed by fascism, leaving it very disorganised. The forces that had been organised in the Aventine Secession represented the last attempt by certain sectors of capital allied with social reformism to restore the liberal rule of law, based on market principles. This test of force lasted from August to October 1924, as the constitutional democratic opposition declined.[38]

The internal debate in the PCd'I was expressed in several provincial congresses between September and November. At the end of September, Bordiga

---

37   Gramsci 1999b, pp. 364–7.
38   Poulantzas 1974.

and Gramsci attended the Naples meeting, in which the former once again refused the latter's invitation to recreate the Livorno leadership. Besides, even though both agreed with the position Trotsky had been defending, namely that social democracy could become the ideological political instrument for the Americanisation of Europe, they yet again disagreed on the issue of the political formula of the united front, which, in practice, Gramsci wished to organise under the slogan of the 'anti-parliament'.

Given the lethargy which held sway over the political situation and the oppositions – thus aiding the reconstitution of fascism – and the ineffectiveness of the call for the formation of 'workers' and peasants' committees' – which the communists had been proposing – on 14 October, during a meeting of the executive commission of the PCd'I, in spite of the resistance that arose particularly among the Neapolitan communists, Gramsci decided to propose the idea of constituting an anti-parliament, formed by all the oppositions:

> For us, such an anti-parliament would be an intermediate phase between Parliament and a Sovietism based on workers' and peasants' committees. The slogan of the constitution of the workers' and peasants' committees is still not understood by the broad masses. That of the anti-parliament will be received as a solution more fitting to the situation's present stage of development.[39]

Gramsci's proposal to subvert the liberal idea of parliamentary representation was only partially accepted, and the idea of anti-parliament as an intermediate stage was rejected. Thus, when Gramsci gave the opening speech to the Central Committee on 18 October, he said: 'We will propose to the oppositions that they call themselves a representative assembly, following the regulations of Parliament ... We will affirm that this assembly will be merely a means of agitation and not a real force until the moment when it decides to base itself on a mass movement and the committees of workers and peasants'.[40]

As it can be seen, Gramsci's political conception, particularly regarding the political formula of the united front, was far more dialectical, flexible and mobile than that of the vast majority of PCd'I leaders and even the Comintern. While Gramsci saw the need to break up the lines of the class enemy without losing one's own autonomy, and to see the movement of the various actors against the overall backdrop of political and social life, the leaders coming

---

39   De Benedetto 1976, p. 138.
40   De Benedetto 1976, p. 146.

from the 'abstentionist', maximalist and even 'ordinuovist' trends remained attached to the cultural assumptions stemming from the traditions of the Italian workers' movement. Besides, the outcome of the Fifth Congress of the Comintern reinforced these various trends, which rested on the crude 'united front from below' formula, the synonymy between 'worker-peasant government' and 'proletarian dictatorship' and even on the idea that 'social democracy is one wing of fascism'.

As expected, the communist proposal was rejected by the democratic oppositions, bringing forth a moment of disorientation not only among party militants but even within the International itself, whose initial suggestion was that the most important thing was to preserve unity against fascism. Manifestations of social discontent and the rapid political exhaustion of the Aventine Secession persuaded the Comintern and the mass of the party that the PCd'I's initial decision to re-enter parliament was more adequate to showing that it was the only force prepared to fight fascism. The result was even greater division among the anti-fascist political forces.

When parliament reopened on 3 January 1925, the régime once again returned to the offensive. Mussolini announced in a speech a strong wave of repression, particularly against communists. Even so, the communists continued to believe that fascism would still tend toward 'normalisation' by means of agreements with the liberal and reformist forces.

During the PCd'I CC meeting called in order to evaluate the situation, Gramsci espoused the idea that the censorship imposed on the press completely buried the activity of the Aventine Secession, which was already tending towards collapse and the formation of a liberal constitutional trend prepared to make a rapprochement with Mussolini. Mussolini, in his turn, attempted to free himself from the most turbulent sectors of the fascist movement, aiming to create a vast conservative party. Still according to this analysis, effective opposition elements in the Aventine Secession were drawing closer to the PCd'I, so there should be an effort to accelerate the dismantling of the PSI and give a new impulse to the slogan of the formation of 'workers' and peasants' committees'.[41] Gramsci's and the PCd'I's position was thus once again among those more to the left of the Comintern, interpreting the united front policy 'from below' and believing that social democracy should be attacked from the left.[42]

---

41   Gramsci 1999b, pp. 381–94.

42   There is a noticeable analogy between the process of differentiation of the communist left within the PCd'I and the formation of the 'centre' group against Bordiga, and that of the KPD, when Thalmann led the formation of a new group dissociating himself from Maslow and Ruth Fischer.

The problem of the ongoing scission within the Bolshevik party was being discussed by the Italian communists for the first time, and Gramsci proposed that the motion to be written

> should contain an exposition of Trotsky's thought: his predictions about American super-capitalism, which will apparently have a European arm in England and bring about a prolonged enslavement of the proletariat under the dominance of American capital. We reject these predictions, which by postponing the revolution indefinitely would shift the whole tactics of the Communist International, which would have to go back to mere propaganda and agitation among the masses. They would also shift the tactics of the Russian State, since if one postpones the European revolution for an entire historical phase ...[43]

Now, such an extreme simplification of Trotsky's thought on the expansive possibilities of Americanism and the role England could possibly play amounts to a distortion of the thought of the author of *Europe and America*, as well as the thought of Gramsci himself, who like Bordiga was not far from this view. Gramsci's stated concern was that, should the revolution in Europe be effectively blocked, the isolation of the USSR would be consolidated, and this would impose limits on the process of the socialist transition. Apparently Gramsci thought that the USSR could be forced to regress to a phase of democratic dictatorship, in the event that the socialist revolution did not spread throughout Europe. Curiously, the criticism aimed at Trotsky could be more properly aimed at Bukharin.

Being a leader of the PCd'I, Gramsci had to move within the correlation of forces that existed within the leadership of the party, influenced by the life of the Comintern and, increasingly, the split process in the Bolshevik leadership. Therefore, his thought could only be expressed in ways strongly conditioned and limited by the circumstances, almost to the point of self-criticism, as in the passage just quoted. Actually, Gramsci needed to widen his base in the PCd'I as well as garner support in the Comintern, and this is why he made an analogy between the behaviour of Trotsky in the RKP(b) and that of Bordiga in the PCd'I. After all, both objectively tended to create fractions within their party and the International, going against the banner of 'Bolshevisation' upheld by the Fifth World Congress and thus breaching party discipline and fracturing its unity, which had to be emphasised at this crucial moment. The matter of unity

---

43   Gramsci 1999b, p. 392.

would be extremely important for the PCd'I. However, referring to the RKP(b), Gramsci recalled that 'the lack of party unity, in a country in which there is only one party, splits the state'.[44]

While Gramsci awaited the moment when he would head for Moscow, where he was to be part of the Italian delegation to the Fifth Enlarged Plenary of the ECCI, he began to put into practice the project he conceived in Vienna of creating a correspondence school for party staff. At the end of February, he finally went to Moscow to see the consolidation – which had already been coming into focus – of the ideological identification between Trotsky and Bordiga as a 'deviation' from 'Leninism'. The document produced by the meeting established a connection between the theoretical views of Trotsky and Bordiga, and between this pair's views and a variant of Second International tradition, thus constraining the next national congress of the PCd'I to 'decide whether it approves the policy conducted by the Central Committee of the Party beginning with the Fifth World Congress, according to the International; also, it must express its choice between Bordiga's tactics and Leninism'.[45]

Thus Gramsci's theoretical elaboration and political activity were shaped by the need he felt to associate himself primarily with the Comintern and the RKP(b), which were then undergoing a clear and institutionalised theoretical regression, and to distance himself from Bordiga and his conception of the proletarian revolution in the West. Gramsci, however, could remain comfortably in that position while still being influenced by Sorel's notion of the separation between the world of labour and the capitalist state, and also, to a certain extent, by Bordiga's notion that the foundation of the PCd'I was something entirely new.

When he returned to Rome after two months, Gramsci tried to give Jules Humbert-Droz, still the main Comintern representative for Romance-language countries, an update on the Italian situation. He said, 'we found, upon our return, a situation greatly changed to our disfavour, not in terms of our influence over the masses, but with regard to the greater difficulties presented to our work by the government and by the CGL'.[46]

As the government was about to promulgate a law against anti-fascist organisations, the CGL, in an attempt to gain legitimacy in the eyes of the régime, began to outlaw communist initiatives. In spite of that, the communists had a good result in the trade-union elections, and were also able to carry out significant public manifestations on 1 May. As for the socialists, however, their break

---

44   Gramsci 1999b, p. 392.
45   Agosti 1974–9, vol. 2, p. 314.
46   Gramsci 1992, p. 417.

was only further aggravated. Likewise, there were new episodes in the internal struggle between the Bordigist opposition and the majority of the Central Committee.

On 16 May in the Chamber of Deputies, Gramsci made his only ever parliamentary speech, a few days after having passed on to the CC the reports from the Fifth Enlarged Plenary of the ECCI and the calling of the Third National Congress of the PCd'I. His speech focused on criticising the so-called Mussolini-Rocco law, which was supposedly a matter of striking against the freemasons as a secret organisation. Gramsci's argument developed along two lines, on the historical significance of the Italian Masonry and on the real intentions behind the bill in question. This was Gramsci's opportunity to present an outline of his understanding of the relation between the Italian state and the representation of the various social classes.

Beginning with the foundational weakness of the Italian bourgeoisie, Gramsci stated that the Masonry was 'the only real and effective party the bourgeois class had for a long time', devoted to fighting the enemies of the unitarian state, which were mainly the Vatican and the Jesuits, representing the 'old semi-feudal classes'. While the Masonry acted as an effective support for the liberal-bourgeois state, the Church boycotted elections and organised armed bands in the countryside, ready to confront the expected advance of the proletariat within liberal democracy. Gramsci then affirmed that 'the rural classes who were represented by the Vatican in the past are now mainly represented by Fascism'.[47]

Gramsci enumerated Italy's lack of raw materials and colonies as well as the Southern question as 'the greatest weaknesses of national life'. In his analysis, 'Italy has been nothing but a means of expansion for non-Italian financial capital', thanks to the mass emigration of its workforce. The bourgeoisie had two chances for articulating social alliances with a view to solving the problems of state weakness and class domination. The first appeared as 'the attempt to establish an alliance between the industrial bourgeoisie and part of the Northern labour aristocracy, with the purpose of subjecting the Italian peasant mass, especially from the Mezzogiorno, to this bourgeois-proletarian formation'.[48]

At the same time, 'in Southern Italy the ruling class is corrupted, and the mass is controlled by the *mazzieri*'. There was the alternative proposal of establishing 'an alliance between the Northern industrialists and a certain vague rural democracy, especially from the South, on the terrain of free trade'.[49]

---

47   Gramsci 1978, pp. 75–85.
48   Gramsci 1978, pp. 75–85.
49   Ibid.

According to Gramsci's reasoning, both these alternatives aimed at broadening the narrow original foundations of the Italian state, whereas fascism, with its alleged 'revolution' and the law that targeted the Masonry, 'fights against the only efficiently organised force the bourgeoisie ever had in Italy, in order to overcome it in the occupation of jobs given by the state to its servants'. Thus it only aimed at replacing the administrative personnel of the liberal-bourgeois state with new personnel, and then reaching an agreement. The true goal of the law would be to impose the greatest barriers to the autonomous organisation of the working class and the peasantry, and also to the revolution – which could only be brought about by these allied forces – that could solve the nation's problems.[50]

Strangely, in his speech Gramsci returned to the understanding that there was a close link between fascism and the agrarian ruling classes. Perhaps for that reason, he was unable to grasp the fact that fascism was approaching its goal of broadening the bases of the state by means of an alliance between Italian financial capital and the petit bourgeoisie which would encompass the whole of the propertied classes in Italy, going beyond the existing bourgeois alternatives and assimilating liberalism into fascism.

Gramsci also did not realise that mass emigration transformed Italy not only into an arena for the expansion of non-Italian financial capital, but for Italian financial capital, too, which soon would claim its colonies. It is possible that at the heart of Gramsci's concerns lay the state bureaucracy, largely formed by intellectuals coming from the intermediate agrarian strata, as he would later explain.

Gramsci himself made a negative evaluation of the meaning and the content of his speech. As he wrote to Giulia Schucht,

> The Fascists did me a favour, such that, from a revolutionary point of view, I began with a failure. I speak in a low voice and so they gathered around me to listen and let me say what I wanted, interrupting me all the time so that I would lose my thread, but they were not there to sabotage me ... I, however, could not concentrate on answering them, and so I was part of their game, because I got tired and was unable to continue with the tone I had wanted to use in my speech.[51]

---

50   Ibid.
51   Gramsci 1992, p. 420.

4   On the Way to the Third Congress of the PCd'I

In his May 1925 report to the CC, in preparation for the Third Congress of the PCd'I, Gramsci made a preliminary assessment of the situation of the party, emphasising the theme of 'Bolshevisation' and the related problem of factionalism, as perpetrated by Bordiga's group. With the purpose of demonstrating the need for 'Bolshevisation', he noted that 'The crises which all the parties of the International have passed through since 1921, that is, since the beginning of the period characterised by a slowing down of the rhythm of revolution, have shown that the overall composition of these parties was not very solid ideologically. The parties themselves oscillated, with often very violent shifts from right to far left; this produced the most serious repercussions on the entire organisation, and general crises in relations between the parties and the masses'.[52]

Possibly under the influence of Lenin's *Left-Wing Communism, an Infantile Disorder*, Gramsci recalled that the situation of the communist parties of the West was similar to that of the Bolsheviks before the war. However, unlike Russia, 'In Western Europe, by contrast, an increasing division of labour arose between the trade-union organisation and the political organisation of the working class. In the trade-union field, the reformist and pacifist tendency developed at an ever-increasing pace ...'[53]

The Italian case was probably even more dramatic, because the communists were in a situation in which they had to fight for the right to compete for the leadership of the trade-union centre with the reformists. Besides, regarding the party, there was still the problem of the absence of a new theoretical synthesis that could guide revolutionary policy and find its place within an international framework. Gramsci also criticised the extreme left, but he avoided repeating the (absurd) attacks of the document coming from the recently concluded plenary of the ECCI, which stated that Bordiga had shifted to the right of the Comintern and that he and Trotsky were acting together. The three main trends converging at the formation of the PCd'I in Livorno still existed, and this created enormous difficulties for the 'realisation of the two political principles which characterise Bolshevism: the alliance between workers and peasants, and the hegemony of the proletariat in the anti-capitalist revolutionary movement'.[54]

---

52   Gramsci 1999b, p. 406.
53   Gramsci 1999b, p. 407.
54   Gramsci 1999b, p. 414.

Gramsci was apparently convinced that so-called 'Bolshevisation', with its emphasis on organisation through workplace cells and the end of party fractions, together with an intense effort toward the ideological training of cadre and more profound political debate, would be able to help the PCd'I overcome its known limitations. The centrality of the factory, emphasised in the notion of 'Bolshevisation', converged with Gramsci's previous view and connected it to the establishment of a revolutionary mass party.

Actually, Gramsci himself had decided to go further on the path he had taken in his first stay in Moscow, which implied conceiving in the best possible way the insertion of Italy's national problems within the international context of the socialist revolution. Bordiga, for his part, and with good reason, believed that 'Bolshevisation' would bring the bureaucratisation of the communist movement.

Precisely as a reaction to Moscow's identification of Bordiga's position and the rightist platform in the Comintern, a leftist trend began to form in the PCd'I, becoming official on 1 June with a letter signed by a 'Committee of Understanding between the Elements of the Left'. Soon afterwards, an open letter from Amadeo Bordiga to the ECCI affirmed the existence of a leftist fraction within the PCd'I.[55]

Thus a fierce and intense polemic began, lasting until the Third National Congress of the PCd'I, during which Gramsci developed his conception of the revolutionary party. Gramsci's path had been marked by Sorel's view of socialism as an act of culture engendered from the working class's spirit of separation from the order of capital and the politics of the intellectuals. Hence his opposition to any separation between the working class and those who claimed to represent it in the party or in liberal institutions. The scission with reformism embodied a moment of this vision, and the convergence with Bordiga was possible thanks to his conception of the radical opposition between the proletariat and capital's state.

However, it was still necessary to break with Bordiga's view of the vanguard political party, which preserved the scission between the working class and its intellectuals. The conception of the party developed by Gramsci, therefore, distanced itself from the social-democratic tradition, which placed the working class within the sphere of action of capital, and also distanced itself from that conception of the vanguard party that reasserted the dominance of politics and set the working class back within the scission proper to the order of capital.

---

55   Spriano 1967, pp. 453–6.

Conditioned by the political situation of the Comintern and the RKP(b), Gramsci frequently based himself on Lenin's formulations, even though a few of his important observations ended up suggesting the preservation of the scission between economics and politics as well as between workers and intellectuals, especially concerning the management of production. Actually, even though many of Gramsci's formulas on the questions of the party and revolutionary class consciousness were close to the ideas of Rosa Luxemburg, they had already been 'anathematised' and remained in the twilight zone of Gramscian elaboration. All in all, for Gramsci the party was part of the class, a historical process within which the anti-capitalist struggle developed, as well as a tool for creating a new relationship between class and material production and between class and culture, materialising a new hegemony.

Lenin's death provided the occasion for Gramsci to present considerations on how his thought on the revolutionary party had developed. From the peremptory statement that 'every state is a dictatorship', Gramsci derived another statement: 'So long as a state is necessary, so long as it is historically necessary to govern men, whichever the ruling class may be, the problem will arise of having leaders, of having a "leader"'.[56]

The essential question of political science lies in the general problem of the state, dictatorship, the government of men, the 'leader'. However, specifically in the proletarian dictatorship, 'Are the leader and the party elements of the working class, are they a part of the working class, do they represent its deepest and most vital interests and aspirations, or are they an excrescence or simply a violent superimposition?'[57]

The answer to this question advances the notion that the revolutionary political party is the best part of the class, which, throughout a relatively long period of class struggle, selects its 'leaders', that is, its own intellectual stratum. Therefore, the class organically engenders its conscience and its intellectuals. This does not mean that these intellectuals cannot leave the class with which they had organic links and take on different interests and a worldview close to that of the ruling classes.

Bureaucratised social-democratic reformism would be an excrescence, and Caesarist forms, such as fascism, a superimposition. Gramsci does not seem indifferent to the theme of the bureaucratisation of the institutions of the workers' movement, already proposed by Robert Michels and merely resumed by Trotsky, in a quite different situation. The fundamental difference was that 'The

56   Gramsci 1999b, p. 292.
57   Ibid.

dictatorship of the proletariat is expansive, not repressive. A continuous movement takes place from the base upwards, a continuous replacement through all the capillaries of society, a continuous circulation of men'.[58]

Therefore the proletarian dictatorship, being a transitional state that aims at finishing with 'leaders', should be led by a party that tends to make 'leaders' or intellectuals of every man. It seems undeniable, then, that Gramsci's constant concern with the centrality of the factory and of production, as well as the masses' self-activity, which engenders consciousness and selects its own intellectuals, is closer to Rosa Luxemburg than to Lenin, for whom consciousness comes from outside production through the action of revolutionary intellectuals who bring to the class their vision of social and state totality. From Lenin and Bolshevism, however, Gramsci took the notion of a centrally disciplined and structured organisation, prepared to face extraordinary situations, from merciless repression to a situation of insurrection.

In the months that followed Gramsci's return from Moscow and the announcement of the formation of a 'committee of understanding', Gramsci's political activity was intense on many fronts. It was necessary to defend the party organisation and its connections with the masses from the renewed fascist offensive. The fight for the right to create communist fractions within the trade unions and the CGL was a decisive element in the ideological struggle against the maximalist PSI and for the united front policy from below which then shaped the PCd'I. It was necessary to avoid the formation of a leftist fraction that could split the party, a danger to be faced energetically and uncompromisingly.

Gramsci's political action then aimed at strengthening the party both organically and ideologically, with a view to the establishment of the conditions to resist fascism. The purpose of the united front strategy was to create a social coalition between the working class and the peasantry that could oppose fascism and capitalism. For that, it was necessary to attract the social base of the PSI and Catholic Populars, and this implied a fierce ideological debate, especially with the maximalist leaders. At the end of May, the ECCI exhorted the PCd'I to 'take particular care to expose the sabotage to the united front policy done by socialists and maximalists ... The workers want the united front of all revolutionary elements; it is necessary to show them, with facts, that the socialist leaders are sabotaging the united front'.[59]

---

58   Gramsci 1999b, p. 296.
59   Spriano 1967, p. 465.

According to this orientation, and aiming at giving a rapid response to the initiative of the Aventine opposition, which had made an appeal to King Vittorio Emanuele III for the return of constitutional normalcy, the PCd'I presented a proposal which was clearly not acceptable as a set of common goals for all anti-fascist parties: '1. worker control over industry, the only way to fight the plutocracy financing Fascism; 2. land for the peasantry, that is, to fight the landowners; 3. to fight for the constitution of a republican assembly arising from the workers' and peasants' councils, which then will organise all the anti-fascist and anti-monarchist forces'.[60]

In his polemic against the maximalist PSI, Gramsci aimed to attract the working-class base of that party to the communist refoundation and the scission with capital, exposing the 'opportunistic' nature of maximalism itself. Considering the maximalists' assertion that the workers' party should 'obey the will of the masses', Gramsci rejected this on the grounds that 'the Communist Party "represents" the interests of the whole of the working mass, but only "acts out" the will of a specific part of the masses, the more advanced part, that part (the proletariat) which wishes to depose the existing régime with revolutionary means and establish communism'.[61]

Pointing to the isolation of the PSI, Gramsci insisted on the importance of internationalism, and said that, according to the Comintern programme, the PCd'I 'fights on two fronts: against Fascism and the Aventine oppositions (two fronts is just a way of saying it, because they are actually the same bourgeois front), and for the autonomous action of the revolutionary proletariat, in order to organise the struggle of the poor against the rich around the revolutionary proletariat, the only force able to break up reaction and establish a new state and its dictatorship'.[62]

Gramsci tried to base his understanding of the themes of the scission, communist refoundation, the party, and the united front, on Lenin, but a large part of his Sorelian formation was still present, and quite possibly Rosa Luxemburg's influence as well. His very understanding of the operation of the united front from below preserved the consistency of this paradoxical juxtaposition. Besides, his formulation was strongly conditioned by the harsh actual conditions of political action, which included a difficult battle within the PCd'I and the persistent tactical undecidedness of the Comintern. In Gramsci, the theme of the scission and the anti-politicism present in Sorel are subverted as the need

---

60   Spriano 1967, p. 464.
61   Gramsci 1978, p. 239.
62   Gramsci 1978, p. 241.

to create a new politics that acts out moral and intellectual reform. The party would educate the masses in the spirit of separation, such that 'the task befalling us Communists is to fight spontaneity, to lead the workers' movement away from trade unionism's spontaneous inspiration to seek refuge under the wings of the bourgeoisie and, on the contrary, lead them to the wings of revolutionary Marxism, that is, communism'.[63]

Gramsci frequently called the leftist fraction of the PCd'I a variation of maximalism, not only because of its practical ineffectiveness, but also because it defended the existence of organised fractions within the party. Amidst the harshness of the debate, Gramsci recalled a statement from the Fifth Enlarged Plenary of the ECCI, which had a certain impact on the party grassroots, saying: 'Bordiga's position is the same as that of the whole of the right of the International when he demands a right to fractions and to organised trends'.[64]

Gramsci's argument was firmly resolved to seek legitimacy in 'Leninism' and in the political support of the ECCI, while Bordiga insisted on the preservation of the autonomy and specificity of an 'Italian left' within the context of the West. For Gramsci, it was always essential that a theoretical synthesis and ideological unity were reached, having 'revolutionary Marxism' as its axis. Bordiga, on the other hand, believed the essential thing was to defend the plurality of ideological conceptions. However, once it had been acknowledged that organised fractions were against party regulations, which had been set at the Fifth World Congress, a decision was taken to end the debate that had been going on in the pages of *L'Unitá*. The discussion was passed over to the party grassroots, initiating the congress process.

The disagreements that could be cleared up during the congress debates revolved around the conception of the party, its historical origins, its relationship with the working class, its organisational form, and its international insertion, rather than concerning the party's own political orientation. The form in which the united front policy was being acted out in practice was not too different from that formal critique Bordiga insisted on denouncing as one of Lenin's mistakes in his analysis of the class struggle in the West. The differences in their evaluation of fascism had the same origins, because while Gramsci pointed to the novelty of fascism and its support base among the petit-bourgeois mass, Bordiga insisted on seeing in the régime the general historical trend of the crisis of the bourgeoisie. Party militants came to the view that a solid and centralised

---

63   Gramsci 1978, p. 246.
64   Gramsci 1978, p. 234.

organisation with an important international connection should be assured, rather than defending the autonomy of a national tradition that would not be able to resist fascism.

Gramsci took part in several conferences in preparation for the Third Congress of the PCd'I, including those in Milan and Naples, important cities where the opposition of the extreme left was particularly significant, and he also taught a course for the political formation of youth entering the party. Amidst his intense political activity, Gramsci matured the ideas that would be espoused in the project for the theses of the CC majority, to be presented to the congress. In September, the theses were finished with the help of Togliatti and especially Grieco, and were certainly submitted for the Comintern's inspection. They were initially spread through inner-party channels and only later were they partially published in the party press.[65]

In the beginning of November, as a consequence of a failed attempt on Mussolini's life, there came a new repressive wave, which put an end to the remaining legal spaces where the workers' movement had maintained some margin of autonomy. The CGL was suspended and the opposition press and the Aventine parties were strongly hit. The crisis of the PSI was particularly serious, as it abandoned the Aventine in September, without returning to parliament. The attempt by Pietro Nenni to approach the PSU, which had just been banned, and to converge with international social democracy, proved a failure which led to him being fired from the PSI leadership.

Not only in Italy, but in France, too, the balance of political forces shifted to the right, leading to the failure of the reformist government coalition, then formed by socialists and radicals. In this context, the Comintern understood that the united front policy should also aim at a rapprochement with the social-democratic leaders. In the case of Italy, at the end of November the PCd'I received direct criticism from the International, in a letter signed by Jules Humbert-Droz, saying that 'the way the Party used the tactic of the united front appears to us as stemming from a certain fear of addressing directly the leadership of the maximalist party and from a certain reserve regarding the united front tactic itself'.[66]

---

65   Certain parts of the *Lyons Theses* were more widely read, such as those parts known as the 'Theses on the Italian Situation', which can be found in various publications. The first complete publication only appeared in 1990, in a volume presenting the material referring to a conference named *Le Tesi di Lione: Riflessioni su Antonio Gramsci e la storia d'Italia* [*The Lyons Theses: Thoughts on Antonio Gramsci and Italian History*].

66   Spriano 1967, p. 467, note 2.

The criticism from the International came a few days before the meeting of the CC that aimed to analyse the new conditions emerging for communist activity, at the same time as the congress process was unfolding. Gramsci drew particular attention to the need for proper organisation in the face of the new conditions presented by the outlawing of the autonomous workers' movement and the repression of the press and the anti-fascist organisations. He observed that fascism was ready to reach its goal of unifying the fractions of the bourgeoisie, 'thus reducing to a minimum any organisational weaknesses of the bourgeoisie itself', so that 'political monopoly corresponds to the complete economic monopoly of the bourgeoisie represented by Fascism'. The seriousness of the situation appeared fully when it was seen that 'Fascism has finally … destroyed every mass organisation, annihilated all effective manifestation of the popular will, and de facto annihilated the representative powers'.[67]

The reversal of this situation would demand an intense organisational and educational activity from the communists amongst the Northern industrial proletariat as well as the peasantry from the South of Italy. Gramsci noted that 'in Italy there is a revolutionary situation when the Northern proletariat is strong; if the Northern proletariat is weak, the peasantry follows the petit bourgeoisie; and reciprocally the peasantry of Southern Italy serve as an element of strength and revolutionary impulse for the Northern proletariat. The Northern workers and the Southern peasants are, therefore, the two immediate revolutionary forces (eighty percent of the peasants of the South are controlled by priests) to which we must direct our attention'.[68]

The worker-peasant alliance was thus the fulcrum of the united front in Italy, which had to oppose the bourgeoisie organised by fascism and possibly even oppose a 'labour aristocracy' bureaucratised and controlled by capital. Gramsci had a clear view that Italy was the weakest link in the imperialist chain, that its bourgeoisie was organically weak and dependent on England and the USA.

This political position was made public in the pages of *L'Unitá*, where a strong attack on the PSI was followed by a clear conclusion:

> The fundamental problem which the Communist Party must set out to resolve in the present situation is that of leading the proletariat back to an autonomous position as a revolutionary class; free from all influence of counter-revolutionary classes, groups and parties; capable of collecting around itself and leading all the forces which can be mobilised for the struggle against capitalism …

---

67   Gramsci 1978, p. 477.
68   Gramsci 1978, p. 478.

> The Communist Party must systematically combat and unmask those groups and political parties which are vehicles for the influence on the proletariat of other classes, and of non-revolutionary social categories. It must strive to remove from their influence even the most backward strata of the working class, so that a united front of class forces may arise from below.[69]

Comparing the Humbert-Droz letter, which brought the suggestion that the PCd'I should approach the PSI in order to resist the consolidation of the fascist régime, to Gramsci's intervention on the CC and this article, it is clear that two different conceptions of the united front policy were here in conflict. These two conceptions actually express two different strategies for the struggle against capital, and not variations on tactics used on one or another occasion. In this aspect, the policy of the PCI was still to confront the PSI directly, aiming at drawing its working-class base to the revolutionary arena. What had changed was that while Bordiga understood the political formula of the united front as something innocuous at best, Gramsci saw the policy of a united front from below as an effective anti-capitalist strategy.

The organisation of the working masses within a spirit of cleavage from capital and the bourgeois state would take place by means of the material construction of an antagonistic subjectivity inside the factory, the other workplaces, the unions and various socio-cultural groups. Here we also find elements of continuity with Sorel's thought, with a clear distinction between the world of workers' politics and bourgeois politics, between the liberating nature of the former and the oppressive character of the latter. For Gramsci, the formula of the united front served the revolutionary strategy of creating a civil society within the world of associated labour that would be antagonistic to the rule of capital. In short, it was the creation of a new hegemony.

The problem was that the Comintern oscillated between two possible strategies for the united front: one, which Gramsci tried to define, investigating its concrete steps and partial goals, within the concrete reality of Italy and in the perspective of the European socialist revolution, and another strategy which implied forms of unity among the workers' parties within the established order. Briefly, the crux of the matter had to do with deciphering the enigma of social democracy, but the International's lack of decisiveness would be a cause for new misunderstandings with the PCd'I.

---

69   Gramsci 1999b, pp. 425–6.

CHAPTER 4

The Strategy of the Anti-Fascist United Front

1   The 'Lyons Theses' and the Theory of the Socialist Revolution in
Italy

The political situation in Italy meant that the Third National Congress of the
PCd'I had to take place clandestinely in the French city of Lyon. In the meeting
in preparation for the congress, Gramsci espoused the main points that should
guide the debates, seeking to counter the theses of the 'extreme left' minority,
led by Amadeo Bordiga, with the theses from the majority of the CC, which
he represented. He began insisting on the importance of the 'Bolshevisation'
of the party, according to the intervention presented during the Fifth World
Congress and Fifth Enlarged Plenary of the ECCI, which was seen as 'a question
of combating every deviation in the doctrine and practice of the revolutionary
class struggle'.[1]

This statement was dangerous, in view of the subsequent events in the life
of the RKP(b) and the Comintern. It aimed to highlight the fundamental points
of disagreement between the political orientation which was being developed
and those defended by the opposition. In spite of the occasional harshness
of his choice of words, Gramsci's goal still was to create a new 'theoretical
synthesis', because this was the way he understood 'Bolshevisation'.

Gramsci presented the problem of the disagreements among Italian communists as revolving around three fundamental points: '1. the problem of relations between the central leadership of the party and the mass of comrades
enrolled in its ranks; 2. the problem of relations between the central leadership
and the working class; 3. the problem of relations between the working class
and the other anti-capitalist classes'.[2]

The solution to these problems 'is necessary for the working class to become
the class that leads the anti-capitalist struggle; for the Communist Party to lead
the working class in this struggle; and for the Party to be structured internally
in such a way that it can fulfil this its basic function'.[3]

The two first problems are organisational, with implications for the nature
of the party and its class character. Gramsci's explanation once again suggests

---

1   Gramsci 1999b, p. 428.
2   Gramsci 1999b, p. 429.
3   Gramsci 1999b, p. 429.

that the question of the workers' revolutionary consciousness was seen as arising from its class position, and it also pointed to the risk of the formation of an intellectual social stratum disconnected from the class. This was a theme already present, though in different form, in Sorel, Luxemburg and the late Lenin.

Gramsci insisted that the party should be seen as '"part" of the working class', that it should seek 'to raise the political level of the masses', and also that 'the organisers of the working class must be the workers themselves'. From this position came his emphasis on the political unification of the working class and on its organisation in the workplace. In Gramsci's critique, the theoretical position of the 'extreme left' was wrong to see the party as an '"organ" of the working class', because in placing the elements of which the party was comprised all on the same level, regardless of their social origin, it was 'not concerned to safeguard the proletarian character of the Party', and thus put the intellectuals in a special position, as 'the most politically and socially advanced elements'.[4]

Besides seeking the unification of the working class, the communists should also unite every anti-capitalist class, because

> In no country is the proletariat capable of winning power and keeping it with its own forces alone. It must therefore obtain allies: in other words, it must follow a policy that will enable it to place itself at the head of the other classes who have anti-capitalist interests, and guide them in the struggle to overthrow bourgeois society. The question is of particular importance for Italy, where the proletariat is a minority of the working population and geographically distributed in such a manner, that it cannot presume to lead a victorious struggle for power unless it has previously resolved very precisely the problem of its relations with the peasant class.[5]

Even though Gramsci did not explicitly refer to the political formula of the united front, at that point his understanding of the question was very clear. He wished to unite the working class under the leadership of the communist party, ensuring its autonomy and its antagonistic position. For that, it would be necessary 'to disintegrate the Opposition, socially and thus politically, in order to deprive it of the base it had among the masses'. This would also be achieved

---

4   Gramsci 1999b, pp. 429–30.
5   Gramsci 1999b, pp. 431–2.

through a bitter polemic – especially with the leaderships of groups based on the workers – always aiming to counter the 'labour aristocracy' phenomenon and to create a united front from below, and always bearing in mind 'a fundamental problem ... that of overthrowing Fascism'.[6] The creation of workers' unity would take place at the same time as a relationship was established with the peasant masses, as well as a confrontation with the reactionary force of the Vatican and the clerical influence especially present in the South of the country. Thus would be forged a united front of the masses: anti-fascist, anti-clerical, anti-capitalist.

Fascism should be seen as a combat organ of the bourgeoisie, but also as a social movement. According to Gramsci, Bordiga's mistake had been to consider only the former aspect of the problem. However, as it concluded its project of organic unification of the bourgeoisie, fascism forced communists to pay attention to 'the different stratifications of the bourgeois class' and to 'examine the stratifications of Fascism itself', so that a more adequate tactic could be found, one that sees that 'it will be within Fascism itself that the conflicts which cannot express themselves in other ways will tend to re-emerge'.[7]

If fascism appeared as a solution for the inner contradictions of the bourgeoisie, it was also proof that 'The Italian situation is characterised by the fact that the bourgeoisie is organically weaker than in other countries and maintains itself in power only insofar as it succeeds in controlling and dominating the peasantry. The proletariat must struggle to tear the peasants from the bourgeoisie's influence, and place them under its own political guidance'.[8]

Surely Gramsci was mistaken about the dimensions of this alleged weakness and the organisational capacity of the Italian bourgeoisie, as he also imagined that the anti-clerical struggle could soon achieve rapid successes – though he did have a more complex view of the bourgeoisie's forms of control. Before, he had tended to agree with the idea that fascism and a liberal-conservative coalition would work as two alternative ways for capital to preserve its power. Now he thought that the fall of fascism could mean the passage from 'a reactionary situation' to 'a democratic situation'. In the first, the struggle to organise the party would prevail, and in the second, the struggle to organise the insurrection. Everything suggests Gramsci had the Russian revolutionary process in mind, from the fall of the Tsar to the rise of the Bolsheviks to power.[9]

---

6 Gramsci 1999b, p. 434.
7 Gramsci 1999b, p. 453.
8 Ibid.
9 Gramsci 1999b, p. 455.

Once again, it should be noted that Gramsci and the PCd'I were among the parties more to the left within the context of the Comintern. The overwhelming majority achieved by Gramsci within the party (from the Como conference to the Third Congress) cannot be really understood without taking into account the Comintern's turn to the left and the possibility of attracting the mass of the party to political positions that were well to the left. Besides, it was Gramsci himself who said that 'the Party leadership ... is still basically the same one that was elected by the Livorno and Rome Congresses',[10] indicating that the 'theoretical synthesis' he sought had something of Bordiga's contribution, especially the spirit of separation from the state and reformism, something he also took from Sorel.

In the CC majority theses for the Third Congress of the PCd'I which regarded the international situation, which were inspired by the interpretations provided by the Fifth World Congress of the Comintern and the Fifth Enlarged Plenary of the ECCI, the understanding that the PCd'I and quite probably Gramsci had of the perspectives of capitalism became very clear. At that moment, there was to be a 'relative stabilisation' within the framework of successes for the offensive of capital against the proletariat, even though the general trend was the crisis of decadent capitalism, especially in Western Europe. The tendency toward decline in Europe was counteracted by the rise of the USA and also South Africa and Australia. The observation that the Anglo-American world had the best chances within the socio-cultural order generated by capital was also noteworthy.[11]

For Gramsci and the Italian communists, the European situation was still objectively revolutionary. They had assimilated a more leftist understanding of the notion of 'relative stabilisation'. This interpretation was very close to that of Zinoviev, president of the Comintern, who, during the period of the Italian congress, had already switched to the opposition in the RKP(b). This understanding held that it would be impossible for capital to exit its crisis through the development of the forces of production, thus leading to the expectation that there would later be an offensive against the working and living conditions of the proletariat, the result of which would only be the worsening of the crisis and the creation of revolutionary possibilities.

Even the possibility that the market could be enlarged by using the colonial periphery was seen as not very favourable for demographic reasons (in South America) as well as political ones (in East Asia). So, Trotsky's analysis on

---

10   Gramsci 1999b, p. 436.
11   Cafagna et al. 1990, p. 109 ff.

Europe, which predicted a phase of peaceful democratic development, with a decisive contribution from social democracy and the growing influence of the USA, was apparently mistaken, considering that the conservative and reactionary forces were gaining strength. However, Trotsky's view that the revolutionary situation was still ongoing held firm.[12]

The theses also declared that the battle between the USA and England for control of the world market was the most important contradiction within imperialism. They also highlighted the Chinese Revolution, then developing at a fast pace, saying that both the workers' movement and the movement of national liberation converged within it, allied in a 'united revolutionary front, going from workers and peasants to the middle bourgeoisie and the intellectuals'. This united front, which did not include the 'national bourgeoisie', would assume, however, a working-class and peasant nature as the revolutionary movement advanced.[13]

It also should be noted that the document highlights the importance of the worker-peasant alliance in the USSR, as well as the existence of a 'workers' and peasants' government'. Thus, in view of what had been going on in the formulation of a revolutionary theory for Italy, there was here a strong emphasis on the revolutionary role of the peasantry within the international framework, and also an insistence on the propulsive role which the USSR could and should play in reinforcing the workers' movement. This was a goal that the USSR would 'reach by developing and reinforcing itself, economically as well as politically'.[14]

For Gramsci, then, the reinforcement of the worker-peasant alliance in the USSR was not in contradiction with the strengthening of the worker-peasant alliance in the development of the Chinese Revolution, nor with the resumption of the proletarian revolution in Europe, as the specific Italian national case was also centred on this same social and political alliance. Through this path, his formulation came close to Bukharin's, though there was a decisive difference: the Russian leader tended to see the 'capitalist stabilisation' as a longer phase, anchored in the restructuring of capitalist production, whereas Gramsci and the Italian communists continued to believe that the 'stabilisation is a temporary and merely apparent episode in the situation', as war and revolution remained the decisive elements.[15]

Gramsci's view of the crisis of capitalism never came close to some 'catastrophist' analyses, replete with the 'economism' he had chosen as his main

---

12   Cafagna et al. 1990, pp. 121–4.
13   Cafagna et al. 1990, pp. 127–8.
14   Cafagna et al. 1990, pp. 128–31.
15   Cafagna et al. 1990, p. 135.

theoretical opponent. However, his understanding of the capitalist crisis would undergo a deep revision in the *Prison Notebooks*, in which he understood bourgeois class rule's enormous capacity for stabilisation.

Thus it can be seen that Gramsci's originality lies, in every circumstance, in his capacity critically to assimilate theoretical contributions coming from a context of conflict, and thus to formulate a new synthesis. Gramsci had been determinedly applying himself to learning from the formulations of the Bolshevik leadership group ever since his first stay in Moscow, passing over the process of organic scission and theoretical regression that was now reaching its climax within the RKP(b). Meanwhile, though, Gramsci hailed the fact that 'the victory of the left-wing trends at the Fifth World Congress meant a victory of the revolutionary forces against the residues of social-democratic opportunism on the organisational terrain'.[16]

The theses referring to national and colonial problems once again highlighted the importance of the worker-peasant alliance, rendering the historical conditions of this united front explicit: 'the poor and middle peasants, during the period of the proletarian struggle against capitalism, and in the subsequent period of the proletarian dictatorship, become allies of the working class'.[17] These theses pay great attention to Yugoslavia and the Balkans in general, highlighting the need for an alliance between the working classes of both Italy and Yugoslavia.[18]

The theses on the Italian political situation and the party considered Italian capitalism and the Italian bourgeoisie to be weak; but they state that 'Capitalism is the predominant element in Italian society, and the force which is decisive in determining its development. This fundamental fact means that there is no possibility of a revolution in Italy that is not the socialist revolution'.[19]

Industrialists were seen as weak owing to the lack of raw materials, which forced them to make economic concessions to the great landowners, who prevailed over a large mass of poor labourers. Between these two ruling strata there was a large and diverse petit bourgeoisie, formed by artisans, professionals and

---

16   Cafagna et al. 1990, p. 132.

17   Cafagna et al. 1990, p. 135.

18   It should be remembered that there was great closeness between the Italian and Yugoslavian communist guerrillas at the end of the anti-fascist war, and as such the PCd'I oscillated between developing the revolution in the North using the support of the Yugoslav popular army and retreating so as to preserve the national integrity of Italy. This last position prevailed, having been defended by Togliatti against Mauro Scoccimarro.

19   Gramsci 1999a, p. 468.

civil servants. From the fact that the alliance between the industrial class and the great landowners had a territorial basis, there resulted the impossibility that any social class other than the proletariat could play an effective role in uniting the country. Thus the petit-bourgeois attempt to give new strength to the Italian state had to be seen as a precarious one. The conclusion was that the concrete socio-historical conditions in Italy made the country the weakest link in the imperialist chain, in which the worker-peasant alliance was of crucial importance: 'In Italy, there is a confirmation of the thesis that the most favourable conditions for the proletarian revolution do not necessarily always occur in those countries where capitalism and industrialism have reached the highest level of development, but may instead arise where the fabric of the capitalist system offers least resistance, because of its structural weakness, to an attack by the revolutionary class and its allies'.[20]

In their analysis of the fascist régime, the theses reasserted all the formulations proposed by Gramsci in the previous years, considering that 'Fascism, as a movement of armed reaction which set itself the task of fragmenting and disorganising the working class in order to immobilise it, fitted into the framework of traditional Italian ruling-class policies, and into capitalism's struggle against the working class'.[21]

Therefore, in its origins, fascism had received the assistance of the old ruling classes, especially the traditional landowners. 'Socially, however, Fascism found its base in the urban petty bourgeoisie, and in a new rural bourgeoisie thrown up by a transformation of rural property in certain regions', which reached ideological and organisational unity in paramilitary groups and the fascist party, and thus 'allowed Fascism to conceive and carry out a plan of conquest of the state, against the old ruling strata'.[22]

Fascism appeared as a new way of conceiving the unification of the Italian ruling classes, replacing the typical agreements and compromises of the liberal state with the 'project of achieving an organic unity of all the bourgeoisie's forces in a single political organism under the control of a single centre, which would simultaneously direct the party, the government and the state'.[23] However, the attainment of the organic unity of the bourgeoisie demanded the gradual overcoming of the liberal-bourgeois oppositions, articulated in a few organs of the press, political groups and the Masonry, and also the displace-

---

20   Gramsci 1999b, p. 471.
21   Gramsci 1999b, p. 477.
22   Gramsci 1999b, pp. 477–8.
23   Gramsci 1999b, p. 478.

ment of the traditional ruling classes and the aggravation of the exploitation of the peasant masses of the South, which tended to be close to the petit bourgeoisie.

The communists correctly saw that fascism was attempting to unify the bourgeoisie organically and replace the traditional state personnel with new elements from the petit bourgeoisie; but even so, they believed the crisis of the régime to be approaching. However, the communists were not the only ones to entertain such an illusion. All the anti-fascist forces were immersed in it.

Given the obvious difficulties faced in completing the tasks they proposed, their analysis of the situation may suggest a paradox. The motor forces of the Italian revolution were taken into consideration: '(a) the working class and the rural proletariat; (b) the peasantry of the South and the Islands, and the peasantry in the other parts of Italy'. The conditions for the revolution would exist, on the one hand, when the proletariat achieved a high degree of organisation and willingness to fight, and, on the other hand, when it could seal an alliance with the peasantry, separating them from the petit bourgeoisie, which began to give massive support to fascism. So, 'the problem of breaking the alliance of the peasantry with the reactionary forces must be posed, to a great extent, in other western European countries too, as the problem of destroying the influence of Catholic organisations on the rural masses'.[24]

Besides, the PCd'I identified a chain of reactionary forces that, starting from fascism, also comprised the anti-fascist political groups – including the reformist and maximalist trends of Italian Socialism – and ended in the CGL leadership. The forces identified with liberal democracy tended to put themselves forward as alternatives to fascism, but that goal was conditioned to putting the brakes on the development of the mass movement. Therefore, an anti-fascist united front policy that involved all these forces would in fact contribute to an operation seeking to defend the capitalist system.

For the Italian communists, given the assumed permanent revolutionary situation, anti-fascist and anti-capitalist goals necessarily tended to be confused. The communists' goal should be 'transforming "revolutionary democratic" movements into working-class, socialist revolutionary movements'. And this owing to 'the impossibility for the régime installed by Fascism to undergo radical limitations and transformations in a "liberal" and "democratic" direction, without a mass struggle being unleashed against Fascism that will inevitably culminate in a civil war'.[25]

---

24   Gramsci 1999b, p. 484.
25   Gramsci 1999b, p. 506.

At a moment which the communists believed to be of political preparation for the revolution, when ideological unity was indispensable, extreme-left positions could not be accepted, as they separated the party from the masses and preserved factionalism. Nor could it tolerate those that defended the democratic united front, which was oblivious to the fact that 'social-democracy, although it still to a great extent conserves its social base in the proletariat, must so far as its ideology and the political function it fulfils are concerned, be considered not as a right wing of the working-class movement, but as a left wing of the bourgeoisie, and as such must be unmasked in the eyes of the masses'.[26]

A party that aimed at making the proletariat achieve full political autonomy had to be organised from the basis of production and to identify itself exclusively with the working class, without pushing aside those anti-capitalist intellectuals and peasants that bridged the divide with the strata of rural workers. Much more than an imposition from the Comintern, 'The practice of the factory movement (1919–20) has shown that only an organisation adapted to the place and system of production makes it possible to establish a contact between the upper and lower strata of the working masses (skilled workers, unskilled workers and labourers), and to create bonds of solidarity which eliminate the basis for any phenomenon of "labour aristocracy"'.[27]

It was precisely from the productive process that 'The "united front" of anti-fascist and anti-capitalist struggle which the communists are striving to create must aim at being an organised united front, i.e. at being based on bodies around which the masses as a whole can regroup and find a form'.[28]

Thus, 'The slogan of workers' and peasants' committees must be considered as a synthetic formula for all the Party's activity, insofar as it proposes to create an organised united front of the working class'.[29]

Besides being a strategy aimed at the formation of a revolutionary united front of the working masses, the tactic of the united front was also considered adequate to 'unmask[ing] so-called proletarian and revolutionary parties and groups which have a mass base'.[30] This being so, the leadership and the organisation of the PSI itself should be seen as enemies, given that what was at stake was the political direction of the working masses.

In view of the formation of the united front, the agitational activity of the party should converge to the slogan of the 'workers' and peasants' government'

---

26   Gramsci 1999b, p. 490.
27   Gramsci 1999b, p. 496.
28   Gramsci 1999b, pp. 507–8.
29   Gramsci 1999b, p. 508.
30   Gramsci 1999b, p. 509.

as a means to draw the most backward masses to the terrain of the struggle for the dictatorship of the proletariat. However, it was underscored that this 'is an agitational slogan, but only corresponds to a real phase of historical development in the same sense as the intermediate solutions ...'[31]

In the terrain of factories and trade unions, the united front of the working masses must 'stick to the very place of production, the factory'. The experience of the 'internal commissions', forged in 1919–20 by the Turin workers' movement, should attempt to subsist wherever possible and to resurface whenever conditions allowed. However, given the difficulties that fascism imposed on autonomous trade-union organisation, agitational committees should be organised as a means for constructing the united front that would be materialised in the workers' and peasants' committees. And although 'different from the internal commissions as regards to form, they are analogous in substance, because they too are organs for the aggregation and representation of the whole of the working mass from the workshops, and for mobilisation in the terrain of class, with the purpose of reaching immediate goals and preparing ever vaster struggles'.[32]

The understanding both of the political formula of the united front and the content of the slogan of the 'worker-peasant' government thus followed the logic established at the Fifth World Congress of the International. The adjustment in the political orientation of the Comintern, which had become apparent in the previous months and once again placed stress on the united front also 'from above', was no longer taken into consideration. Humbert-Droz's interventions in the congress only suggested greater attention to the maximalist party and the possibility of a rapprochement, but his words found no audience.

The new national leadership was composed by the ninety percent majority that supported the theses presented by the CC, including the old 'right', and by the ten percent that supported the theses defended by the 'extreme left'. The Executive Political Committee was composed of Gramsci, Togliatti, Terracini, Scoccimarro, Grieco, Ravera and Ravazzoli, while other important names such as Bordiga, Leonetti, Serrati and Malfi remained on the CC. It was decided that Togliatti, an important leader, should represent the PCd'I before the ECCI, considering the delicate moment the RKP(b) was facing in the process of the scission within its leadership, but also that Bordiga should go to Moscow.

Gramsci's evaluation of the congress results was very positive. The party had approved 'Bolshevisation', creating a new Central Committee, which incorpor-

---

31   Gramsci 1999b, p. 512.
32   Cafagna et al. 1990, pp. 222–3.

ated a large majority within a political orientation that tended to be a new organisational and theoretical synthesis. The questions of centralisation and democratic unity should, from that moment on, be seen as matters of revolutionary ethics, in spite of the resistance from a reduced 'extreme left' and Angelo Tasca's almost isolated presentations in defence of some of the theses that were seen as 'rightist'.[33]

In the text assessing the results of the congress, which Gramsci dictated for publication in *L'Unità*, he stated – confirming the theoretical nature of the problem – that the united front was a question that had to do with 'the relations of political leadership between the most advanced part of the proletariat and its less advanced fractions',[34] and also with the relationship between the proletariat and the other objectively anti-capitalist classes, especially the peasantry. On this particular matter, he emphasised the pressing need to act so that the peasantry would apply itself to achieving an autonomous organisation, considering 'the most recent events of Italian life, which have caused the Southern petit bourgeoisie to go over *en masse* to Fascism'.[35]

2   The Third Congress and the New Lines of Division

In spite of Gramsci's optimism, soon fascist persecution became more serious, and several disagreements in the new party leadership made their appearance, the effects of which were particularly felt in what came from Moscow. These disagreements would not have been important if they had not been more and more wrapped up in the problem of the worsening of fascist repression and the climax of the internal disputes of the RKP(b).

Independent trade unionism was living out its final days. The anti-fascist press was nearly silent. The Aventine political parties were close to collapse. Police violence was frequent. The fascist régime was thus rapidly consolidating itself. It simultaneously eliminated the final traces of the liberal institutions and took over the state machine, to which it subordinated the Partito Nazionale Fascista itself, as well as its militias. The process was concluded by the end of

---

33   Angelo Tasca defended the thesis that the 'workers' and peasants' government' could arise from a united front of anti-fascist parties which could find their institutional expression in parliament. The analogy with the position espoused by Togliatti and the PCd'I at the moment of the fall of fascism in 1944–5 should be noted.

34   Gramsci 1999b, p. 526.

35   Gramsci 1999b, p. 539.

1926, when every anti-fascist party and political organism was outlawed, and whatever remained of the liberal parliament was abolished.

From the beginning of the process of fascistisation in 1921 until the consolidation of the régime by the end of 1926, the industrial bourgeoisie was able to re-establish factory discipline, suppress the right to strikes, reduce salaries, increase working time and destroy autonomous trade unionism, pursuing its goal of establishing a form of rationalisation in production. The policy of the Confindustria, aiming at the scientific organisation of labour, needed an environment of cooperation among the classes, which social reformism was unable to provide. However, the fascist project of subordinating the working class to the state as well as nationalist discourse were able to associate themselves with the productivist impulses required by big industry.

The expression of this convergence had already been presented with the so-called 'pact of Palazzo Vidoni', from October 1925, which granted the monopoly of workers' representation to the fascist trade union. Thus fascism approached 'Fordism' and was accepted by various corporate designs from the Catholic world, even though these stemmed from a different conception and theoretical matrix.[36]

The scientific organisation of labour redefined workers' inferiority within the productive process, all the while remaining attached to the fascist project of reorganising the state. Thus the lowering of living standards, the imposition of factory discipline and the intensification of work formed a complex whole. In January 1926 the Ente Nazionale Italiano per la Organizzazione Scientifica del Lavoro (ENIOS) was created, converging with the interests of the industrial bourgeoisie. Its purpose was to spread Taylorism in the country's industry. From this point onward the assembly line would become more generalised, and there would also be standardisation of materials used and a consequent increase in productivity. As such, in Italy, Taylorism and Fordism advanced through the process of the accumulation of capital.[37]

Even though the factory dictatorship was extremely harsh, the communists were able to organise a few dozen 'Committees of Agitation', understood as organs of the united front. The role of this form of organisation and its relation to the trade union question brought about a certain polemic with the ECCI delegation to the Third Congress of the PCd'I, which continued at the Sixth Enlarged Plenary in February. Togliatti was in Moscow, representing the PCd'I and leading the Italian delegation to the Sixth Enlarged Plenary of the

---

36   Dubla 1986, p. 99 ff.
37   Dubla 1986, pp. 104–8.

ECCI, and there he sought to overcome the International's differences with the party, insisting that greater emphasis should be given to political action for the defence of trade union liberties and to the alliance with the maximalists, especially after the PSI had joined the Anglo-Russian Trade-Union Committee.

Besides asking the party to carry out the decision taken during a trade-union conference of the PCd'I on 20 December 1925, which corrected the congress theses and created a closer link between 'committees of agitation' and 'committees of trade-union defence', Togliatti took on board the suggestion from the Sixth Enlarged Plenary of the ECCI that they should propose to the maximalists a united trade-union front. Togliatti's suggestions were accepted by the PCd'I leadership, though they explained (not very convincingly) that they had no knowledge of the minutes from the trade-union conference. In practice, a choice had been made in favour of the original congress theses.[38]

Louder still was the disagreement within the Italian delegation to the Sixth Plenary of the ECCI, between Bordiga and Togliatti – a dispute that would also bring consequences for the majority of the national leadership. Bordiga, possibly trying to establish a front with 'left' and 'extreme left' oppositions in the Comintern, in line with Trotsky's orientation, began a heated debate with Stalin on the essential points of disagreement among communists, during a meeting of the general secretariat of the RKP(b) with the Italian group. During the plenary meeting, it was Togliatti himself who rebutted Bordiga's views, which insisted on the specificity of the West and on the inconsistency of the formula of the united front. Togliatti, for his part, defended the PCd'I and the International's policy.[39]

Even though Bordiga had been nominated by the Third National Congress of the PCd'I for the Executive Committee in Moscow, together with Togliatti,

---

38   Vacca 1999, pp. 22–3. We are not convinced by Giuseppe Vacca's effort to give the impression that there was a seed of strategic disagreement between Togliatti and Grieco, on the one hand, and Gramsci and Scoccimarro, on the other, as regards trade-union policy and the united front. The idea of a united front 'from above' with the PSI was consistent with the wishes of Humbert-Droz, but not with those of Togliatti or Gramsci, even though it corresponded to the specific policy of the FGCI (the communist youth). What can be seen is Togliatti's concern to keep the Italian communists' stance within the majority of the International. It is also known that the policy of the trade-union united front with the maximalists and the socialist youth was already present at the time when Bordiga was running the party.

39   In the face of the enormous diversity in their theoretical-political understanding and national situations, the effort to unite the left and extreme-left oppositions within the Comintern never seemed realistic.

the events at the Sixth Plenary of the ECCI led to a dispute. Given Bordiga's conduct in the International meeting – he even challenged the legitimacy of the recent PCd'I congress – and also the various discussions among the Russian opposition groups, which also included the Italians in exile there, Togliatti understood that 'the Party must consider the danger of fractionist activity in Moscow, as it ponders the suitability of sending Bordiga here next summer', because 'it is necessary to examine whether since, as I believe, all hopes of bringing Bordiga back are lost, it would not be better to continue the tactic of isolation'.[40]

The political commission of the PCd'I reaffirmed a month later the congress's decision to send Bordiga to Moscow, even though everyone was stupefied by his attitude during the Sixth Plenary. Bordiga's return to Italy was a signal for his followers also to question the legitimacy of the Third Congress, at the same time as the composition of Russia's 'united opposition' progressed, an opposition that would remain at a distance from extreme left fractions. These, for their part, were facing strong pressure, even including expulsions, such as Karl Korsch's expulsion from the KPD. The prevailing orientation in the Comintern and especially in the PCd'I was still to avoid extreme measures, but the tensions only increased, particularly after the formalisation of the 'opposition bloc' in the RKP(b) at the end of June.

Then the Comintern's Presidium asked the PCd'I to be more strict with the Bordigist opposition, considering that they did not even acknowledge the validity of the Third Party Congress. So, Togliatti's position, opposed to Bordiga travelling to Moscow, was very much supported. At the same time, the political leadership of the PCd'I reaffirmed its desire to 'prevent expulsions as much as possible', at the same time that it would 'not tolerate factional activity, whatever the cost'.[41]

Even though there were disagreements between Togliatti and the political secretariat of the PCd'I – especially Gramsci and Scoccimarro – on the best way to deal with Bordiga's opposition, everyone remained within the terrain of the orientation given by the Third Congress. This can be seen in the discussion about the international political situation in that first half of 1926, a theme that also gave rise to disagreements between the group active in Italy and its Moscow representative. Replying to a letter from Togliatti, which talked about the great expectations created by the British general strike, Mauro Scoccimarro wrote on behalf of the political secretariat: 'It is true that the English strike, the

---

40   Vacca 1999, p. 191.
41   Vacca 1999, p. 319.

French crisis and the *coup* in Poland are events that push the situation towards a revolutionary crisis, but I don't believe we have already come to that point'.[42]

We can see that Togliatti had a very optimistic view of the revolutionary perspectives for the coming period, a position that was shared by most Italian communist leaders. The positions of Togliatti and the political secretariat on the tactic of the united front were also in agreement. At that moment, the PCd'I was attempting to influence the grassroots of the PSI, such that it would turn to the left and an element favourable to the united front would arise from the existing connections between the youth organs of both parties. The goal was always to break and disorganise the PSI.[43]

There was emerging, among the Italian communists, a way of carrying out the united front policy that was less clumsy and sectarian than that employed in other countries, criticising and debating with the socialist leaders ideologically and programmatically, at the same time as seeking a rapprochement with the youth and grassroots and intermediate layers of maximalist socialism. However, the best results in the united front policy were being achieved through contacts with the Catholic left.

Not every letter from Togliatti to the PCd'I and vice-versa reached its destination, so there was a certain political disorientation. It seems that only in the second half of July was the PCd'I leadership fully informed of the decision taken by the Comintern's Presidium regarding the cancellation of Bordiga's trip to Moscow. Besides asking for clarifications, the PCd'I sent a letter confirming the party's position (which did not correspond to Togliatti's). Not only did the political secretariat of the PCd'I declare its total disagreement with the Comintern Presidium's decision, but it also insisted that Bordiga had not asked to go to Moscow, and, instead, that 'we, still following the same political line regarding the extreme left, have shown our comrade Bordiga his duty to work for the Party and the International', as a member of the Executive Committee of the PCd'I.[44]

This letter also recalled that 'during the Party Congress we made the extreme left take part in the CC; then we made them work for the party. In the last Plenum of the EC(CI), comrade Ercoli (Togliatti), from the tribune, invited comrade Bordiga to collaborate with the Communist International and work in its central organs'.[45]

---

42   Vacca 1999, p. 318. Togliatti's letter was never found. It must also be recalled that, at this
       point, the PCd'I's understanding of the 'capitalist stabilisation' corresponded to that of the
       Fifth World Congress of the Comintern, which derived from Zinoviev's formulation.
43   Vacca 1999, p. 319.
44   Vacca 1999, pp. 354–6.
45   Ibid.

Then it denied that the idea to send Bordiga to Moscow was a premeditated way of getting him away from Italy so as to facilitate the struggle with the extreme left. The letter concludes with the suggestion that open debate should not be feared, and that this would be the best way to deal with 'Bordigism'.

Thanks to the PCd'I's insistence, the question was left open, such that it would be resolved in the Seventh Enlarged Plenary of the ECCI, set to take place in November and December.[46] Togliatti apparently thought that given the worsening of the Italian crisis, it was more important than ever that the PCd'I should be in tune with the majority positions of the RKP(b) and the International, and not leave itself vulnerable to the internal opposition, whether the process led to the revolution or the reinforcement of the counter-revolution. Mauro Scoccimarro, Gramsci and the political secretariat of the PCd'I as a whole understood that the democratic dialectic and the search for a theoretical-practical synthesis, constantly redefined by the movement of the real, were part of the very essence of the revolutionary party, which could not dispense with any of its elements without undermining the communists' organisational and political effectiveness.

This difference in perspective had implications especially for the understanding of the party's national role and its international connections. It also concerned the problem of how the national sections and the theoretical and political components of the Comintern should relate among themselves in the international process of the socialist revolution, which had the formula of the united front at its core. This implicit problem – whether it would be convenient for Bordiga to be in Moscow – returned in a more explosive manner in October.

Until then, the political leadership of the PCd'I had preferred not to address questions that implied a disagreement on perspectives on the development of the socialist revolution in the USSR, limiting itself merely to condemning the factional behaviour of the 'united opposition'. Togliatti, having a clearer view of the goals of each of the tendencies fighting in the RKP(b), and certain that a scission was virtually inevitable, believed that the PCd'I should discuss as soon as possible the contrasting positions and give complete support to Bukharin's and Stalin's majority, even though the decision from the Sixth Enlarged Plenary

---

46   For this occasion, Bordiga was once more appointed as a delegate of the PCd'I, together with Togliatti and Tasca, though he did not get to Moscow, having been detained by the fascist police, who seized his passport. On the other hand, from the end of July, the PCd'I took disciplinary measures against various members of the extreme left, who were suspended for insisting on not accepting the political orientation expressed by the Third Congress. Among those were Fortichiari, Reposi, Perrone and Vercesi. See Pistillo 1996, p. 47.

of the Comintern – not to bring the debate on the Russian question to other sections of the International – was still in force.

The opening text of the discussions of the Leadership Committee of the PCd'I, which met on 2 and 3 August, followed the previous decision not to discuss the internal problems of the RKP(b), and so the debate was restricted to an analysis of the situation in Italy and Europe. Gramsci then presented his efforts to bring the tactic of the united front to Italy – a very significant theoretical advance. The role of the 'committees of agitation' was to set the masses in motion and to join them together in the united front. However, these masses were the social base or sphere of influence of parties who also spoke to the workers, so the form in which they organised themselves and their followers should be taken into account in order to establish the line of political action in view of the united front.

Gramsci noted that the democratic and social-democratic parties were very loosely organised, but that they generally comprised three strata: an upper stratum, comprising intellectuals and parliamentarians, with links to the ruling classes; an lower stratum, comprising workers, peasants and the urban petit bourgeoisie, making up the mass of the party and its sympathisers; and an intermediate stratum, 'which maintains the link between the leading group at the top, and the mass of members and those influenced by the party'. Gramsci's diagnosis pointed out that it was precisely 'on a significant part of these middle strata of the various popular parties that the influence of the movement in favour of a united front was making itself felt. It was in this middle stratum that there was occurring this molecular phenomenon of disintegration of the old ideologies and old political programmes, and that the beginnings of a new political formation on the terrain of the united front could be seen'.[47]

Thus, in the political formula of the united front as conceived by Gramsci, there was no place for agreements between party leaderships, as he considered that they were in one way or another ingrained in the bourgeois state. The dispersion of the masses, on the other hand, made the organisation of a united front of the masses something extremely complex. Hence the reason why the united front should be based on the intermediate strata of the parties that spoke of popular and working-class representation. These were cadres specialising in political activity who had a direct representation in the social movement. The youth were another key element for the creation of the united front: since they were by definition in a formative phase, they could come to agreements with the leaderships of analogous organisations from other parties.

---

47   Gramsci 1999b, p. 544.

The policy of a united front of the working masses, as conceived by Gramsci, was neither 'sectarian' nor 'isolationist', because it was precisely the connection with the masses and its anti-capitalist bent that would define its shape. The essential point was to undermine the influence the existing organisations had on the masses and their molecular disintegration. If Gramsci believed every strategic agreement with the party leaderships of the democratic opposition to be ineffective, he attributed remarkable importance to the possible adherence of a member of the Catholic Action to the programme of the proletarian united front. This was because this organisation was seen as 'an integral part of fascism. It tends through religious ideology to give fascism the agreement of broad masses of the people. And it is destined in a certain sense, in the minds of a very strong tendency within the Fascist Party (Federzoni, Rocco, etc.), to replace the Fascist Party itself in its function as a mass party and organism for political control of the population'.[48]

Gramsci thus intended to battle with fascism itself for the leadership of the working masses, especially because he saw two trends in the régime: one, mentioned above, which desired a stabilisation agreement among the state institutions, the monarchy and the army, and also the Church; the other trend, however, represented by Farinacci, was the expression of the contradiction between agrarians and industrialists and the contradiction between the petit bourgeoisie and capitalism. There was no dispute that 'the fascism of today typically represents the clear predominance of finance capital over the State: capital which seeks to enslave all the country's productive forces' or that 'the fact of the total enslavement to America to which Italy has been subjected by the fascist government'. This is why Gramsci saw the pertinence of the slogan of the 'United Soviet States of Europe'[49] (bringing back a famous polemical position of Trotsky's).

Economic difficulties could provide a political arena for the disaggregation of fascism, but Gramsci also understood, as he had since 1922, that the bourgeoisie had, besides fascism, another means to prevent the possible development of the proletarian revolution: a more or less democratic liberal constitutional régime. And Gramsci realised that 'a certain regroupment is taking place in the democratic field, of a more radical character than in the past', spreading republican ideology among the intermediate strata of the parties, so crucial for the united front policy, and which could eventually take power in case the

---

48   Gramsci 1999b, pp. 545–6.
49   Gramsci 1999b, pp. 547–8.

régime collapsed. And this because 'Though it is true that, politically, fascism may be succeeded by a dictatorship of the proletariat ... it is nevertheless not certain, and not even probable, that the passage from fascism to the dictatorship of the proletariat will be a direct one'.[50]

Never did Gramsci sacrifice the autonomy and the antagonism of the working class and the united front, even when his analysis took into account the possibility that intermediate phases would have to take place in the social and political process leading to the socialist revolution.[51] Gramsci believed the army's and the civilian bureaucracy's position could be decisive, in the face of a possible crisis, to 'bring the republican democratic coalition to power ...', capable of checking the revolution'. However, faced with this possibility, the communists would either have to 'reduce to a minimum the influence and organisation of the parties which may constitute the left coalition, in order to make more and more probable a revolutionary collapse of fascism', or 'strive to make the democratic interlude as brief as possible'.[52]

The effort to particularise the Italian situation and the united front policy would have to be mediated by the insertion of Western European capitalism within the international context. The axis of the reflection is composed of the following problems: 'Is the period of so-called stabilisation over? What point have we reached, with respect to the capacity of the bourgeois order for resistance?'[53] In the evaluation of the correlation of forces and the particularisation of political tactics, a first point of discrimination had to be placed in the difference between advanced capitalist countries and states on the periphery of capitalism, even if aspects from both groups could be seen in France and Czechoslovakia. Gramsci proposes, as an analytical criterion, that the first step should be the acknowledgement that

---

50   Gramsci 1999b, pp. 550–1.

51   The emphasis is valid to the extent that this document is one of the most widely used in the 'new readings' of Gramsci, which seek clues for the idea that he was a convinced democrat, thus giving legitimacy to policies developed in other times and even other places. One such example of a retrospective reading can be found in the excellent introduction to Gramsci's political thought, written under the influence of 'Eurocommunism', by Carlos Nelson Coutinho, at the point where he calls 'still narrow' Gramsci's formulation of the republican constitutional assembly based on workers' and peasants' councils, because it prevented 'the alliance with anti-fascist and republican democratic-bourgeois sectors'. The author did not realise at the time that it was not narrowness but a different political strategy that rejected such an alliance. See Coutinho 1981, p. 50.

52   Gramsci 1999b, pp. 551–2.

53   Gramsci 1999b, p. 553.

in the advanced capitalist countries, the ruling class possesses political and organisational reserves which it did not possess, for instance, in Russia. This means that even the most serious economic crises do not have immediate repercussions in the political sphere. Politics always lags behind economics, far behind. The state apparatus is far more resistant than is often possible to believe; and it succeeds, at moments of crisis, in organising greater forces loyal to the regime than the depth of the crisis might lead one to suppose.[54]

Such would be the case of the USA, Britain and Germany. In the states of the periphery, such as Italy, Portugal, Spain and Poland, 'a broad stratum of intermediate classes stretches between the proletariat and capitalism: classes which seek to carry on, and to a certain sense succeed in carrying on, policies of their own, with ideologies which often influence broad strata of the proletariat, but which particularly affect the peasant masses'.[55]

The turn to the left seen by Gramsci, especially in the countries of the periphery and in the trade-union struggles in Britain, led him to believe that 'we are entering a new phase in the development of the capitalist crisis. This phase takes different forms, on the one hand in the countries of the capitalist periphery, and on the other in the advanced capitalist countries'. However, in every case, 'For all the capitalist countries, a fundamental problem is posed – the problem of the transition from the united front tactic, understood in a general sense, to a specific tactic which confronts the concrete problems of national life and operates on the basis of the popular forces as they are historically determined'.[56]

Even at the risk of being labeled an *ordinuovist* he suggests that 'one of the most important problems we face, especially in the major capitalist countries, is the problem of factory councils and workers' control – as the basis for a new regroupment of the proletarian class, which will permit a more effective struggle against the trade-union bureaucracy'.[57]

The experience of the factory councils in the Turin of 1919–20 could be considered a demonstration of the organic capacity of the working class, manifested particularly in

---

54   Gramsci 1999b, p. 554.
55   Gramsci 1999b, p. 554.
56   Gramsci 1999b, p. 556.
57   Gramsci 1999b, p. 556.

1. Capacity for self-government of the mass of workers ... 2. Capacity of the mass of workers to maintain or exceed the capitalist order's level of production ... 3. Limitless capacity for initiative and creation of the working masses.[58]

From this conviction, in which we hear the echo of Sorel and Luxemburg's formulations, came the insistence that 'In Italian society, which has attained the highest degree of capitalist development which it historically could attain, given the conditions of time and place, only one class is revolutionary in a complete and permanent sense: the industrial proletariat'.[59]

Gramsci and the leadership of the PCd'I took from this reading the political orientation of the anti-fascist and anti-capitalist united front, which, in refusing to take part in the democratic coalition proposed by republicans and socialists, instead insisted on the slogan of the 'Republican assembly on the basis of workers' and peasants' committees'. The belief that the achievement of socialism was a current question and that the proletariat was the only force able to lead Italy down the socialist path led Gramsci to argue that the alliance proposed was impossible, because 'The Republican Concentration is working to subordinate the proletariat to other social forms – which in practice can only be capitalism'.[60] Gramsci also affirmed that such was the political orientation followed by the communists since June 1923, when Matteotti had been murdered.

Considering that the so-called capitalist stabilisation was unsteady and nearing its end, and that the intermediate social strata were turning to the left, Gramsci believed the moment had come to strengthen the united front throughout Europe, while always remaining attentive to the various countries' national specificities. Whatever the context, however, the united front should emphasise its mass nature and antagonism towards capitalism. It is obvious that, in a situation like this, even though Gramsci did not even touch on the subject, the political and ideological support of the International and the USSR would be an element of the greatest importance, and hence the need to avoid fissures in this area, preserving especially the unity of the Bolshevik leadership.

---

58   Gramsci 1999b, pp. 566–7.
59   Gramsci 1999b, p. 571.
60   Gramsci 1999b, p. 574.

3   Gramsci and the Russian Question

The worsening of the social and political situation in the USSR provided the opportunity for every opponent of the Russian Revolution to present their harshest criticisms.[61] Gramsci, then, avoided taking a stance or even mentioning the crisis in the Bolshevik leadership, and tried to defend the process of the socialist transition in the USSR, thus setting the fundamental assumptions on which he would base himself. Even though Gramsci placed his hopes in the socialist revolution in Europe resuming within the short term, everything leads us to believe that he conceived of the first phase of the socialist transition using the hypotheses indicated by Lenin and Bukharin, which included the consolidation of the worker-peasant alliance and the NEP. Since the agrarian question was at the core of the ongoing polemic in Russia and among the opponents of the historical project represented by the Soviet state, and since it also had consequences for the specific circumstances of the Italian revolution, Gramsci applied himself to this theme with greater attention.

This was Gramsci's opportunity to make more explicit a few of his ideas of a more general nature concerning the problem of socialist transition. As he tried to distinguish the emergence of bourgeois domination from the initial phase of socialist transition, he highlighted that 'even before taking power, the bourgeoisie was able to train itself in the administration of the state, developing an experience of many centuries', whereas 'the proletariat cannot, while the bourgeois regime lasts, better its own administrative capacities and create its own morality'. Surely the situation in Italy was better than in Russia, in this regard, given the example of the 'occupation of the factories'.[62]

Thus the socialist transition would be a long apprenticeship, not only in the management of the productive process, with the assimilation of the most advanced science and technique, but also a process of creating a new morality for social relations. Surely in America, where science and technique involved the productive process as a whole and even the workforce, the process of socialist transition would start from a much more advanced point and the taking of power would also be specific in other senses.

In the Russian case, Gramsci attempted to recover Lenin's formulation from the dawn of the revolution, when the Bolshevik leader stated that socialism was not the immediate goal. For Lenin, in fact, the Russian Revolution could take

---

61   Indeed, between 1926 and 1927, with criticism coming from various ideological positions, the opinion that the USSR was going to restore capitalism became increasingly widespread.

62   Gramsci 1978, pp. 313–15.

place as a democratic radicalisation of the bourgeois revolution, having as its immediate goal the control of production and its distribution throughout the working class, the confiscation and nationalisation of land, and the creation of a national bank controlled by the soviets, which would take the place of the bourgeois state's instruments of oppression. These transformations, even though they remained within the terrain of capitalism, would act as a strong stimulus to the world socialist movement, even working as a possible prologue to the international socialist revolution. The Russian Revolution would put the country on the path of the socialist transition, though doubtless from a much more backward starting point.[63]

In answering the usual argument from both leftist and social-democratic critics (who shared in having a limited corporatist view of the working class) that the NEP, with its tolerance for small and medium agrarian property, would inevitably lead to some form of agrarian capitalism, Gramsci argued that in the USSR the 'force of the state and the collectivised industrial and financial economy'[64] would prevent such an outcome. He made use of Lenin's and Bukharin's thought on how the socialist transition would proceed in the countryside through the grouping-together of small family holdings into cooperatives for production, sales and consumption. This would be the path for the future industrialisation of the countryside and the formation of large agro-industrial enterprises, which would make it possible to dilute the peasantry and market production within a working class more and more educated and trained in the administration of things, so that 'the bond between workers and peasants through industrial economy and agrarian economy will take place with the industrialisation of the land'.[65]

The key to the problem of the socialist transition in the USSR, on which Gramsci insists, is the countryside, which the revolution had declared to be collective property, and the use of which had been granted to the rural workers, according to their own needs. However, in the present situation there was only one thing to ensure: that 'the socialist elements in politics and economics prevail over the capitalist elements, so that the development of the former is constantly greater, and therefore one cannot speak of capitalism in the Soviet state, and should rather speak of a process towards the complete realisation of a communist society'.[66]

---

63   Ibid.
64   Gramsci 1978, pp. 315–19.
65   Gramsci 1978, p. 319.
66   Gramsci 1978, p. 320.

The fact that social differentiation was developing in the countryside was inevitable, but the strength of the alliance between the working class and the poor and wage-earning peasantry would prevent the possible political and economic strengthening of the richer peasantry, which could have an interest in the restoration of capitalism. Besides, Gramsci argued that 'the industrialisation of agricultural production is inevitable, but it is in the very interest of the peasant classes that it occurs through collective forms, and not under capitalist management'.[67]

These remarks by Gramsci on the beginning of the process of the socialist transition in the USSR find their international dimension not only in the possibility that the peasantry may be assimilated into the working class through the action of capital, enlarging the reserve industrial army, but through the action of the working class as well. At first, the peasantry arises as an allied class and then as a class that must be absorbed as the productive forces advance in the transition phase. However, the essential point for ensuring the transition process itself is, rather than the generalisation of the proletariat, that the working class prove 'capable, both organically and as mass, of managing production'.[68]

Gramsci saw the possibility of the socialist revolution and its 'civilising' potential precisely in those organic capacities that were present in the working class and that would find free expression in the liberating process of the socialist transition. Gramsci's suggestion that the working class's fundamental alliance should be with the poor peasantry is noteworthy, as is his insistence that the self-organisation and the self-government of the masses would be the condition both for achieving the socialist revolution and the advance of the socialist transition.

However, since the working class was itself divided into conflicting strata, and as it tended to assimilate portions of the peasantry, there was a need for the political party as an element for the education and promotion of the historical interests of the class, as an expression of the self-government of the working masses and therefore of a non-state arising from a counter-power. The inherent concern in this reasoning, opposed to any process of bureaucratisation affecting the self-government of the masses, is to indicate the contradictions that emerge in the process of the socialist transition.

The sudden worsening and conclusion of the conflict within the Soviet leadership, and also the decision to promote the discussion of the Russian question in the Seventh Enlarged Plenary of the ECCI, set to begin on 15 November, finally

---

67   Gramsci 1978, p. 322.
68   Gramsci 1978, p. 340.

provoked Gramsci to write a letter to the Central Committee of the RKP(b) on behalf of the political secretariat of the PCd'I. His goal was still that the letter could influence positively the development of the Fifteenth Conference of the RKP(b), which should precede the Enlarged Plenary of the ECCI.[69]

Gramsci's letter describes with great clarity some of the basic ideas of his conception of the revolutionary process and his political science, espousing from another angle the connection that exists between national specificity and international generality. Most of all, in Gramsci we find the conviction that polemic, even if harsh, is a constitutive element of the revolutionary dialectic embodied by the party. Thus, 'having achieved a greater ideological and organisational homogeneity through these discussions, the Party would be more prepared and more equipped to overcome the various difficulties associated with the ruling of a workers' state'.[70]

However, taking the debate to the limits of a scission had inevitable 'international repercussions', which would benefit 'class enemies', whose desire was to see the disintegration of the dictatorship of the proletariat. According to Gramsci, the Western working-class masses would 'wish to see in the Republic of the Soviets and in the ruling Party a single combat unit working within the general perspective of socialism', because this was the condition for the RKP(b) to continue being accepted as the 'leading party of the International'. Besides, the open conflict in the RKP(b) would benefit the 'bourgeois and social-democratic parties', which wished to 'fight the influence of the Russian Revolution, the revolutionary unity that is constituting itself in the whole world around the CP of the USSR'. Statements from the leaders of the opposition such as 'the state of the soviets is becoming a pure capitalist state' would be particularly harmful.[71]

To Gramsci, this split process, which was nearing its tragic conclusion, was in absolute contrast with the effort defined by the Fifth World Congress seeking the establishment of 'Bolshevised' parties. At least in Gramsci's understanding,

---

69   The correspondence between Gramsci and Togliatti, especially from October 1926, gave rise to an intense historiographical and political debate, based on memories and ever richer documentary sources. A certain instrumentality can be detected in the analysis, given the importance of the political effects of the relationship between Gramsci and Togliatti within the tradition of Italian communism as a whole. The documentation recently brought forth contradicts the established belief that Togliatti had taken the initiative of not sending Gramsci's letter to the CC of the RKP(b), going against a party decision. Among the studies on this theme, some of the more recent deserve mentioning: Canfora 1990, pp. 293–316; Natoli 1991, pp. 407–25; Fiori 1991; Pistillo 1996; Vacca 1999.

70   Vacca 1999, pp. 404–11.

71   Ibid.

that would require the creation of a democratic and unitarian dialectic within a party closely associated with the working class and the movement of the real, both nationally and internationally. So, the coming scission 'would once again put success farther from the organic unity of the world workers' party'. And this would happen fundamentally because 'it seems to us that the violent passion for the Russian questions makes you lose from sight the international aspects of the Russian questions themselves, and makes you forget that your duties as Russian militants only can and should be fulfilled within the framework of the interests of the international proletariat'.[72]

Up to this point, Gramsci emphasised the international dimension of the process of the scission within the Bolshevik leadership. After the letter, he compared the national situations of the USSR and Italy, so as to be able to generalise the concrete problems proposed by the socialist transition. Gramsci recalls that in Italy, just as in Russia, the 'rural masses' comprise most of the working population. He notes, however, that in Italy, in spite of the presence of a more lively industrial sector, 'all the problems intrinsic to the hegemony of the proletariat will surely present themselves to us in a form more complex and acute than that in Russia itself, because the density of the Italian rural population is far greater, because our peasants have a very rich organisational tradition ..., because among us the organised Church apparatus has two thousand years of tradition and specialised itself in the propaganda and organisation of the peasants in such a way as there exists in no other country'.[73]

It was precisely his analysis of Italian specificity that allowed Gramsci to declare as 'fundamentally just the political line of the majority of the Communist Party of the USSR', and that 'the majority of the Italian Party will follow it, should it become necessary fully to pose this question'.[74] It can be seen, therefore, that Gramsci supported the political orientation of the majority of the CC of the RKP(b) regarding the essential theme of the hegemony of the proletariat and the worker-peasant alliance in the process of the socialist transition, especially in relatively backward countries, even though such a position would only be affirmed in cases where it was absolutely necessary. This anticipated the position that would be taken in the Seventh Enlarged Plenary of the ECCI.

The criticism directed at the 'united opposition' was that its positions attacked 'the principle and the practice of the hegemony of the proletariat', and that they also affected 'the fundamental alliance between workers and

---

72   Ibid.

73   Ibid.

74   Ibid.

peasants'. Using the tone of an invocation, Gramsci insisted on a theme that would become permanent in his political thought, that of 'corporatism'. The socialist transition, especially in countries where the productive forces were little-developed, demanded precisely that if the proletariat were to maintain its hegemony over the working masses as a whole, it would have to have living standards inferior to those of strata more distanced from revolutionary political power.

In the advanced capitalist countries, in which the working class had achieved better standards of living, reformism and trade unionism arose as manifestations of the 'corporatist spirit'. In every case, however, 'the proletariat will not become the ruling class without overcoming this contradiction by sacrificing corporate interests, it cannot preserve its hegemony and dictatorship if, when it becomes dominant, it does not sacrifice these immediate interests in the name of the general and permanent class interests'.[75]

Gramsci sharply pointed out that 'in the ideology and the practice of the opposition bloc the whole tradition of social-democracy and trade unionism is once again reborn, that which until now prevented the Western proletariat from organising itself as a ruling class'. Acknowledging the role and the importance that Trotsky, Zinoviev and Kamenev had in the revolutionary process, Gramsci suggested that all factional activity cease, but also that the majority should avoid taking 'excessive measures'.[76] Gramsci, indeed, indicated that the most adequate path would be precisely that followed by the PCd'I as it dealt with Bordiga's extreme leftist trend.

In the note Gramsci attached to the letter, he informed Togliatti that he was authorised to 'review the text' as long as its essential ideas were preserved, and that 'because we wish to help the "majority" of the CC, you can reach agreements with others in sharing the responsibility for these changes'.[77] Togliatti showed the letter to Bukharin, Manuilsky, Kuusinen and Humbert-Droz and sent an urgent telegram to Gramsci stating that 'the uneasiness expressed in your letter no longer corresponds to the present situation of the Russian party'.[78]

Indeed, given the lack of results from the united opposition's agitation among the party base, which rendered it virtually isolated, it felt obliged to give in and to promise to end its factional activity. Even so, the question was far from being resolved – the opposite of what Togliatti seemed to imagine when

---

75   Ibid.
76   Ibid.
77   Vacca 1999, p. 402.
78   Vacca 1999, p. 413.

he suggested that 'Since I am quite familiar with the situation, I propose that the letter should no longer be sent, as it would be untimely in the current state of affairs'.[79]

Soon, Togliatti wrote a letter to the Political Secretariat of the PCd'I and also a private letter to Gramsci. In the first, he described in greater detail the reasons why he believed Gramsci's letter would be untimely: 'The leaders of the opposition would use it to refute some of the conditions imposed on them, to ask for other conditions, to create delays, causing clear harm to the Party'. According to Togliatti, the leaders of the opposition hoped that certain sectors of the basis of the party would send 'a generic appeal to unity and to the responsibility of the leaders'. This was precisely the goal of Gramsci's letter, but Togliatti, on the contrary, believed that 'if that had happened, it would have been harmful to the party, because it would have meant, actually, the beginning of a revision in the line of the cc and a too harsh discussion in a too short time'.[80]

Togliatti seems to have put himself on a course that aimed at wrecking the opposition, exactly what Gramsci had warned the majority of the cc of the RKP(b) against doing. Togliatti was also advancing a concealed criticism of the behaviour of the majority of the PCd'I from the process of the Third Party Congress up until the dispute about Bordiga's trip to Moscow. Besides, Togliatti indicated that Gramsci's letter could lead it to be supposed that the opposition would find support for its positions in the PCd'I or in other sections of the International. Finally, he insisted that they wait for Humbert-Droz's trip to Italy.

Togliatti's personal letter to Gramsci is far more incisive, explaining the disagreements. While Gramsci gave priority to the importance of the democratic unity of the Bolshevik leadership and its revolutionary dialectic, seeking new theoretical and practical syntheses, for Togliatti 'the problem of the correctness or otherwise of the line being followed by the majority of the Central Committee' prevailed, especially considering that, from that moment on, 'the unity of the Leninist old guard will no longer be – or will only with difficulty be – realised in a continuous manner'. In this situation, any appeal to party unity could only be harmful, as the focus would shift from internationalism to the study of Russian questions, whereas the Italians would be able to offer 'a contribution – on the basis of our revolutionary experience – towards fixing and confirming the correct Leninist line in the solution of the Russian problems'. Thus, 'the best

79   Ibid.
80   Vacca 1999, pp. 414–19.

way of contributing to overcoming the crisis is to express one's own support for that line without putting any limits on it'.[81] A few days later, Manuilsky sent Gramsci a letter, in which he sought to reassure him and persuade him that there was no point in sending his letter, stating that 'there is no more danger of a split within the RKP(b)'.[82]

Even though using the excuse of persistent difficulties in the transmission of information, the Political Secretariat of the PCd'I would send a telegram a few days later, signed by Camila Ravera (Micheli), stating that 'it was good not to send the letter to the RKP'.[83] This meant that the Political Commission of the PCd'I, even if apparently upset, accepted the decision coming from a superior instance of the Comintern, which Togliatti had consulted. On 1 November, Togliatti confirmed that he had received the telegram and kept hold of the letter.[84]

Gramsci, however, on the same day that the telegram stopping the delivery of the letter to the CC of the RKP(b) was sent, decided to give a personal answer to Togliatti's letter, stating: 'I am sure that I also express the view of the other comrades'. Togliatti was then accused of considering the problem merely from the point of view of the parties as apparatuses and not 'also the great working masses, which are politically stratified in a contradictory fashion, but which as a whole tend towards unity'.[85]

The USSR would be a fundamental element for the construction of a united front of the working masses from across the whole world, precisely because this region had chosen the path of the socialist transition. But it should be seen as a complex and unstable terrain, which the conscience of the masses would find hard to understand. This is why Gramsci insisted that 'the question of unity, not only of the Russian party but also of the Leninist nucleus, is therefore a question of the greatest importance in the international field. It is, from the mass point of view, the most important question in this historical period of intensified contradictory process towards unity'.[86]

Given the importance of the unity of the so-called Leninist nucleus in the configuration of a united front of the working masses from across the whole world, Gramsci stated that 'our aim is to contribute to the maintenance and creation of a unitary plan, in which the various tendencies and personalities can

---

81   Gramsci 1999b, pp. 584–7.
82   Vacca 1999, pp. 426–7.
83   Vacca 1999, p. 434.
84   Vacca 1999, p. 440.
85   Gramsci 1999b, p. 590.
86   Gramsci 1999b, p. 591.

draw closer and merge, even ideologically'. The struggle for party unity – under-stood as a synthesis of conflicting positions – was, in Gramsci's understanding, the core of the so-called 'Leninist line'. It naturally followed that this was also his understanding of what the 'Bolshevisation' of the Comintern should be. Gram-sci concluded by saying that the significance of the Bolsheviks taking power was not so much the great propulsive force emanating from the USSR, but rather 'the conviction (if it exists) that the proletariat, once power has been taken, can construct socialism'.[87]

The background disagreement that seems to oppose Gramsci to Togliatti in this epistolary debate is that whereas the former insists on the centrality of the united front of the working masses across the world, of which the USSR would be just one important element to the extent that the proletariat displayed the organic capacity to build a new order, the other inverted the argument and believed the USSR to be the essential propulsive force of the united front. This latter was a proposition that would be consolidated during the Seventh Plenary of the ECCI, set to take place before the end of that year, and which ran against the thesis of the feasibility of the construction of socialism in an isolated USSR.

The meeting of the CC of the PCd'I was set to take place between 1 and 3 November on the outskirts of Genoa. It was due to discuss, among other points, a position on the Russian question, which would be taken to the Sev-enth Enlarged Plenary of the ECCI. However, a failed attempt on Mussolini's life on 31 October sparked repression against each and every anti-fascist organ-isation, causing many people's absence from the meeting. Gramsci himself was detained in Milan and forced to return to Rome, where he began to be closely followed by the police.

So no one knows what would have been Gramsci's position on the Russian question, even though it is possible to imagine that he could have insisted on the ideas presented in his recent letters, as these were in a profound sense con-sistent with the whole theoretical-political elaboration he was then maturing. We could conclude that Gramsci's positions would have expressed support to the positions of the majority of the CC of the RKP(b), though with some reser-vations over the feasibility of the notion of 'socialism in only one country'. They would also have insisted on the importance of keeping the 'united opposition' as part of the leadership's work.

The plenary meeting of the CC, as always, was preceded by a meeting of the Political Commission in the presence of Humbert-Droz, in which the path that the debate should take was decided. In Gramsci's absence, the opening remarks

---

87   Gramsci 1999b, pp. 591–4.

were made by Mauro Scoccimarro (Morelli), who repeated in broad terms the same assessment of the Italian situation as had been made in the previous meeting of the party's CC, which had taken place in August. He reaffirmed the fact of the 'control, at present fully exercised, of the government and the Fascist Party by the agrarian-industrial bloc, in which financial capital and the steel industry associated with it obtain an ever more dominant position'. He insisted that the communists' political activity should aim at the working-class base of the parties of the Republican Concentration, accentuating the ideological debate, but without cutting contact with the 'more advanced elements', such as to be able to engage in joint actions.[88]

The opening exposition on the Russian question was made by Jules Humbert-Droz, who once again asked the PCd'I to assume a clear position in favour of the majority line of the CC of the RKP(b) in the dispute against the 'united opposition'. Surprised by the offensive of the fascist régime, and without the presence of Gramsci, who was supposed to present the party's position, the communist leaders seem to have responded only evasively.

Ruggero Grieco's exposition, longer and more articulated, gave some insight into the position and the mood of the communist leadership. He stuck by the idea that the problems affecting the RKP(b) should not be taken to the whole of the Comintern, as they referred to a matter of political tactics, and not one of principle. The most important questions to be debated was theoretical-political in nature: 'the question of whether it is possible to build socialism in only one country; the relation between workers and peasants, and so on'.[89]

Grieco argued that the lack of information had prevented any deeper discussion of the Russian questions within the CC of the PCd'I, and that Gramsci was responsible for giving this meeting a detailed exposition on the subject, as well as for presenting a proposal for a motion. However, considering the Humbert-Droz report, 'now we are able to take a position and so we do: we must say we agree with the political line followed by the majority of the Russian CC'.[90]

After this peremptory statement, Grieco advanced the position of the leadership, as espoused by Gramsci, regarding the criticism aimed at the theses of the 'united opposition'. He stated that this was a heterogenous bloc, but that

> naturally, the important thing is that the hegemony of the proletariat be preserved in Russia. But for us the hegemony of the proletariat does not

88   Canfora 1990, pp. 304–10.

89   Canfora 1990, pp. 311–13.

90   Ibid.

mean the control of all classes by one class. If the working class, which doubtless faces grave trials and sacrifices, began to fight the peasants, this would mean the disintegration of the worker-peasant bloc, the basis of proletarian power, and a step towards the defeat of the workers' state.[91]

In Grieco's speech, we can clearly see his conviction in the ideas defended by Gramsci in recent pieces on the USSR and in the whole elaboration the PCd'I had been developing on the importance of the worker-peasant alliance. However, he referred to differences regarding

> the question of whether it is possible for socialism to be built in only one country [that] has been discussed in the RKP for a year and a half. We hesitated a year and a half ago in the face of Trotsky's stance. Perhaps some of the comrades still hesitate today. So we want every comrade to have, as much as possible, sufficient elements to see the question clearly. Essentially, what is necessary is to watch the development of the socialist economy of the USSR and see whether it goes at a faster pace than that of the private economies.[92]

The PCd'I leadership voted support to the political line of the RKP(b) CC majority, a position that would then be taken by the Italian delegation to the Seventh Enlarged Plenary of the ECCI. At Humbert-Droz's request that the position of the CC of the PCd'I be recorded in a document, Grieco answered that

> this document was perhaps written by Gramsci, who had been tasked by the Political Commission and would have brought it here. This is why we appeared at the CC without a resolution. Anyway, we can provide this written document, shortly.[93]

Here, it is possible to see a much lesser degree of confidence. For the Italian communists, the focal point of the matter seemed to lie in the question of whether the USSR was heading towards some form of capitalist restoration, or whether it would be possible to proceed with socialist transition by means of the NEP and the worker-peasant alliance – though without any doubt that the socialist revolution was still of an international nature. Thus the main

---

91   Ibid.
92   Ibid.
93   Canfora 1990, pp. 315–16.

question was that of the role of the peasantry in the socialist transition, and how it could be transformed into part of the working class. The problem of the complete realisation of socialism in only one country was thus a false alternative, because it assumed not only the stagnation of the revolution in the West, but also the construction and permanence of a strong socialist state in a situation dominated by imperialism. Such an understanding of the problem explains the common belief in the leadership circles of the International and RKP(b) that the PCd'I leadership nurtured sympathies for Trotsky.

It is not known whether Gramsci had really written a draft resolution on the Russian question or whether at the end of the meeting the CC wrote some short and hurried note (which was never found), but the Italian communists' reticence, here, is evident. The fact remains that Gramsci's letter was never made official and fell into the void, though the previously stated reluctance to spread the problems of the internal struggles of the RKP(b) to other parties persisted, postponing the whole discussion to the Seventh Enlarged Plenary of the ECCI. As such, these problems would be discussed in a proper international forum, and the party grassroots would not be enveloped by doubts and divisions, which could paralyse political action at a moment as dramatic as could be imagined.[94]

Even though the PCd'I declared support for Stalin's and Bukharin's majority, this came with the excuse that the different elements of the problem still required greater clarification, which would be provided by Gramsci. In fact, the Italian communists seemed very reticent about accepting the theoretical and political implications presented by the notion of 'socialism in only one country'. Even though they agreed with the emphasis on the worker-peasant alliance and the NEP, the idea of dividing the world into two areas and the possibility of completing the socialist transition in only one country or region of the planet seemed unacceptable, also because such theses suggested a significant delay in the revolutionary process in the West and even a fundamental change in the united front tactic.

---

94   The existing information about this meeting can be fruitfully accessed in the introduction to Vacca 1999, pp. 8–13 and 141–9, even though we cannot share its interpretation, given its obvious exaggeration of the actual disagreements between Togliatti and Gramsci, and the inexistent polarisations between Gramsci and Scoccimarro, on the one hand, and Togliatti and Grieco on the other. See too Canfora 1990, pp. 293–318; Pistillo 1996, pp. 97–102; and Pistillo 2001, pp. 15–31. In her criticism of Giuseppe Vacca, Pistillo tends to go in the opposite direction, diluting the disagreements between Togliatti and the majority of the Political Committee, suggesting the acceptance of the theory of 'socialism in only one country'.

In fact, there was already a tendency in the Comintern, in the face of the worsening of the situation in France and Italy, to value a rapprochement with social democracy within the framework of a political united front of party leaderships. At the same time, the PCd'I maintained a perspective of revolution in the short term, at least in the peripheral zones of Europe: Spain, Yugoslavia and Italy itself.

Gramsci and the leadership of the PCd'I had been constructing, in an autonomous and internationalist manner, a theoretical and practical conception that could be identified with the communist refoundation undertook by Lenin and the Bolsheviks. So it is understandable that the process of theoretical regression and splitting of the Bolshevik leadership had a negative impact on this process of refoundation, and so did the objective conditions of the offensive of capital under fascism, broadening the scope of political disagreements that could have been isolated and creating antinomies between analyses of reality that could have been synthesised on a higher level.

In this context, we can see signs that Togliatti was adjusting to the ongoing logic of the process of the scission and the theoretical regression that was taking place within the Bolshevik leadership, which had as its most evident implications the notion that minority ideas had no rights within the party, that the International should be completely in tune with the majority of the RKP(b), and that the construction of socialism in the USSR had become the main propulsive force of the international socialist revolution. An important consequence of this scenario was the trivialisation of the political formula of the united front and the political initiative of the communists, now transformed into mere coadjutants of the socialist construction of the USSR.

Gramsci, on the other hand, was accustomed to the logic of the communist refoundation and did not accept the premises or the implications of the thesis of 'socialism in only one country', to which Bukharin and Togliatti had submitted in the heat of the immediate political struggle. For Gramsci, the USSR was a decisive moment in the international revolution because it was there that the socialist transition had begun. However, the preservation of the worker-peasant alliance, in this case, and the creation of a united front of the working masses of the world, to be constructed according to the specificities of each country, anticipated a rather complex, changing and multifaceted world scenario, with surprising advances and retreats.

4   The Agrarian Question as a National Question, and the Problem of
       the Southern Intellectuals in the United Front

While Gramsci developed his polemic in the party press about the actual content of the Russian post-revolutionary social form, and tried to use Comintern
channels to bear a positive influence that might help prevent the imminent
scission in the Bolshevik leadership, in Italy he tried to enable the party to take
the most appropriate course toward the realisation of the worker-peasant alliance. The socialist tradition, the political culture of which had remained in a
subaltern position relative to the liberalism and positivism that fed Italian capitalist development, paid little attention to the agrarian question.

    In his writings from 1918–21, Gramsci saw the agrarian-peasant question in
Italy as being strongly analogous with Russia. Assimilated by the bourgeois
state, the peasant masses remained subject to economic and cultural forms of
a feudal nature, but the circumstances of the imperialist war, as

> Four years of the trenches and exploitation of his blood have radically
> changed the peasant psychology. This change occurred especially in Rus-
> sia, and was one of the essential factors in the revolution. What industri-
> alism had not brought about in its normal process of development was
> produced by the war.[95]

However, Gramsci's and the *L'Ordine Nuovo* group's perception that the workers' movement had to be closely connected with the rural masses was put
aside during the first years of the PCd'I. This was because Amadeo Bordiga,
the most influential communist leader at the time, strongly emphasised the
revolutionary role of the industrial proletariat, and even denied the existence
of the Southern question in Italy, a view related to the lack of value he saw in
the political formula of the united front.

    It was precisely the political formula of the united front – as it established
the link between the new tactic proposed by the Comintern for resisting the
offensive of capital, and the policy of socialist transition by means of state
monopoly capitalism induced by the NEP in the USSR – that made it possible
for Gramsci to resume his reflections on the agrarian and peasant question.
This proved to be the key for understanding Italy's specific national situation in
the context of the international socialist revolution, and the guiding thread of
his analysis of fascism, reformism, the revolutionary party and every question

---

95   Gramsci 1999a, p. 133.

regarding the political formula of the united front and the revolution in Italy. Thus we can see that the attention Gramsci devoted to the Southern question put him on the fast track to the trend of communist refoundation, especially as it put him close to Lenin's method of reflection.

An agrarian conference of the PCd'I, held in the suburbs of Bari on 12 September 1926, tried to improve the guidelines for political action previously presented at the Third Party Congress. It noted both the crisis of the political organisations present in the South and fascism's difficulty in stabilising its base. The autonomous organisation of the Southern peasantry and alliance with the medium intellectual strata, with their tendency toward radicalisation, appeared crucial to blocking possible bourgeois efforts to lead the process of overcoming fascism and, on the contrary, to establishing a workers' and peasants' united front that anticipated the socialist revolution.[96]

Intellectuals such as Piero Gobetti, Carlo Rosselli, Guido Dorso and Tommaso Fiore believed that the only possible solution to the Italian Southern problem would be based on the popular masses and the middle intellectual strata of the South, opposing the centuries-old domination by the feudal landowners, even though a major role would also be attributed to the Northern working class in the liberation movement as a whole. This Southernist stance, which presented a proposal for a national bourgeois-democratic revolution to complete the *Risorgimento*, was promoted by publications such as Piero Gobetti's *La rivoluzione liberale*[97] and Carlo Rosselli's and Pietro Nenni's *Il quarto stato*.[98]

---

96   See the introduction by Francesco Biscione in Gramsci 1996b, pp. 1–6.

97   Piero Gobetti was a collaborator of *L'Ordine Nuovo*. In 1922 he created the magazine *La rivoluzione liberale*. In April 1924, Gobetti, then 23, published the book *La rivoluzione liberale: saggio sulla lotta politica in Italia*, in which he critically analysed every Italian political trend and proclaimed his anti-fascism. He argued for the creation of a new ruling class, able to found a modern state based on the 'industrial vanguard' of the North, and which could provide a solution to the question of the South, promoting its industrialisation. The points of convergence with the communists are very obvious. See Gobetti 1995. On the close links between Gobetti and Gramsci, see Spriano 1977.

98   Carlo Rosselli (1899–1937) was influenced by the Southernism of Gaetano Salvemini and the reformist trend of Italian socialism. During his stays in England, he became close to Fabian socialism. He collaborated on magazines such as *La rivoluzione liberale* and *Critica sociale*. He joined the PSU in 1924. In March 1926, together with Pietro Nenni, who represented a social-democratic trend associated with the Second International, he founded the magazine *Il quarto stato*, which brought together a wide range of anti-fascist intellectuals. In 1928, in prison, Carlo Rosselli wrote the book that synthesised his political ideas: *Liberal Socialism*. See Rosselli 1997.

Guido Dorso's book, *La rivoluzione meridionale*, published in 1925 by Casa Gobetti Editore, sparked great debate about the Southern question, bringing together intellectual leaders from various anti-fascist currents. Dorso located the distant roots of the division of the Italian peninsula in the era of the wars between the Roman Republic and Epirus and Carthage, which took from the South its role as the provider of grain. The disintegration of the Roman Empire, the establishment of the Longobardi in the North and the subsequent effort by Charlemagne to recreate the Empire left aside the South, making possible the Benevento Ducat, and after that, the feudal reign of the Normans.

The Angevin conquest (1266–1441) 'gave all directing faculties, all forms of spiritual activity to Naples, the great and glorious parasite, always increasing ...' From then on, with the exception of the short Aragonese period (1442–1503), 'the Mezzogiorno, offered to the Florentine bankers as a colony for economic exploitation, rescued by feudalism, impoverished by the rise of Sicily and the consequent wars, began to be precipitated into ruin ...'[99]

The feudal and colonial regression that took place under the Habsburgs' viceroyalty was aggravated by the Spanish practice of leasing. The efforts by some monarchs of the Bourbon dynasty to impose absolutism after 1734 were at the roots of what later became the agrarian bourgeoisie. However, it was the Neapolitan revolution of 1799 that gave the rural bourgeoisie its greatest impulse for becoming the dominant class. After they had been restored to power, the Bourbons' insistence on imposing an absolutist monarchy still had to face the resistance of the rural bourgeoisie, just as it earlier had to face the power of the feudal barons. The liberal and conservative ideal that the Neapolitan rural bourgeoisie was unable to find in its own king was, instead, discovered in the Northern region of the Piedmont, with which it allied itself, so that, 'in substance, the Southern liberals found in Piedmontese centralism the legal and bureaucratic embodiment of that political ideal, towards which they had in vain sought to push the Bourbons' absolutism'.[100]

Once local political power had been conquered, the rural bourgeoisie began to oppose any anti-feudal action coming from the newly unified state, in exchange for accepting the political norms emanating from the Northern ruling class. From then on, the Mezzogiorno was transformed into a 'colony exploited by the Northern capital then being formed' and into a 'market for leases by the Northern industrial plutocracy'. Emigration provided the only escape for demographic growth. Dorso saw the reasons for the backwardness of South-

---

99   Dorso 1972, pp. 110–11.

100   Dorso 1972, p. 115.

ern Italy in the 'immobility of its economic-feudal structure, derived from the legislative debris of feudalism, which still endured, and in the lack of modern legislation'.[101]

Guido Dorso and the *La rivoluzione liberale* group believed that the great task at hand was to create the cultural conditions for the formation of a new ruling class in Italy. This conclusion derived from their analysis of the existing political forces, all of them backward or immature, such that 'the task of fighting for the modern state is, for now, restricted to very small cultural minorities, without precise political goals'.[102] Sceptical towards state action and the existing political parties, Dorso understood that 'it is necessary also to confront the problem scientifically, including in the political arena, in order to try to strengthen with Jacobin intransigence the scarce elements of the solution that already do exist, even if in a tendential and latent state'.[103]

Even though he believed the *La rivoluzione liberale* group to be 'the only truly liberal faction existing in Italy',[104] Dorso broadly acknowledged the role of the communists in seeking to resolve the concrete problems of the country and the Mezzogiorno. In the optimistic analysis of Guido Dorso, the *L'Ordine Nuovo* group and the experience of the factory councils 'were the first attempt to adhere to the revolutionary reality of the country', with the goal of 'forming the new ruling class within the old one, and later making it break out from its formative cocoon at the appropriate time', something that would demand 'a long period for the practical elaboration of ideas and political formations in order to maintain a revolutionary position appropriate to the present economic and social reality of the country'.[105]

However, the complete overcoming of the reformist socialists' conception would only be realised through an acknowledgement of the need to destroy the bureaucratic-centralising state and solve the Southern question. Thus, Dorso believed, when the communists acknowledged that the true revolutionary forces of Italy were in the Mezzogiorno, they would take up their place 'in the first line among the Italian liberal movements'.[106]

As a consequence of the organisational work and theoretical elaboration of the PCd'I, Gramsci attempted to write an essay or a series of articles specifically discussing the Southern question and its importance for defining the motor

---

101   Dorso 1972, pp. 206–7.
102   Dorso 1972, p. 171.
103   Dorso 1972, p. 209.
104   Dorso 1972, p. 171.
105   Dorso 1972, pp. 189–91.
106   Dorso 1972, p. 195.

forces of the Italian revolution, with the purpose of empowering the party and establishing a dialogue with possible allies and also with political adversaries. Written mostly during the month of October, the text was entitled *Some notes on the Southern question and on the attitude of communists, socialists and democrats*. As Gramsci was arrested, it remained unfinished.[107]

As Gramsci himself tells us, 'These notes were initially stimulated by the publication of an article on the Southern question by "Ulenspiegel" in the 18 September issue of the journal *Quarto Stato*, and by the somewhat comical editorial presentation which preceded it'.[108] The text comments on Guido Dorso's book, including the analysis of the communists' position regarding the Southern question. Looking to inform his polemic with its editorial group, Gramsci takes up much space espousing the positions of the 'Turin communists' on the Southern problem. He recalls that 'the fundamental concept of the Turin communists was not the "magical formula" of dividing the big estates, but rather the political alliance between Northern workers and Southern peasants, to oust the bourgeoisie from state power', so that 'in the proletarian camp, the Turin communists had one undeniable "merit": that of bringing the Southern question forcibly to the attention of the workers' vanguard, and identifying it as one of the essential problems of national policy for the revolutionary proletariat'.[109]

However, the obstacle to be confronted was precisely the dissemination of bourgeois ideology among the proletariat. The positivism that guided the Northern industrialists and exerted great influence on the ideology of the Socialist Party indicated that the causes of the social backwardness of the Southern region were natural and biological in nature. Thus, besides having to 'modify the political stance and general ideology of the proletariat itself, as a national element which exists within the ensemble of State life and is

---

107   The handwritten text was collected by Camila Ravera, who sent it to Paris, where it reached Togliatti. Publication was delayed while the result of Gramsci's trial was awaited, and then while the political struggle within the USSR between Stalin and Bukharin developed and led to the crisis of the NEP. The publication of Gramsci's unfinished essay – on the pages of the January 1930 *Lo Stato Operaio*, the PCd'I magazine, with the title that became famous: 'Alcuni temi della questione meridionale' – came after the new Stalinist political line had imposed itself. A copy of Gramsci's piece can be found at the Fondazione Istituto Gramsci di Roma and in Gramsci 1978, pp. 137–58.

108   'Ulenspiegel' is the pen name of Tommaso Fiore, and the editorial comment dissociates itself both from Dorso's book and Fiore's commentary, directing its criticism at the communists. See Gramsci 1999b, p. 595.

109   Gramsci 1999b, pp. 597–8.

unconsciously subjected to the influence of bourgeois education, the bourgeois press and bourgeois traditions', the communists had to face up to the socialists and the authors of the so-called positivist school, through which, 'Once again, "science" was used to crush the wretched and exploited; but this time it was dressed in socialist colours, and claimed to be the science of the proletariat'. And this took place precisely in Turin, 'where war-veterans' reminiscences and descriptions of "banditry" in the South and the Islands had most powerfully influenced the popular traditions and outlook'.[110]

Gramsci brings back a series of examples of how, even before the war of 1914, the Turin proletariat effectively reacted against such anti-Southern prejudices and how, soon afterwards, the communists developed a germ of political practice opposed to the bourgeois ideology prevailing at the time. The relevance of the Southern question in Gramsci's analysis is focused on the choice of the Italian ruling classes to create 'a capitalist/worker industrial bloc' instead of 'a rural democracy, i.e. an alliance with the Southern peasants'.[111]

Thus socialist reformism offered the chance for the working class to enter the life of the state, even if this was to the detriment of the Southern peasant masses. The origins of revolutionary syndicalism lay in the clash with such reformist politics, thus suggesting the possibility of the realisation of a bloc joining together the working class and the peasantry. In clearer terms, 'syndicalism is a weak attempt on the part of the Southern peasants, represented by their most advanced intellectuals, to lead the proletariat', to the extent that its leadership was comprised of Southern intellectuals opposed to state centralism and foreign trade barriers, having as its ideological essence 'a new liberalism, more energetic, more aggressive, more pugnacious than the traditional variety'.[112]

Gramsci found in emigration and free trade the explanation for the gradual passage of the socialist intellectuals to the political camp of the bourgeoisie. Colonialist expansion, presented as the solution for the problem of emigration and Southern poverty, made their support for 'nationalism' possible. On the other hand, the social differentiation of the Northern peasantry, with the increase in the number of manual labourers, gave the Southern syndicalists a new chance for political and cultural insertion, while at the same time the bourgeoisie invested, through the Catholics, in a rapprochement with the peasantry.

---

110   Gramsci 1999b, pp. 599–600.
111   Gramsci 1999b, p. 607.
112   Gramsci 1999b, pp. 607–8.

In the aftermath of the war, in the face of the advance of the popular masses, the bourgeoisie invested in the corporate-liberal project to fit the working class within the state. As the autonomous workers' movement was defeated in Turin, 'with the help of the CGL, i.e. of corporative reformism', and 'through the subordination of the working-class political party to government policies', eventually

> The Turin proletariat will no longer exist as an independent class, but merely as an appendage of the bourgeois State. Class corporatism will have triumphed, but the proletariat will have lost its position and role as leader and guide. It will appear to the mass of poorer workers as privileged. It will appear to the peasants as an exploiter just like the bourgeoisie, because the bourgeoisie – as it has always done – will present the privileged nuclei of the working class to the peasant masses as the sole cause of their ills and their misery.[113]

Resistance to this project provided the basis for the development of the communist party in Turin, even though it is possible to note its presence in other regions of the North as well. Thus, for Gramsci, the prevalence of bourgeois ideology in the workers' movement was expressed in reformism materialised as class corporatism, which emptied out the workers' autonomy, and in prejudice against the South. While reformist socialism accepted corporatism, revolutionary syndicalism, for its part, even though it acknowledged the need for the peasantry to ally itself with the working class, was easily attracted by the liberal and expansionist economic policy applied by the Italian bourgeoisie.

It is from this general crisis in the political and cultural leadership of the subaltern classes, including revolutionary syndicalism and reformist socialism, that communism arose as an alternative. It must be recalled that, in spite of his immense idiosyncrasies, Gramsci had always been an opponent of reformist socialism, having taken more nourishment from the revolutionary syndicalist trend (including its liberal aspects), and not least because of its Southernist focus.

However, from 1929 on, according to Gramsci, 'The Turin communists posed concretely the question of the "hegemony of the proletariat": i.e. of the social basis of the proletarian dictatorship and of the workers' State'. This would indicate an awareness that 'The proletariat can become the leading [*dirigente*] and the dominant class to the extent that it succeeds in creating a system of class

---

113   Gramsci 1999b, pp. 610–11.

alliances which allows it to mobilise the majority of the working population against capitalism and the bourgeois State. In Italy, in the real class relations which exist there, this means to the extent that it succeeds in gaining the consent of the broad peasant masses'.[114]

However, there is a condition for that to happen:

> The proletariat, in order to become capable as a class of governing, must strip itself of every residue of corporatism, every syndicalist prejudice and incrustation. What does this mean? That, in addition to the need to overcome the distinctions which exist between one trade and another, it is necessary – in order to win the trust and consent of the peasants and of some semi-proletarian urban categories – to overcome certain prejudices and conquer certain forms of egoism which can and do subsist within the working class as such, even when craft particularism has disappeared.[115]

And also, 'They must think as workers who are members of a class which aims to lead the peasants and intellectuals. Of a class which can win and build socialism only if it is aided and followed by the great majority of these social strata'.[116]

Surely Gramsci is here referring to the need to overcome the cultural tradition of the Italian subaltern classes and create a new culture capable of generating a new hegemony, for which the political formula of the united front would seem to be of strategic importance. Gramsci also anticipates the social composition of the revolutionary united front, and also of the new historic bloc that would lead the socialist transition. It is impossible not to perceive in these lines the shadow of the polemic between Gramsci and part of the Italian press about the direction of the USSR, and also his particular view of the disagreements plaguing the Bolshevik leadership.

The fundamental importance of the realisation of the worker-peasant alliance requires a working knowledge of the specificity of the agrarian and peasant question. So it is that 'In Italy the peasant question, through the specific Italian tradition, and the specific development of Italian history, has taken two typical and particular forms – the Southern question and that of the Vatican. Winning the majority of the peasant masses thus means, for the Italian proletariat, making these two questions its own from the social point of view;

---

114   Gramsci 1999b, p. 598.
115   Gramsci 1999b, p. 605.
116   Gramsci 1999b, pp. 605–6.

understanding the class demands which they represent; incorporating these demands into its revolutionary transitional programme; placing these demands among the objectives for which it struggles'.[117]

In spite of its particularities, as a whole 'The South can be defined as a great social disintegration. The peasants, who make up the great majority of its population, have no cohesion among themselves'.[118] For Gramsci, still, 'Southern society is a great agrarian bloc, made up of three social layers: the great amorphous, disintegrated mass of the peasantry; the intellectuals of the petty and medium rural bourgeoisie; and the big landowners and great intellectuals'.[119]

Gramsci essentially restricts himself to a brief description of the social stratification of Southern Italy, not making any reference to the regional productive process or its economic connections with the North of the country, except for in his comments on economic policy. Even the social and economic conditions of the peasantry are not the direct object of greater attention. Even so, he highlights that 'Any accumulation of capital on the spot, any accumulation of savings, is made impossible by the fiscal and customs system; and by the fact that the capitalists who own shares do not transform their profits into new capital on the spot, because they are not from that spot'.[120]

Aiming, rather, at locating the forms by which the political power of the big landowners was organised, his concern is focused from the outset on the question of the intellectuals and the state bureaucracy. Gramsci remarks that the development of capitalism created a new type of intellectual: 'the technical organiser, the specialist in applied science'. In Southern Italy, however, there prevailed the old type of intellectual, 'the organising element in a society with a mainly peasant and artisanal basis. To organise the State, to organise commerce, the dominant class bred a particular type of intellectual'.[121]

This is the type of intellectual that 'provides the bulk of the State personnel; and locally too, in the villages and little country towns, it has the function of intermediary between the peasant and the administration in general'. The Southern intellectual has its origins in the rural bourgeoisie, that is, 'the petty and medium landowner who is not a peasant',[122] but who provides land in a partnership or lease. This stratum is characterised, at the same time, by revulsion for and fear of the working peasant. Besides civil servants and military

---

117   Gramsci 1999b, pp. 598–9.
118   Gramsci 1999b, p. 599.
119   Gramsci 1999b, p. 613.
120   Gramsci 1999b, p. 619.
121   Gramsci 1999b, p. 614.
122   Ibid.

bureaucrats, churchmen also comprise a very important fraction of the traditional intellectual stratum, intervening in economic life as land administrators or usurers.

This intellectual mass, which comprises the state bureaucracy, establishes the link between the Southern peasant and the great landowner. This link is established by political groups and parties organised by intellectuals who act on the peasant mass, but who are controlled by the great landowners and the political personnel acting at a national level. This is how 'a monstrous agrarian bloc which, as a whole, functions as the intermediary and the overseer of Northern capitalism and the big banks'[123] comes into existence.

Thus we see that Gramsci broadens and redefines the notion of intellectual. For him, the structure of the intellectual class is comprised of a mass of intellectuals, who carry out a decisive role in the stabilisation of the social order. A fracture in this social stratum could be crucial for the success of a socialist revolutionary process. So it is that 'Over and above the agrarian bloc, there functions in the South an intellectual bloc which in practice has so far served to prevent the cracks in the agrarian bloc becoming too dangerous and causing a landslide'.[124]

However, the social disintegration that characterises the situation of the peasants can also be used to refer to the intellectual and cultural world, considering that we here see a great concentration of intelligence and culture in restricted groups of great intellectuals, while at the same time there 'does not exist any organisation of middle culture ... there do not exist small or medium reviews, nor publishing houses around which medium groupings of Southern intellectuals might form'.[125]

The Southern intellectuals who sought a radical solution to the Southern question had to organise themselves outside of the Mezzogiorno. However, every cultural initiative that took place in Italy from the beginning of the twentieth century until the moment Gramsci was writing, would have some influence from Southernism, albeit a Southernism limited by the reflection of the great Southern intellectuals: Giustino Fortunato and Benedetto Croce. In Italy,

since modern conditions of civilization rendered impossible any mass religious reform, the only historically possible reformation has taken place with Benedetto Croce's philosophy. The direction and method of

---

123   Gramsci 1999b, p. 617.
124   Gramsci 1999b, p. 619.
125   Gramsci 1999b, p. 620.

thought have been changed and a new conception of the world has been constructed, transcending Catholicism and every other mythological religion. In this sense, Benedetto Croce has fulfilled an extremely important 'national' function. He has detached the radical intellectuals of the South from the peasant masses, forcing them to take part in national and European culture; and through this culture, he has secured their absorption by the national bourgeoisie and hence by the agrarian bloc.[126]

Gramsci acknowledges that the *L'Ordine Nuovo* group itself was originally connected with this intellectual formation, even though they 'represent at the same time a complete break with that tradition and the beginning of a new development'. In practice, such a rupture took place in the moment when the Turin communists 'posed the urban proletariat as the modern protagonist of Italian history, and hence also of the Southern question'.[127]

Another fraction that detached itself from the intellectual formation that prevailed among the Southernists and recognised the proletariat's social position was the trend represented by Piero Gobetti and Guido Dorso. In Gramsci's assessment, Gobetti's conception 'is to a great extent related to syndicalism and the way of thinking of the intellectual syndicalists. In it, the principles of liberalism are projected from the level of individual phenomena to that of mass phenomena'.[128] Through these intellectuals, a link could be established between the proletariat and those intellectuals who came from the terrain of capitalist technique and adopted a leftist position, as had been attempted during the Turin factory occupations movement.

Even considering this piece's rough and particularly unfinished nature, the absence of any reference to Bordiga's group, which allied itself to the *L'Ordine Nuovo* group to found the communist party, is noteworthy. It is even more noteworthy when we consider its original nature as a Neapolitan and anti-Crocean group. This gap may be explained if we remember that for the leftist communist trend the Southern question did not exist, not even as a perspective for the much discussed worker-peasant alliance. So it was that Gramsci, from this point of view, saw the Bordigist trend as a variation of the positivism of the socialist tradition. Another absent element, which would almost certainly be discussed at another moment, was the Catholic Church, the Vatican question, and also the analysis of the positions of other political and cultural groups.

---

126   Gramsci 1999b, p. 621.

127   Gramsci 1999b, p. 621.

128   Gramsci 1999b, p. 622.

Gramsci knew how important it was to break up the intellectual bloc that had Benedetto Croce as its leading point of reference, and he also knew how difficult it would be to forge a revolutionary intellectual stratum closely connected with the working class. Hence the need to fight for an organic fracture in the mass of intellectuals and for the formation of a leftist trend, orientated toward the industrial proletariat. The fraction that detached itself from the intellectual bloc should take part in the united front the communists were trying to build.

At the same time that Gramsci attempted to give the communists' political action a focus, seeking to attract to the united front the intermediate strata of the workers' and petit-bourgeois parties – their intellectual mass – he also emphasised the need for an alliance with the Southern intellectuals who acknowledged the historical role of the proletariat, such that the peasant masses could do the same thing. So it was that 'The proletariat will destroy the Southern agrarian bloc insofar as it succeeds, through its party, in organising increasingly significant masses of poor peasants into autonomous and independent formations. But its greater or lesser success in this necessary task will also depend upon its ability to break up the intellectual bloc that is the flexible, but extremely resistant, armour of the agrarian bloc'.[129]

Here, Gramsci uses a broader conception of the worker-peasant alliance, because the inclusion of the question of the intellectual mass touches on the theme of the historic bloc, which implies themes such as the organisation of production and the state during the transition period, and also the essential question of the organisation of the subjective sphere. Thus, the political formula of the united front found, in Gramsci, new solutions and a theoretical development that the International as a whole was unable to achieve.

---

129   Gramsci 1999b, p. 624.

Conclusion

Gramsci's arrest, on 8 November 1926, interrupted a theoretical-political elaboration that had been developing on the basis of practical, day-to-day revolutionary activity, but would be resumed some time later in the harsh prison environment. Only then, by re-reading Marx – in a very peculiar situation – and establishing a critical dialogue with the variety of intellectual components that contributed to his own thought, would it be possible for him to make a radical critique of the hegemonic culture in Italy, expressed in Croce's work, as well as an (indirect) critique of the theoretical regression of the communist refoundation. Together with his critique of Americanism, these would be the conditions for fascism to be defeated and for the revolutionary process in Italy to be resumed.

As we saw, Gramsci's starting point lay in the anti-positivist inspiration present in the revisionist universe of late nineteenth-century Marxism, recovering Hegel's dialectics, but also certain aspects of the more advanced liberal-democratic reflection. Among the various contributions that converged to form Gramsci's political thought, the first that we must highlight is Benedetto Croce, as a promoter of the recovery of idealist dialectics, and the second Georges Sorel, who placed emphasis on the 'spirit of cleavage' of the working class with regard to the bourgeois world, but reproduced the scission between economic and politics typical of this latter, as well as of liberalism and reformism. In a more general sense, Gramsci came from a Southern intellectual trend that contested the current oligarchic order, which, based on liberalism, aimed at completing the work of the Risorgimento, transforming Italy into a democratic republic.

Though on the left-wing fringe of this cultural terrain, Gramsci associated himself with revolutionary syndicalism, especially insofar as he acknowledged the need to liberate the peasantry by means of a rapprochement with the industrial working class (which was itself largely of a migrant and rural background). It was through the world of labour that Gramsci established contact with the PSI, and not the other way around. His relationship with the PSI became closer when this group offered the Russian Revolution its support and sympathy.

In the rich experience of the Turin workers' movement – especially that which brought the factory councils to life, with a view to a means of control over the productive process that went beyond the logic of capital – Gramsci really lived the 'spirit of cleavage' that pervaded the working class at the time, not only in Italy but in various parts of the globe, especially in Central and Eastern Europe, under the influence of the revolution that emerged in the

Russian East. The perception that the main social institutions of the working class, namely the trade union and the party, tended to situate themselves within the bourgeois world and to preserve the foundations of the broken order of capital – the relations of the private appropriation of social production – led Gramsci to invest in the centrality of the factory and control of the productive process as the foundations for antagonism toward the power of capital.

The revolutionary experience of the factory councils was broadly identified with similar experiences in Russia, Germany, Austria, Hungary and Britain. A struggle for the liberation of the working masses clearly did seem to be underway. But the social isolation of this fraction of the working class, and the beginning of the counter-offensive of capital, unveiled the limits and the crisis of revolutionary syndicalism and socialist reformism in Italy and everywhere else. Gramsci's position was already very peculiar within this context, as he did not deny a role to the workers' party, so long as it maintained its *raison d'être* as a representative of class antagonism.

So his theoretical-political position came close to Sorel and also to Luxemburg, in spite of the many differences between the two revolutionaries. Both nurtured great sympathy for and identification with the Russian Revolution, and also believed the question of the self-activity of the masses and their capacity to create their own institutions to be fundamental. It is very likely that Gramsci saw in Luxemburg's formulations and in the Spartakist experience (and also in Karl Korsch) an important theoretical connection, linking together the mass strike, the workers' councils and the formation of the revolutionary party.

The observation that both the CGL and the PSI tended to be assimilated by the bourgeois state and that the mere control of production was not by itself able to promote the emptying-out of the political power of capital led Gramsci to aim at a complete scission with liberalism and reformism and its social base, and at the construction of a new political party as the privileged instance of working-class antagonism and the perspective of totality. This was how he took the path of the recently founded Communist International and of his encounter with Lenin.

The foundation of the communist party demanded the convergence of the *L'Ordine Nuovo* group, the majority group from *Il Soviet*, and a small group of 'maximalists', all originating from the PSI. The preservation of the 'spirit of cleavage' and the construction of a workers' party of a national character and associated with the perspective of the international socialist revolution guaranteed this political agreement.

The need to confront the fascist movement and preserve the unity and the legitimacy of the PCd'I before the International kept Antonio Gramsci and

Amadeo Bordiga united. Bordiga's view of the party and the revolution was very peculiar. Bordiga believed the vanguard party should be formed by all those who possessed the knowledge of the science of revolution and made an effort to spread it during workers' struggles, until there was an identification between class and party in a situation of capitalist crisis. Fascism was, for him, a variation of capitalist reaction at that moment of crisis, and its defeat was identified with the socialist revolution. Now, this formula, besides disregarding mediations, also preserved the scission that exists in the order of capital between manual and intellectual labour, the simple and the knowledgeable. Gramsci could not identify himself with such a position, out of respect for his own background.[1]

Gramsci and Bordiga separated during the dispute in the PCd'I and Comintern. The International's effort to establish mass communist parties in Western Europe was connected to a loss of spirit and the subsequent defeat of the international socialist revolution, the implication of which was the emergence of the political formula of the united front. The application of this tactic in Italy suggested a new scission in the PSI, which should assimilate that party's 'maximalist' majority into Comintern ranks, and, afterwards, involve the forging of a new alliance of anti-fascist political forces. The PCd'I, in its turn, preferred to believe that the united front would be merely a tactic aimed at the socialist workers, one that would only be adopted in the trade unions and among the youth.

As the threats of a Comintern intervention and the disintegration of the original PCd'I leadership – with its subsequent replacement by a maximalist majority allied to Angelo Tasca's communist right wing, the goal of which would be the imposition of the tactic of the united front – both increased, Gramsci realised that Bordiga's resistance was innocuous. Indeed, his resistance only brought forth latent theoretical weaknesses regarding the party-form and, principally, the problem of social alliances and the international dimension of the Italian revolution. Thus, distancing himself from the alleged national tradition of the Italian left, claimed by Bordiga, Gramsci drew closer to the formulations of the Bolshevik leadership, especially Lenin's, without however abandoning the theoretical inspirations that had led him to the camp of separation from the order of capital and with the subaltern formulations within the political culture of the workers' movement.

The earlier theoretical elaboration that had developed Gramsci's aversion to reformism and positivism had not been able to accumulate sufficient strength

---

1   It must be recalled that Gramsci had inherited from Sorel a perspective that was very critical of 'Jacobinism', identified with 'Blanquism' in terms of the prominence attributed to the vanguard over the masses in the fight for political power.

to overcome Bordiga within the camp of the communist scission opposed to the trends then prevalent in the workers' movement. Now, however, during his stay in Moscow, he came closer to Lenin's theoretical conceptions and had the Comintern's organisational backing in taking a qualitative leap theoretically, one that placed him within the trend of the communist refoundation, which had mainly been opened up by Rosa Luxemburg and Lenin.

It was precisely in the political formula of the united front that Gramsci found the guiding thread of his revolutionary praxis. From the beginning, his conception sought its own orientation within the theoretical entanglement arising within the Comintern and its main parties. This was due, in the first place, to the novelty and thus the immaturity and imprecision of the notion of the united front, and, later, the theoretical regression that affected the majority of the communist movement after Lenin's death and the dissolution of the Spartakist group.

The political formula of the united front emerged in Germany in 1921 from an initiative by Paul Levi and Karl Radek that expressed the idea of creating a new form of unity for the working class, which at the time was seriously affected by the consequences of the war and the attempted revolution of 1919. From the outset, the dispute that arose opposed those who accepted collaboration with social democracy and those who did not. This formulation assumed that the offensive of capital was to be relatively strong and lasting, and so the united front tactic should unite every working-class organisation, especially trade unions and parties – a stance that would initially be defensive, but that could provoke a counter-attack. Therefore, the struggle for the political hegemony of the workers' movement should also make use of the institutions of liberal-bourgeois democracy.

The trend that opposed itself to this formulation ended up taking two different varieties. One represented by Brandler and Thalheimer believed that collaboration with social democracy could take place whenever it was necessary to organise the working class within the factory and autonomous institutions, fighting the power of capital, or even externally to support a social-democratic government with leftist positions or under threat from conservatives. In this case, it was understood that the political formula of the united front was a defensive tactic in the face of the offensive of capital and that it should last until the revolutionary movement could – shortly – return. In this case, an alliance should be sought with the social-democratic working mass, with the purpose of showing that the revolution had been momentarily defeated because of the inherent connection that the reformist leaders had with the bourgeois order.

The second variety of opposition, more reticent toward this political formula, believed that there was no possibility of collaborating with social democracy, only with its working-class base in the process of the common struggle. The counter-revolutionary role of social democracy would be demonstrated by its willingness to participate in coalition governments with the bourgeois parties. The united front 'from below' could, then, be a strategy that aimed at 'unmasking' the social-democratic leaders and attracting the majority of the workers to the camp of the socialist revolution. This being so, there was little consideration of the effectiveness of the offensive of capital on production and the state and of to what extent the united front should be a long-term solution.

Soon emerged a new disagreement, which ultimately expressed the strategic duality just mentioned, on the real content of the political slogan of the 'workers' government' or 'workers' and peasants' government'. On one side there were those who believed that, as a corollary of the tactic of the united front 'from above', this should be an intermediate goal to be achieved still within the framework of bourgeois domination, maybe opening a path for the socialist transition within democracy. Others believed it was merely synonymous with 'proletarian dictatorship', since a real workers' government could only be born out of the opposition to bourgeois democracy.

These divergent positions manifested themselves throughout the whole of Western communism in different hues, but the core of the theoretical and practical problem was in Germany. There are signs that Gramsci opposed Paul Levi's and Karl Radek's formulation and identified more with Brandler and Thalheimer, having criticised precisely the compromises made with Radek in the period before October 1923. After having supported the removal of these leaders, Gramsci expressed his support to Thalmann, because he saw in him an alternative united front policy that privileged the centrality of the factory and autonomous workers' organisation. In the theoretical-political dispute that took place within the PCd'I, it can also be said that Angelo Tasca defended the political formula of the united front as understood by Levi and Radek, whereas Bordiga always opposed this formulation, avoiding any type of compromise.[2]

The Comintern's strategic indecisiveness stemmed from the difficulty to forge a truly international leadership, able to deal with the questions related to the crisis of capital and the state. The theoretical regression and the process of the scission affecting the Bolshevik leadership, as well as the absolute impossibility of reaching a theoretical synthesis in Germany, caused the Comintern to

---

2 In polemical terms, we could say that Tasca's understanding of the political formula of the united front, which followed Radek, was victorious within the communist party after the 'svolta di Salerno' (1944) promoted by Togliatti, even though he used Gramsci's name to give legitimacy to this political line, which became the 'via italiana al socialismo' (1956) and later the 'Eurocommunism' of the 1970s.

oscillate between two different strategies. The ambiguity was disguised by its peripatetic journey across different situations and analyses of particular cases. As we have seen, Zinoviev, president of the Comintern, performed countless tricks in order to keep together these profoundly different conceptions.

Symmetrically, in Russia, also in 1921, the New Economic Policy was announced, with the goal of restoring the worker-peasant alliance. Thus, even as a logical consequence of this, the political formula of the united front started to be understood, especially in countries with less capitalist contamination, as a worker-peasant alliance or bloc. Such was the case not only in Russia, but also in Italy and other European countries, besides those countries in the colonial periphery.

In the USSR, the implications of this strategic theoretical ambiguity were of decisive importance. Strictly speaking, after Lenin's death, only Bukharin had a united front strategic perspective. Little by little he realised that the offensive of capital could last a long time in the West, such that the communist movement would have to fight a resistance battle and accumulate forces by means of the united front policy with a view to intermediate goals such as the 'workers' government', derived from the coalition between communists and social democrats. In the USSR, on the other hand, the preservation of the worker-peasant alliance and the development of the NEP would be fundamental. State monopoly capitalism would be the path of the socialist transition in the USSR, but this could be the appropriate direction for the West as well. The NEP would be able to bring even peasants to socialism, even if that demanded a deep and slow material cultural change.

Other important political actors of the Bolshevik leadership saw in the political formula of the united front a tactical resource. For Trotsky, the united front was a defensive tactic that should last so long as no progress was made on the path of insurrection. Regarding the USSR, only a working class strengthened in a rapid industrialisation process could prevent the bureaucratisation of the party and the state, as well as contain the risk of a capitalist restoration in the countryside and contribute to the indispensable spread of the international socialist revolution.

Stalin favoured the NEP and the united front policy while he maintained his alliance with Bukharin. But he never had the same conception of the socialist transition. For Stalin, the worker-peasant alliance should last while the Soviet state was not strong enough to unleash an accelerated development of the productive forces and subject the peasantry to 'socialisation'. His idea was that there existed the possibility of rapid progress in the socialist transition in the USSR, and also that it was possible for a strong socialist state to exist in the middle of the world preponderance of capitalist imperialism. Hence his theses antithetical to those of Lenin, on the aggravation of the class struggle and the strengthening of the dictatorial state during the period of transition.

Zinoviev attempted to keep a balance between these two different positions, but he remained very far from reaching any form of theoretical synthesis. In his position as president of the Comintern and a major leader of the RKP(b), Zinoviev's responsibility was immense, and he was, together with Stalin, the greatest expression of the theoretical regression of the Comintern, even though, as we have seen, on many occasions his positions were close to Gramsci's regarding the international context.

The theoretical regression in Bolshevism could have been compensated in Germany if the Spartakist leadership had not been scattered by its confrontation with social democracy and the internal struggles of the Comintern itself. The vast riches of German Marxism were not able to bring forth any alternative for the communist refoundation. As Rosa Luxemburg and Lenin made their untimely disappearances, the refoundation of revolutionary praxis could now only flourish marginally and incompletely, in countries that were relatively backwards from the point of view of capitalism, Hungary and Italy, with the political and intellectual trajectories of Lukács and Gramsci respectively. It was not by chance that these authors were the most sophisticated elaborators of the political formula of the united front, making this strategic theoretical conception the distinctive mark of the second phase of the communist refoundation.

Certainly, those authors who made up the camp of the communist refoundation of the twentieth century had diverse theoretical matrixes, even if they all took the work of Karl Marx as their basic reference. They also diverged in their stances or theoretical approaches regarding several important questions. What we tried to show in these pages was precisely the specificity of Gramsci within the context of the communist refoundation in the period preceding his imprisonment. This is why an association was made among the political and cultural climate of Europe, which gave rise to the communist refoundation in Central-Eastern Europe, the crisis of the workers' movement, the war and the international socialist revolution, and with the particular Italian environment and Gramsci's own surroundings. Thus it can be seen that the original Southernism, replete with democratic liberalism, became a Southernism placed within the international context of the socialist revolution, projecting the periphery to the core of the future.

Gramsci attempted to elaborate a particular theoretical synthesis that made him an extremely important political actor and author of the communist refoundation. Between 1919 and 1926, Gramsci discussed various problems related to the united front, from the scission to how to deal with the intellectuals. From Sorel and Luxemburg he kept the theme of the scission between the world of labour and capital, and also trust in the autonomy and the self-activity of the masses, the implication of which is the creation of self-generated institutions that make their antagonism toward the order of capital clear. Naturally, Sorel's notion of the 'general strike' is not the same as Luxemburg's 'mass political strike', but both were connected in the political practice of the *biennio rosso* of 1919–20. The centrality of the factory and the social relations of production are permanent elements of Gramsci's thought, also inherited from Sorel and Luxemburg. These elements are essential for understanding Gramsci's later formulations on the united front policy.

Believing, like Rosa Luxemburg, that socialism is an act of culture that revolutionises the relations of production in opposition to the political power of capital and its set of intellectual, political and managerial representatives, Gramsci thus necessarily sought a workers' party arising from class struggle and the rebellious and antagonistic elements present in popular culture. A party that would be the filter through which the best fraction of the antagonistic class could be selected and become the educator of the masses, forging its own intellectuals and attracting part of the intellectuals opposed to the bourgeois order.

What united Gramsci and Bordiga was the need to split with reformism, this being the organised expression of bourgeois ideology within the workers' movement. What separated them was the difference in their conception of the revolutionary party. Gramsci believed that revolutionary consciousness originated in itself, in the antagonism toward the order of capital. However, Bordiga radicalised and one-sidedly understood Lenin's formulation about the origin of revolutionary consciousness being 'outside' the immediate class struggle and carried by external revolutionary intellectual activity, the only activity capable of conceiving the social totality, thus overcoming corporatist trade-union consciousness.[3]

From Lenin Gramsci basically took the idea of the need for a strongly centralised and organised party, able to face trials such as the fascist onslaught, but also able to prepare the insurrection. Again from Lenin, a decisive element in Gramsci's synthesis was his assimilation of the need for the worker-peasant alliance, both for achieving the revolution and consolidating the socialist transition and the social basis of the workers' state. This meeting point between

---

3   'Class political consciousness can be brought to the workers only from without, that is, only from outside the economic struggle, from outside the sphere of relations between workers and employers. The sphere from which alone it is possible to obtain this knowledge is the sphere of relationships of all classes and strata to the state and the government, the sphere of the interrelations between all classes' (*What is to be done?*).

Lenin and Gramsci is particularly important as it suggests the overcoming of Gramsci's originally narrow Southernism in favour of Lenin's universalising proposition, which would also equip him better to understand Americanism.

Much like Lenin, who began by criticising *narodnik* thought, Gramsci criticised the Southernism that placed the peasantry at the core of social transformation. By contrast, both Lenin and Gramsci proposed that the factory working class should lead the socio-political alliance of workers and peasants. It must also be said that the proposal of the worker-peasant alliance is a fundamental element for distinguishing the praxis proposed by the communist refoundation, and especially the political formula of the united front.

In this trend, to the extent that Bukharin followed Lenin's programme, developing his reflection on the NEP and the worker-peasant united front as a necessary base for the proletarian dictatorship in the initial stages of the socialist transition, Gramsci, for the purpose of reflecting on both the agrarian-peasant question in general and the specificities of Russia and Italy, did take on board Bukharin's influence. Gramsci disagreed with Bukharin, however, on the idea that capitalism in the West was recovering its strength and heading for a lasting offensive, the result of which should be a policy favouring the united front with social democracy. He agreed even less with Stalin's view of 'socialism in only one country', to which Bukharin capitulated.[4]

In his analysis of the context of international politics, Gramsci was almost always close to the sectors more to the left of the communist movement. His assessment that the revolutionary process was a permanent presence in Europe led him very close to Trotsky's views, especially regarding the relationship between Europe and America and the role to be played by social democracy. The penetration of Americanism into Europe would be helped by social democracy, fascism being merely an emergency solution for the bourgeoisie, which would anyhow submit to America's designs. This process only could be stopped by a European socialist revolution.[5]

---

4 It was only in the prison years that Gramsci acknowledged Lenin's intuition that the international socialist revolution had been exhausted, perhaps for a long time, since 1921. Soon Bukharin came to a similar conclusion. It is also known that Gramsci strongly criticised Bukharin's communism in his *Prison Notebooks*, even though he focused on the young, pre-1921 'leftist communist'. Actually, Gramsci takes the *Popular Manual on Historical Materialism* as a prime and pioneering example of the theoretical regression that would affect the communist movement, the obvious expression of which is the effort to systematise Marxism, just like Stalin and Zinoviev did, following in Bukharin's footsteps.

5 In the *Prison Notebooks*, Gramsci developed a critical assessment of Trotsky's internationalist perspective and the notion of 'permanent revolution' in the West that, to a certain extent, also served as a self-criticism.

Even Zinoviev contributed to the maturation of Gramsci's and the Italian communists' political theory, even if in a rather crude manner. The President of the Comintern believed that 'capitalist stabilisation' was precarious and so, too, the revolutionary situation in the West. The tactical implication of this reading was that social democracy was seen as a bourgeois intrusion in the workers' movement, and the united front policy should expose this and thus bring the working class as a whole to the camp of revolution.

Armed with such varied theoretical resources, and facing the reality of fascism, which was then growing and consolidating itself, Gramsci created a promising and sophisticated theoretical synthesis, as can be seen in his development of the political formula of the united front. For Gramsci, the core of the united front should be based on the social forces antagonistic to capital, especially the working class and the poor peasantry. These subaltern classes should organise themselves autonomously, according to their own experience, creating their own social institutions, which would give materiality to the antagonistic subjectivity then developing itself. The revolutionary party would be the element of coordination, centralisation and dissemination of this antagonistic subjectivity – a filter for everything that was more advanced and developed within the working class.

However, this process of constituting a new hegemony and a new state would demand an operation that would besiege and wear down capital and the bourgeois state, driving wedges between them whenever possible. The capitalist production process would be a privileged camp for political action, with the resulting need for workers' organisation in the workplace and the effort to win control of production and self-management. Considering that the PSI and the CGL were social institutions that had been assimilated by the bourgeois state and that expressed the strength of bourgeois ideology within the working class, their deconstruction and the resulting attraction of their social support base to the camp of the antagonistic forces, then organising themselves through their own institutions, was crucial for the success of the revolutionary united front policy.

This would be achieved by setting temporary goals that could attract the intermediate cadre of the political parties with a working-class and popular base. This would affect the stability of these parties, breaking the transmission channels between their social base and the political leaders whose private interests meshed with the state. Actually, the intermediate cadre was made up of the true organisers of the masses, their intellectuals.

This formulation of Gramsci's is very much consistent with the aforementioned need to attract to the united front those Southern (Southernist) intellectuals who acknowledged the socio-historical importance of the working class, and with the goal of dismantling the ruling Southern intellectual bloc. Since the intellectuals who connected the big intellectuals of the ruling class and the peasant mass to a large extent held positions in the state (civilian and military) or Church bureaucracy, they were part of the very structure of the state. And since the Southernist intellectuals who could take part in the united front tended to migrate to the North, the task of organising the peasants had to begin from a very primitive stage, making use of the spirit of rebellion present in the Mezzogiorno.

The greatest difficulty presented by this policy lay in attracting significant portions of the petit bourgeoisie, which was suffering greatly from the war and living in a situation of imminent social decline. The reason for that was that fascism consolidated itself precisely by recycling and expanding the state bureaucracy, increasing the number of the mechanisms for the repression and state organisation of the subaltern classes, thus assimilating to the bourgeois state a substantial segment of the masses. As Gramsci observed, this marginalised the Masonry and the old liberal tradition inside the bourgeois state machine, while at the same time the working class was subjected to state corporatism. Thus fascism could provide a new intellectual stratum of managers from the domain of capital.

It may be concluded that the success of the united front policy did not depend on a possible anti-fascist alliance with the liberal-democratic parties, which were going through a serious crisis of representativeness. It was more important to analyse the contradictions that existed in the mass support of fascism, as an internal crisis could leave part of that petit-bourgeois mass open to rapprochement with the proletariat at the moment when the intrinsic connection between the régime and big capital became visible. Gramsci had already clearly understood that, whereas the Russian Revolution was made against a feudal-absolutist state, the revolution in the West would be made against a liberal state form, the crisis of which could lead either to the socialist revolution or to fascism, or even some form of 'democratic' state that assimilated the petty bourgeoisie, the trade-union and party bureaucracy of the working class, recreating the rule of capital.[6]

---

6 In a certain sense, the end of fascism in 1945 effectively pointed to the second path, with the construction of a democratic-republican state that, as it recreated bourgeois hegemony, assimilated the trade-union bureaucracy and the political representation of the working class. However, because of the hegemonic participation of the communists in the anti-fascist resistance, the resulting situation could also be seen as the achievement of a transitory goal on the path of the socialist revolution, which, in the end, as we know, did not happen.

For Gramsci, however, the proletarian democracy and the socialist transition began from the first moment of emergence of the social antagonism materialised in the anti-fascist and anti-capitalist united front. It would be within the very process of resistance to fascism, guided by the political formula of the united front, that a new social form based on the self-government of the producers, with their own institutions and a new subjectivity, would be constructed. The centrality of work, the revolution, democracy and socialism were all intertwined in the effort to understand and transform social life. This set the terrain for Gramsci's later elaborations, indicating the need for a new civil society, the material and subjective expression of a new hegemony, antagonistic to capital, as the foundation of a new historic bloc with liberated work at its core. A hegemony that tended to be ever more civil and less political.

Now, if Gramsci possessed a political theory far more complex and sophisticated than the vast majority of the leaders of the Communist International, a theory that can be distinguished by the mark of the formula of the united front, and if it really was Gramsci who best understood the process of fascistisation and its meaning, then the question must be posed as to the deeper reasons for Gramsci's arrest (and the arrest of so many other PCd'I leaders) and the consolidation of fascism. Setting aside contingent or psychological explanations, the question that remains has to do with a possible theoretical insufficiency in the interpretation of the movement of the real.[7]

Was fascism underestimated, and did the political formula of the united front, as conceived by Gramsci, demonstrate that fact? If this assertion does hold any truth, there still remains the question of why. Had Gramsci not overcome the idealism and subjectivism of the Crocean formation of his youth? Or did he now assimilate a new subjectivist formula that began to emanate from the theoretical regression of the communist movement? So was Gramsci's greatest weakness that of not having assimilated Lenin (and Marx) fully, or not sufficiently?

The book now reaching its conclusion has tended to indicate a negative answer to all these questions, which have so often been raised in the historiographical and political debate, even though without making any peremptory claims. In fact, the first person to raise all these questions and who provided the best answers, even though necessarily incomplete ones, was Gramsci himself. During the rest of his short life, spent in jail, Antonio Gramsci reflected and improved on his political science, seeking better to understand all the theoret-

---

7   A recent analytical example emphasising psychological aspects of Gramsci's biography is Lepre 1998.

ical questions he had faced between 1919 and 1926 in the labour of his everyday struggles, precisely in order to look into a new horizon and a potentially victorious political orientation.

In prison, Gramsci realised how deep the defeat had been, as well as the resulting need to provide a much more consistent theoretical foundation to the political formula of the united front – though without abandoning the line of reflection and research that originated during his times as a leader of Italian and international communism. From a strictly political point of view, Gramsci saw two great errors of assessment that led him to prison and the communist movement to a lasting defeat – expressions of the solidity of the offensive of capital in the period that followed the defeat of the international socialist revolution.

One essential point was that the profile and the composition of the working class were being changed by the action of capital. The skilled working class that existed in Italy (and also in the USA) by 1920 was undergoing a process of professional impoverishment and loss of autonomy, such that its status as a class socially and culturally subaltern to the rule of the bourgeoisie could be maintained. This meant that the assessment that there was a permanent revolutionary situation had been a mistake, one that turned out to be fatal.

In the *Notebooks*, Gramsci establishes a critical dialogue with all the authors who influenced his political and intellectual formation: Croce, Sorel, Machiavelli, Trotsky, Bukharin and others. His main allies in his vast intellectual enterprise were Marx, Lenin and Labriola, who nourished his theoretical programme, even though he also preserved/overcame much of what had been assimilated by his interlocutors. Thus, he fought the theoretical regression of communism and criticised the ideologies prevailing in Italy; but mainly he analysed the new liberatory possibilities presented to the working class by the productive process of capital, and also pointed to the challenges and immense difficulties that could be foreseen. The specialised worker tended to be replaced by machines, by the scientific organisation of labour, and by economic planning, thus creating a more sophisticated form of exploitation and alienation of labour, but also a new and more advanced terrain from which the socialist revolution would set out.[8]

However, there is nothing that indicates that he abandoned the strategic view presented by the political formula of the united front, which was based

---

8   Baratta and Catone 1989. This book is the result of a seminar on Gramsci's thought that ran absolutely against the trend of similar events, publications and interpretations of that time, which tended to play down the role and the work of the Sardinian, or to make it into an irrelevant 'classic', frozen and limited to the past.

on the alliance of the subaltern classes and their intellectuals with forces that detached themselves from the current order. The path of such a united front would demand the achievement of successive transitory goals, which, in a single movement, would comprise the anti-fascist resistance, the socialist revolution and the realisation of labour democracy. The present debate on the contemporary literature dealing with Gramsci's work certainly still bears its impact in the arenas of political action, perspectives and programme. This is how the possible relevance of the political formula of the united front must be considered, taking into account its strategic value, its contents, and its role in the world of labour, social movements and the revolutionary party.

References

Agosti, Aldo 1974–9, *La Terza Internazionale: storia documentaria*, 6 vols., Rome: Riuniti.

――― 1980, 'Il mondo della III Internazionale', *Storia del marxismo*, vol. 1, edited by Eric Hobsbawm, Turin: Einaudi.

――― 1999, *Bandiere rosse: un profilo storico dei comunismi europei*, Rome: Riuniti.

Anderson, Perry 1976, 'The Antinomies of Antonio Gramsci', *New Left Review* I/100: 5–78.

Antunes, Ricardo 1999, *Os sentidos do trabalho*, São Paulo: Boitempo.

Badaloni, Nicola 1975, *Il marxismo di Gramsci: dal mito alla ricomposizione politica*, Turin: Einaudi.

Baratta, Giorgio and Andrea Catone (eds.) 1989, *Tempi moderni: Gramsci e la critica dell'americanismo*, Rome: Edizioni Associate.

――― 2003, *Le rose e i Quaderni: saggio sul pensiero di Antonio Gramsci*, Rome: Carocci.

Bertelli, Antonio Roberto 2000, *O marxismo e as transformações capitalistas: do Bernstein-Debatte a República de Weimar (1899–1933)*, São Paulo: IAP/IPSO.

Bettelheim, Charles 1979–83, *Class Struggle in the USSR*, New York: Monthly Review Press.

Bobbio, Norberto 1990, *Saggi su Gramsci*, Milan: Feltrinelli.

Boffa, Giuseppe 1976, *Storia dell'Unione Sovietica*, 2 vols., Milan: Mondadori.

Bukharin, Nicolai 1980, *Le vie della rivoluzione (1925–1936)*, Rome: Riuniti.

Cafagna, Luciano et al. 1990, *Le Tesi di Lione: riflessioni su Gramsci e la storia d'Italia*, Milan: FrancoAngeli.

Canfora, Luciano 1990, 'Il verbale di Valpocevera', *Studi storici*, I.

Caprioglio, Sergio (ed.) 1997, 'Gramsci e il delito Matteotti com cinque articoli adeposti', *Belfragor: rassegna di varia umanità*, 3.

Coutinho, Carlos Nelson 1981, *Gramsci*, Porto Alegre: L&PM.

――― 2006, *Il pensiero politico di Gramsci*, Milan: Unicapli.

D'Orsi, Angelo 1998, *Il giovane Gramsci e la Torino d'inizio secolo*, Turin: Rosenberg & Sellier.

――― 2004, 'Antonio Gramsci e la ua Torino', *La nostra città futura: scritti torinesi (1911–1922)*, Rome: Carocci.

De Benedetto, Silvia 1976, 'Gramsci, l'Antiparlamento, la Constituente: due documenti inediti del 1924', *Nuovo Impegno*, 33.

Del Noce, Augusto 1978, Il suicidio della rivoluzione, Milan: Rusconi.

Del Roio, Marcos 1998, *O império universal e seus antípodas: a ocidentalização do mundo*, São Paulo: Ícone.

Dias, Edmundo Fernandes 2000, *Gramsci em Turim: a construção do conceito de hegemonia*, São Paulo: Xamã.

Dias, Edmundo Fernandes et al. 1996, *O outro Gramsci*, São Paulo: Xamã.

Dorso, Guido 1972, *La rivoluzione meridionale*, Turin: Einaudi.

Dreyfus Michel et al. 2001, *Il secolo dei comunismi*, Milan: Marco Tropea.

Dubla, Ferdinando 1986, *Gramsci e la fabbrica*, Bari: Lacaita, 1986.

Fiori, Giuseppe 1991, *Gramsci, Togliatti, Stalin*, Bari: Laterza.

———— 1995, *Vita di Antonio Gramsci*, Bari: Laterza.

Fondazione Istituto Piemontese Antonio Gramsci (org.) 1998, *Il giovane Gramsci e la Torino d'inizio secolo*, Turin: Rosenberg & Sellier.

Fresu, Gianni 2005, '*Il diavolo nell'ampola': Antonio Gramsci, gli intellettuali e il partito*, Naples: Città del sole.

Frosini, Fabio and Guido Liguori (eds.) 2003, *Le parole di Gramsci: per um lessico dei 'Quaderni del carcere'*, Rome: Carocci.

Furet, François 1999, *The passing of an illusion: the idea of communism in the twentieth century*, Chicago: University of Chicago Press.

Gerratana, Valentino 1981, 'Stalin, Lenin e il marxismo-leninismo', in *Storia del marxismo*, vol. 2, edited by Eric Hobsbawm, Turin: Einaudi.

Gervasoni, Marco 1998, *Antonio Gramsci e la Francia: dal mito della modernità alla 'scienza della politica'*, Milan: Unicopoli.

Giacomini, Ruggero, and Domenico Losurdo (eds.) 1999, *URSS: bilancio di un'esperienza*, Naples: Istituto italiano per gli studi filosofici.

Gobetti, Piero 1995, *La rivoluzione liberale: saggio sulla lotta política in Italia*, Turin: Einaudi.

Gramsci, Antonio 1964, *Per la verità (1913–1926)*, edited by Renzo Martinelli, Rome: Riuniti.

———— 1971, *Selections from the Prison Notebooks of Antonio Gramsci*, edited and translated by Quintin Hoare and Geoffrey Nowell Smith, New York: International Publishers.

———— 1973, *Scritti politici*, 3 vols., edited by Paolo Spriano, Rome: Riuniti.

———— 1974, *Socialismo e fascismo (1921–1922)*, Turin: Einaudi.

———— 1975, *Quaderni del carcere*, 4 vols., Turin: Einaudi.

———— 1978, *La costruzione del Partito Comunista (1923–1926)*, Turin: Einaudi.

———— 1992, *Lettere (1908–1926)*, edited by Antonio Santucci, Turin: Einaudi.

———— 1993, *Letters From Prison*, New York: Columbia University.

———— 1996a, *Lettere dal carcere (1926–1930)*, vol. 1, edited by Antonio Santucci, Palermo: Sellerio.

———— 1996b, *Disgregazione sociale e rivoluzione: scritti sul Mezzogiorno*, edited by Francesco Biscione, Naples: Liguori.

———— 1997, *Filosofia e política: antologia dei 'Quaderni del carcere'*, Florence: Nuova Italia.

———— 1999a [1977], *Selections from Political Writings (1910–1920)*, edited by Quintin Hoare, London: Elecbook.

———— 1999b [1978], *Selections from Political Writings (1921–1926)*, edited by Quintin Hoare, London: Elecbook.

———— 2004, *La nostra città futura: scritti torinesi (1911–1922)*, edited by Angelo d'Orsi, Rome: Carocci.

———— 2010, *Prison* Notebooks, translated by Joseph A. Buttigieg, 3 vols., New York: Columbia University Press.

Hájek, Milos 1975, *Storia dell'Internazionale Comunista (1921–1935)*, Rome: Riuniti.

Haupt, Georges 1978, *L'Internazionale socialista della Comune a Lenin*, Turin: Einaudi.

Konder, Leandro 1980, *Lukács*, Porto Alegre: L&PM.

Labriola, Antonio 1977, *Saggi sul materialismo storico*, Rome: Riuniti.

Lenin, Vladimir I., 1972, *Collected Works*, Moscow: Progress.

Lepre, Aurelio 1998, *Il prigionero: vita di Antonio Gramsci*, Bari: Laterza.

Liguori, Guido 1996, *Gramsci conteso*, Rome: Riuniti.

Losurdo, Domenico 1997a, *Antonio Gramsci dal liberalismo al 'comunismo critico'*, Rome: Gamberetti.

———— 1997b, *Dai Fratelli Spaventa a Gramsci: per una storia político-sociale della fortuna di Hegel in Italia*, Naples: Città del sole.

Lukács, György 1928, 'Blum Theses', *Political Conceptology*.

Luxemburg, Rosa 1972, *Selected political writings*, London: Cape

———— 2003, *The Accumulation of Capital*, London: Routledge.

Manes, Sergio (ed.) 1996, *La fondazione del Partito Comunista: documenti i discorsi*, Naples: Laboratorio Politico.

Martorano, Luciano Cavini 2002, *A burocracia e os desafios da transição socialista*, São Paulo: Xamã.

Medici, Rita 2000, *Giobbe e Prometeo: Filosofia e política nel pensiero di Gramsci*, Florence: Alinea.

Mordenti, Raul 2003, *La rivoluzione: la nuova via al comunismo italiano*, Milan: Marco Tropea.

Natoli, Aldo 1991, 'Il PCd'I e il Comintern nel 1926', in Natoli and Pons (eds.) 1991.

Natoli, Aldo and Silvio Pons (eds.) 1990, *Antigone e il prigionero*, Rome: Riuniti.

———— 1991, *L'età del stalinismo*, Rome: Riuniti.

Netto, José Paulo 2002, 'Georg Lukács: um exílio na pós-modernidade', *in Lukács e a atualidade do marxismo*, edited by Maria Orlanda Pinassi and Sérgio Lessa, São Paulo: Boitempo.

Nieddu, Luigi 2004, *Antonio Gramsci: storia e mito*, Venice: Marsilio.

Paggi, Leonardo 1984, *Le strategie del potere in Gramsci*, Rome: Riuniti.

Pinassi, Maria Orlanda and Sergio Lessa (eds.) 2002, *Lukács e a atualidade do marxismo*, São Paulo: Boitempo.

Pistillo, Michele 1996, *Gramsci-Togliatti: polemiche e dissensi nel 1926*, Bari: Lacaita.

———— 2001, *Gramsci in carcere: le difficili verità d'un lento assassinio*, Rome: Lacaita.

———— 2004, *Pagine di storia del Partito Comunista Italiano: tra revisione e revisionismo storiografico*, Bari: Lacaita.

Poulantzas, Nicos 1974, *Fascism and dictatorship: the Third International and the problem of fascism*, translated by Judith White; translation editors, Jennifer and Timothy O'Hagan, London: NLB.

Rosselli, Carlo 1997, *Socialismo liberale*, Turin: Einaudi.

Sader, Emir (ed.) 1982, *Mao-Tsé Tung*, São Paulo: Ática.

Somai, G. 1989, 'Gramsci al Terzo Esecutivo Allargato (1923): i contrasti com l'Internazionale e uma relazione inédita sul fascismo', *Storia Contemporanea*, XX, 5.

Sorel, Georges 1998, *Reflections on Violence*, Cambridge: CUP.

Spriano, Paolo 1967, *Storia del Partito comunista Italiano: da Bordiga a Gramsci*, Turin: Einaudi.

———— 1969, *Storia del Partito comunista italiano: gli anni della clandestinità*, Turin: Einaudi.

———— 1971, *'L'Ordine Nuovo' e i consigli di fabbrica*, Turin: Einaudi.

———— 1977, *Gramsci e Gobetti: introduzione alla vita e alle opera*, Turin: Einaudi.

Trotsky, Leon 1937, *The Lessons of October*, London: Pioneer.

———— 1971, *Europe et Amérique*, Paris: Anthropos.

Vacca, Giuseppe 1998, *Appuntamenti con Gramsci*, Rome: Carocci.

———— 1999, *Gramsci a Roma, Togliatti a Mosca: il carteggio del 1926*, Turin: Einaudi.

Vianna, Luiz Werneck 1997, *A revolução passiva: iberismo e americanismo no Brasil*, Rio de Janeiro: Revan.

Zinoviev, Grigory 1926, *Le léninisme*, Paris: Bureau d'éditions, diffusion et publicité.

Index

Ambrogi, Ersilio 65

Bauer, Riccardo 123
Bela-kun 52
Bernstein, Edward 24
Bombacci, Nicola 35, 38, 39
Bordiga, Amadeo 8, 13, 22, 30, 36, 38, 42,
    62–5, 73, 77, 79–82, 84, 86, 88, 90,
    108, 113, 114, 117, 118, 121, 124, 126–8,
    131, 132, 136, 139, 140, 142, 143, 149,
    152–5, 166, 167, 174, 184, 188, 189, 190,
    193
Brandler, Heinrich 51, 74, 75, 104, 105, 116, 117,
    189, 190
Bukharin, Nicolai 3, 9, 52, 56, 79, 87, 97–101,
    103, 108, 109, 110, 111, 114, 115, 127, 144,
    155, 161, 162, 166, 172, 173, 191, 194,
    198

Croce, Benedetto 2, 7, 24, 25, 28, 29, 183, 184,
    185, 186, 197, 198

Dorso, Guido 175, 176, 177, 178, 184

Eberlein, Hugo 22
Engels, Friedrich 5, 17, 28, 29, 111

Farinacci, Roberto 157
Fiore, Tommaso 175
Fischer, Ruth 74, 116
Fortichiari, Bruno 38, 39, 84
Fortunato, Giustino 183

Gennari, Egidio 39, 81, 84
Gentile, Giovanni 3, 24, 25
Gobetti, Piero 2, 123, 175, 176, 184
Goethe, Johann Wolfgang von 10
Gorter, Hermann 25
Gramsci, Antonio 1–10, 15, 22–32, 34–7,
    39–43, 45–9, 52, 53, 55, 57–68, 77, 79–91,
    96, 97, 100, 101, 104–9, 111–150, 153–190,
    192, 193–9
Graziadei, Antonio 35, 42, 63, 65, 79, 84
Grieco, Ruggiero 3, 80, 84, 112, 137, 149, 152,
    170, 171

Hitler, Adolf 74
Humbert-Droz, Jules 63, 128, 137, 139, 149,
    152, 166–171

Kamenev, lev 102, 103, 115, 166
Kapp, Wolfgang 62, 72
Kautsky, Karl 20
Kolarov, Vasil 63
Korsch, Karl 7, 8, 24, 32, 153, 187
Kuusinen, Otto 166

Labriola, Antonio 7, 28, 29, 198
Landler, Jeno 23
Lassalle, Ferdinand 25, 102
Lazzari, Costantino 50, 66
Liebknecht, Karl 22, 50
Lenin, Vladimir 1, 4, 6–9, 12–15, 17–20,
    25, 27–9, 36, 38, 40, 46, 52, 53, 55, 56,
    68, 69, 76, 82, 87–90, 92, 93, 98–102,
    111, 114–117, 128, 131, 133–6, 141, 161,
    162, 167–9, 173, 175, 187–194, 197,
    198
Leonetti, Alfonso 114, 149
Levi, Paul 42, 50, 51, 52, 55, 116, 186, 190
Loria, Acchille 29
Lukacs, Gyorgy 6, 23, 91, 96, 97, 192
Luxemburg, Rosa 6–9, 12, 16–25, 30–2, 37, 38,
    47, 50, 108, 117, 133–5, 141, 160, 187, 189,
    192, 193

Maffi, Fabrizio 66, 67
Mandolfo, Rodolfo 24
Manuilsky, Dimitri 166, 168
Mao Zedong 111
Machiavelli, Niccolò XI, 7, 26–7, 88–9, 198
Marabini, Anselmo 42
Marx, Karl 1–8, 17, 20, 24, 27–30, 38, 55, 69,
    73, 88, 91, 102, 111, 136, 186, 192, 194, 197,
    198
Maslow, Arkadi 74
Matteotti, Giacomo 122, 160
Michels, Robert 133
Misano, Francesco 38, 39
Mussolini, Benito 3, 48, 67, 126, 129, 137, 169

Nenni, Pietro 137, 175

Owen, Robert   25

Pannekoek, Anton   15
Parodi, Giovanni   39
Pachukanis, Evgeni   90
Piatakov, Giorgi   105
Polano, Luigi   38
Preobrazhensky, Evgueni   97
Proudhon, Pierre-Joseph   27, 28

Radek, Karl   51, 56, 62, 68, 69, 72–5, 79, 87, 98,
    104, 105, 107, 114, 116, 117, 189, 190
Rakosi, Mátyás   67
Ravazzoli, Paolo   149
Ravera, Camila   149, 168
Repossi, Luigi   39
Riboldi, Ambrogio   66
Rosselli, Carlo   175
Rubin, Isaak Illich   90
Ruhle, Otto   19, 20

Salvemini, Gaetano   2, 24, 25, 85
Schucht, Giulia   130
Schucht, Tatiana   10
Scoccimarro, Mauro   79, 84, 122, 149, 153, 155,
    170
Serrati, Giacinto Menotti   35, 40, 42, 48, 50,
    58, 66, 67, 149
Sorel, Georges   7, 8, 14, 25–8, 32, 33, 81, 90,
    128, 132, 135, 139, 141, 143, 160, 186, 187,
    192, 193, 198

Spaventa, Bertrando e Silvio (fratelli,
    Brothers)   28
Sraffa, Piero   119
Stalin, Joseph   3, 4, 98, 101–3, 108–111,
    114, 116, 152, 155, 172, 178, 191, 192,
    194
Stolypin, Piotr   99

Tasca, Angelo   30, 35, 63, 79, 80–4, 113, 114,
    150, 188, 190
Terracini, Umberto   30, 35, 38, 42, 63, 71, 114,
    149
Thalheimer, August   69, 74, 75, 104, 105, 116,
    117, 189, 190
Thalmann, Ernst   74, 108, 116, 190
Togliatti, Palmiro   1, 3, 30, 35, 84, 113, 121, 137,
    149–155, 166–9, 173
Trotsky, Leon   9, 62, 76, 79, 87, 93–8, 101–6,
    111, 114–117, 125, 127, 128, 131, 133, 143,
    144, 152, 157, 166, 171, 172, 191, 194,
    198

Vico, Giambattista   7, 26, 88
Vittorio Emanuele III   135

Zetkin, Clara   52, 69, 74, 79, 106, 107
Zinoviev, Grigory   54, 56, 65, 68, 73, 78, 79, 83,
    87, 98, 101–6, 108, 109, 111, 114–116, 143,
    166, 191, 192, 195

www.ingramcontent.com/pod-product-compliance
Lightning Source LLC
Chambersburg PA
CBHW060037030426
42334CB00019B/2364